ALSO BY CHARLES KIPPS

Out of Focus

COP WITHOUT A BADGE

The Extraordinary Undercover Life of Kevin Maher

Charles Kipps

SCRIBNER

New York   London   Toronto   Sydney

SCRIBNER
A Division of Simon & Schuster, Inc.
1230 Avenue of the Americas
New York, NY 10020

First Scribner trade paperback edition August 2009

SCRIBNER and design are registered trademarks of The Gale Group, Inc.,
used under license by Simon & Schuster, Inc., the publisher of this work.

For information about special discounts for bulk purchases,
please contact Simon & Schuster Special Sales at 1-866-506-1949
or business@simonandschuster.com.

The Simon & Schuster Speakers Bureau can bring authors
to your live event. For more information or to book an event
contact the Simon & Schuster Speakers Bureau at 1-866-248-3049
or visit our website at www.simonspeakers.com.

Manufactured in the United States of America

3   5   7   9   10   8   6   4   2

ISBN 978-1-4391-7711-2
ISBN 978-1-4391-7637-5 (eBook)

Acknowledgments

Over the past several years, I have spent many evenings in a restaurant called Elaine's. I have eaten well, imbibed liberally, and enjoyed the conversation of the proprietor, Elaine Kaufman. If it hadn't been for Elaine, I would never have written this book.

In January 1994, author/screenwriter David Black called me to say he had heard about the extraordinary life of a confidential informant named Kevin Maher. It was a compelling tale, David noted, one that would make a good book, TV show, or movie. David was busy writing a film script and suggested I look into the story. A short time later, I wrote a proposal for *Cop Without a Badge* and delivered it to literary agent Fifi Oscard. Fifi worked diligently to find the best publisher for the material.

David Black and Fifi Oscard have one thing in common. Both were introduced to me by Elaine Kaufman.

Thank you, Elaine.

AND THANKS TO . . .

Jim Doherty and Bobby Colaneri, who spent hours recounting their own stories and provided invaluable research in the writing of this book.

Kevin Maher, who withstood a barrage of questions during a long series of relentless interviews.

Tom Harkins, Bob DeBellis, and Dennis Calo, who were particularly generous with their time.

Private Investigator and former NYPD Detective Mike Struk, who brought Kevin Maher to the attention of David Black.

And, of course, Kent Carroll, who edited a sprawling manuscript and turned it into a book.

Author's Note

This is a true story. Unless otherwise noted, actual names are used. The facts were verified by court records and law enforcement agents.

Whenever possible, more than one source confirmed the conversations in this book. If participants were either unavailable or unwilling to offer comment, the dialogue reflects Kevin Maher's recollection of what was said.

It was my intention that *Cop Without a Badge* be both informative and enjoyable. And while it is non-fiction, I hope it proves as absorbing as a novel. After all, there is only one difference between *Cop Without a Badge* and a work of fiction.

You can't make this stuff up.

COP WITHOUT A BADGE

Chapter 1

THE 1969 PLYMOUTH ROADRUNNER HEMI, ITS BODY TREMBLING FROM the power of the 426-cubic-inch engine that growled underneath the hood, rumbled up the entrance ramp to the northbound lanes of the Bronx River Parkway. The driver was Kevin Maher, a seventeen-year-old Irish kid from the Bronx. Freckled face. Burst of reddish-blond hair. Pale blue eyes. He looked like he should be on a bicycle, not behind the wheel of a two-thousand-pound machine.

A factory standard Hemi was considered to be among the fastest stock automobiles on the highway. But beyond the high-performance design there was another attribute that set Maher's Hemi apart from other cars on the Bronx River Parkway that evening.

It was stolen.

Maher urged the Hemi to eighty miles per hour and swept up beside a 1967 Pontiac GTO. The driver of the GTO, a young Italian man who understood the taunting language of chattering cylinders and roaring manifolds, smiled at Maher. In an instant, the cars charged forward. By the time the Hemi and the GTO thundered past 233rd Street, the Hemi was clocking a hundred miles an hour and the GTO seemed to be going backward. Maher glanced in the rearview mirror and watched as the competition fell away. It wasn't until the GTO quickly darted to the side of the road that Maher saw the flashing lights.

Maher pondered the options: He could face grand theft auto or make a run for it. There wasn't really any choice, he had to run. Besides, a six-cylinder squad car was like a horse and buggy compared to the souped-up Hemi.

Maher pressed the accelerator into the floorboard, the sudden shift in momentum forcing his head back. A hundred and ten now and climbing. A hundred and twenty. He squinted as the dark highway rushed at the windshield, then glanced into the rearview mirror. The cop was right on his tail. How could that be? Maher looked again. It wasn't a basic NYPD squad car at all. It was a Highway Patrol car: a 440 Plymouth Interceptor with a gear ratio ratcheted for speed.

"Fuck!" Maher said aloud.

For many teenagers in the economically ravaged Bronx of the dawning seventies, stealing cars was a pastime. Virtually every Irish and Italian kid who lived there was proficient at ripping out an ignition and cranking up an engine with a screwdriver. They didn't sell the cars, just took them for joy rides and abandoned them. When they were caught—and they almost always were—they generally were treated with leniency by some weary judge. After all, this was the Bronx. People *killed* people in the Bronx. A teen with a stolen car? What the hell?

But Maher was more sophisticated than his teenage buddies who stole cars for the fun of it. The fact was, Maher could turn a stolen car into a lawfully registered vehicle in minutes. All it took was a knowledge of VIN numbers and a couple of "stars."

A car's Vehicle Identification Number is stamped on a small metal tag fastened under the base of the windshield. This number was at the heart of Maher's automotive shell game. Maher would simply replace the VIN number of a stolen car with the VIN number taken from a legitimately owned vehicle.

In this case, Maher actually owned a Roadrunner, which was sitting in the driveway at his father's house. However, as Maher had done with every car he had ever owned, he had driven the life out of it, broken it like a rodeo hotshot on a bull. About the only thing worth salvaging was its VIN number. So Maher drilled the metal tag from his disabled Plymouth and spent the day "shopping." He checked the want ads and went from place to place, kicking tires, test-driving each Roadrunner carefully. Finally, on Undercliff Avenue in the Bronx, he came across a beauty of a vehicle. He drove it around the block a few times, thanked the owner, and went home. At midnight he returned, pried out the ignition, and drove away.

The first thing Maher did after he stole the Hemi was head to Queens, where he knew a guy in a body shop who did "tag jobs," which involved removing the windshield, swapping VIN numbers, and then replacing the windshield. That was the easy part. When the original VIN tag was ripped out, there was no way to keep from destroying the special rivets that held it in place. These rivets, called "stars," were hard to come by and carried a street price of $125 each. But Maher was prepared. He had two "stars" in his pocket. Maher had already switched license plates, so once the "tag job" was done, everything would match. Plates. Registration. Insurance certificate. VIN number. The color was different, of course, but even that was no real problem. Maher would go to the Division of Motor Vehicles the next day and tell them he had painted the car. They would issue a new registration, no questions asked. At that point, since every document was linked to another document, thus creating an illusion of validity, and since DMV records would show that Maher actually *did* own a Roadrunner, there would be no suspicions aroused, giving police no justifiable reason to investigate further. Indeed, once Maher finished the tag job, no one would guess that the stolen Hemi he was driving wasn't the Roadrunner he actually owned. Unfortunately, the body shop owner in Queens was nowhere to be found. And now Maher was racing up the Bronx River Parkway with a shaky VIN number.

Maher checked the rearview mirror again and saw the Interceptor's grill sneering back at him. Maher decided he needed to get to Westchester County in a hurry, where the intricate maze of "communities" would hide him until he cooled off. Each cozy little development was filled with indistinguishable cloned houses and had its own system of streets cutting through perfectly manicured lawns. A fugitive couldn't ask for a better place to get lost.

As Maher planned his escape route into suburbia, he looked up and saw the toll plaza. Since it was late at night, all but one booth had been closed, and that booth was blocked by a Volkswagen. Maher slammed on his brakes and laid on his horn, skidding to a stop behind the Volkswagen. Suddenly, Maher heard a pounding on his car. He turned to see the highway patrolman, gun drawn, banging on his trunk.

"Get out of the car!" the cop screamed, pointing his gun. "Get *out* of the car!"

Maher looked back toward the toll plaza. The driver of the Volkswagen, an executive type, jumped from his car.

"What's going on here?!" the pinstripe yelled at Maher.

Maher shrugged. *Fuck this!* He popped the clutch and, with the screeching of tires and a cloud of smoke from burning rubber, pushed the Volkswagen through the gate. And then he was off again.

Maher spotted the next toll booth a little sooner, allowing him time to point at it like a kamikaze diving for the deck of an aircraft carrier. Panicked toll takers dove for cover as the Hemi blasted through the swing gate like it was made of cardboard. Maher laughed, finding comfort in the knowledge that he was the best there was when it came to driving fast cars. *Everybody* knew Kevin Maher.

Given Maher's skill at stealing cars and his penchant for bragging about his exploits, it was to be expected that he would get to know most of the body shop owners in Queens, particularly those who preferred not to *buy* auto parts. Joey Braccini, for example. So, when a local Queens man named Jimmy Nace introduced Braccini to "an Irish kid who's good with cars," Braccini immediately offered Maher a job.

"If you can get me a 1970 Lincoln Continental," Braccini told Maher, "I'll pay you two-fifty. And if you find me a tan one, that'll save me a paint job. I'll give you five hundred for a tan."

Now that Maher was a "pro," his choice of tools underwent a change as well. Instead of a screwdriver, Maher began using a "dent puller" to extract ignitions. Designed for use by body shops in restoring crumpled automobile fenders, the "slide hammer," as it was also called, consisted of a steel rod with a sheet metal screw attached to one end and a large washer secured to the other end. A cast-iron weight with a center hole slid along the length of the rod. Maher would turn the screw into a car's ignition and then forcefully jerk the weight back until it slammed against the washer, the resulting force easily ripping out the ignition. The mechanical advantage supplied by the slide hammer allowed Maher to be on his way in fewer than thirty seconds.

A short while after Maher began stealing cars for Joey Braccini, Joey's brother Tony was released from prison. A convicted bank robber, Tony had not been rehabilitated.

"I need a wheel man," Tony told his brother Joey.

"I know this Irish kid," Joey offered. "If you can make it from the bank to the car, this kid'll get you away."

Maher lived up to his reputation. Seven times the Braccini brothers hit a bank in the Cross Bay area, and seven times Maher spirited them away. Once, when they were spotted by a bank employee before they even got out of the car, Maher eluded a pursuing squadron of cops by jumping a concrete highway divider and barreling across an overpass bridge in the wrong direction. For his efforts, Maher received payments that ranged from $500 to $7,500.

If Maher had grown up in the Midwest he might have wound up at the Indianapolis 500 taking the checkered flag. But a kid from the Bronx didn't have such heady dreams. The way Maher saw it, the only difference between Indianapolis and the Bronx was that in the Bronx you got the prize *before* you started the race. And to Maher, that was the far better proposition.

The prize on this night was the 426 Roadrunner Hemi. And the race was nowhere near over. For the next hour, Maher led the Highway Patrol car on a chase through five New York counties at speeds topping a hundred and forty miles per hour. The impromptu Gran Prix spilled onto the Sprain River Parkway and off again, over the Taconic State Parkway, and across to the New York State Thruway. Because the highways were so long and straight, Maher was never able to get out of sight of the persistent Interceptor.

Poughkeepsie. Rhinebeck. Kingston. And, of course, more toll booths. The Hemi was going so fast, Maher's sighting of the toll plazas and the sharp crack of the Hemi's grill pulverizing the wooden gates occurred almost simultaneously. Maher would blink, and when he opened his eyes, a blizzard of splinters would swirl over the windshield.

Somewhere near the Catskill Mountains, Maher rounded a curve and spotted three State Police cars blocking his way. Since there wasn't time to react, Maher braced himself for a collision, only this time the obstacle wasn't as flimsy as a wooden toll gate. Maher's heart was pumping now, his face flushed. It was a rush like he had never experienced, a taste of both terror and anticipation at the thought of tempting sudden death. Suddenly, the perspective reversed. It didn't seem as if the Hemi was moving at all, rather the police roadblock was hurtling toward him. And then, accompanied by the crunching of metal and the shattering of glass, the Hemi plowed through the automotive blockade.

Although the Hemi survived the impact, it was now severely damaged. One of the headlights was destroyed and the other was pointing straight up, making it impossible to see the road in the black night. At least the radio was still working. *Shaft* by Isaac Hayes blasted out of the speakers.

The moment the Hemi cleared the roadblock, the State Troopers drew their guns and began firing. The first bullet slammed into the trunk, the second fractured the rear window. Several more rounds pelted the doors.

Who's the baddest mutha . . . Isaac Hayes's growling voice was cut off in midverse as a slug ripped into the radio.

Miraculously, Maher wasn't hit, and the speeding Hemi took him out of range of the troopers' guns within seconds. But now he had another problem. Since he couldn't see the road without headlights, he was forced to slow down. And the Interceptor was somewhere close behind him.

Fortunately for Maher, the state troopers had neglected to radio the highway patrolman as to the location of the roadblock. So when the Interceptor rounded the curve, it collided with the three state vehicles, spinning to a stop on the side of the road.

The Hemi limped off the highway and entered the Catskill Mountains, vanishing into the darkened hills. After more than a hundred miles, the race had ended. And Maher had won.

AT DAWN, MAHER FOLLOWED BACK ROADS TO NEW YORK. HE COULDN'T go to 1607 Cross Bay Boulevard in Queens, where he now lived with his father, because the tags on the Hemi were registered to that address. (Due to Maher's age, the Roadrunner had been registered in his father's name.) So he made his way to the

Bronx, and abandoned the smashed-up Hemi five blocks away from his mother's apartment at 239 East Mosholu Parkway. He carefully wended his way through the neighborhood and sneaked through the back doorway of the apartment building.

"The cops were here," Maher's mother, Agnes, said, her voice edgy. "They said you were speeding."

A moment later, there was a pounding on the door.

"Police! Open up!"

"Tell 'em I'm not here," Maher whispered as he headed down the hall, his eyes sparkling like the eyes of a favorite son. "Okay, Mom?"

Agnes fought back a smile and walked to the front door, opening it to reveal two cops standing in the hallway.

"What do you want?" Agnes challenged.

"We're looking for Kevin Maher."

Agnes looked them straight in the eye. "I told you before, he's not here."

"Yes, he is," a cop said, "We found his car five blocks away."

The two cops swept past her like they were after the FBI's most wanted criminal.

"What are you doing?!" Agnes demanded. "Get out of here before I call the cops."

"We *are* the cops," one of the officers shot back.

The cops conducted a room-to-room search, finally coming upon a closed bathroom door, where they heard the sound of running water.

"Who's in there?" a cop demanded.

"My daughter," Agnes said.

A cop reached for the doorknob.

"No!" Agnes shouted. "You can't go in there!"

The cop twisted the knob and pushed into the bathroom. Someone *was* in the shower. Kevin Maher, no doubt. But then a teenage girl poked her dripping wet head around the shower curtain. She shrieked. And shrieked. And shrieked. The stunned cops backed out of the room.

"You perverts!" Agnes screamed as she showed the cops the door.

Had the cops not been so startled, they might have pulled back the shower curtain and discovered that Susan actually was dressed in a T-shirt and shorts.

Soaked and not the least bit amused, Susan turned off the shower and looked down at her brother, who was lying fully clothed, in the tub. She shook her head: "You *really* owe me this time, Kevin."

EDWARD MAHER KNEW HIS SON HAD DONE MORE THAN MERELY EXCEED the speed limit on the Bronx River Parkway. The cops had run the plates on the Hemi and come up with his home address. An officer had given Edward all the details of the car chase and had emphasized the serious nature of the charges that had been filed against Kevin. For a blue-collar, law-abiding, churchgoing Irishman like Edward Maher, this latest escapade by his troubled son was a hurtful thing. This wasn't kid stuff. This was bad.

Edward Maher married Agnes McNulty in the euphoric 1950s when the memory of war was fading and the promise of peacetime prosperity was beckoning. The first-generation Irish couple settled into the Bronx and started a family: Kevin was born April 18, 1954. Two years later the Mahers had a daughter, Susan. But the marriage was never a good one, and by 1960, Agnes and Edward were separated. Like any six-year-old might be, Kevin was devastated.

Following the separation, Edward seemed always to be locked in a struggle just to survive, sometimes working two jobs. Thus he had little time to spend with his son. Despite the infrequent visits, Kevin worshiped his father and would often resort to fantasy to justify that worship. Although Edward Maher held a series of mundane jobs that included bartender and furniture mover, Kevin made up stories about him.

"My father is a famous cop," Kevin would tell his schoolmates one day. And the next day he might say: "My father is a famous businessman and he's very, very rich."

Naturally, six-year-old Kevin refused to believe his father could have been responsible for the breakup of the marriage, and he blamed his mother, often striking out at her. On one occasion he bought five cigarette "loads" at a novelty shop and packed the tiny gunpowder-coated wooden splinters into one of his mother's cigarettes. When she lit it, the explosion shot flames into her beehive hairdo, which caught fire and sent her screaming around the kitchen.

Maher managed to get through grade school—at St. Anne's and St. Brendan's—but at fourteen his emotional state worsened considerably when his mother moved in with a man named Edward Tierney. Maher saw Tierney as a "drunk" and a "no-good." Whatever Tierney was like, it wouldn't have mattered to Maher. No one could measure up to his father. No one. As far as Maher was concerned, his father was a saint who loved his kids.

Maher stayed away from home as much as possible, and during the summer of 1968 he often went with a neighborhood friend named Eugene Gilhooley to a vacation house Gilhooley's parents owned in Kingston, New York. But even the sojourns to the country turned bad for Maher. On one trip he was blinded in the right eye by a pellet fired from a BB gun. Now there were physical scars as well as emotional ones. He returned home from the trip, his eye bandaged and his self-worth knocked down another notch.

Since Maher and his mother were not getting along, Kevin moved in with his father. Edward's two jobs left Kevin unattended for long hours, so he reluctantly suggested that Maher return to live with his mother. When Maher called his mother, she had some unexpected news. She told her son that she intended to fly to Mexico for a quickie divorce so she could marry Tierney. Maher was inconsolable. *I ain't going back to that bitch*, he fumed as he hung up the receiver.

For the next two months, Edward thought his son was with his ex-wife, Agnes. And Agnes thought her son was with Edward. They never spoke to each other, so they never knew that their son was in neither home. Spending the summer doing whatever he pleased, he sometimes stayed with friends, often ran around all night, usually slept in cars, and only occasionally visited his parents. As for money, he managed to find the odd job that would pay him off the books. A porter, for example, at a seedy hotel.

Maher also hung around the local precinct. He loved the sound of crackling police radios and the nonstop action in the squad room. He idolized the detectives, who dressed well and had a certain heroic air about them. Other than the detectives, the only men in the Bronx who exuded as much style were the gangsters. For an Irish teenager looking to be *somebody*, not just a worker drone in a factory, these were the choices. Maher decided early on he wanted to be a cop. The job offered excitement *and* it commanded respect from the community. Someday, Maher told himself, he would be a detective and make his father proud.

Autumn came, and for most fourteen-year-olds, it meant an exciting event: entering high school. But Maher spent exactly one day in high school and remained a truant until March 1969. All he wanted to do at this point was get out of town. Go somewhere exciting. But how does a fourteen-year-old get out of town?

Eugene Gilhooley, who was nineteen, was about to be drafted into the Army.

"I'm thinking about going to Canada," Gilhooley told Maher. "No way I'm going in the service."

"Don't worry about it," Maher said. "Just give me the papers and *I'll* go."

Exhibiting astonishing resourcefulness, Maher assumed the identity of Eugene Gilhooley and, after forging an eye test, sidestepped the Army by enlisting in the Marine Corps. The youngest-ever marine got away with it for fourteen months before he was found out. So, at fifteen, Maher landed back in the Bronx with a choking sense of hopelessness. And now, at seventeen, he was a fugitive.

MAHER SPENT THE DAY SLEEPING AT A NEIGHBOR'S APARTMENT ACROSS the hall. That night he slipped out the back door of the apartment building and made his way to a subway entrance, where he boarded a Manhattan-bound subway and headed to the apartment of family friend Buddy Hample. Hample lived at 425 East 81st Street, a posh address that was testimony to the financial rewards of being a doorman in New York City, which was his occupation. In fact, East 81st Street was a perfect hiding place for Maher, since the cops wouldn't look for an Irish street kid in such a neighborhood. And Hample didn't mind. While Hample knew Maher was always up to some kind of mischief, he thought this was just speeding.

On December 17, 1971, three weeks after arriving at Hample's apartment, Maher felt safe enough to leave. At 4:00 A.M.

Maher walked up York Avenue and stole a 1966 Oldsmobile Tornado. He checked the want ads and found a wrecked 1966 Oldsmobile on sale for fifty dollars. He bought the wreck, then stopped off to see the insurance broker who held the policy on his Plymouth Roadrunner.

"I want to take the insurance off the Roadrunner," Maher told the broker, "and put it on this Olds."

Maher showed the broker the paperwork pertaining to the *wrecked* Oldsmobile, in which the owner had signed over the title to Maher's father, Edward Maher. A few minutes later, the broker handed Maher an FS1, a proof of insurance card required in New York State. Maher took the FS1 to the Division of Motor Vehicles and, after registering the *wrecked* Oldsmobile, wound up with a *legal* VIN number and *legal* license plates. In fact, *everything* Maher had done pertaining to the wrecked Olds was perfectly legal. Next came the sleight of hand. Maher bolted the *legally* obtained plates on the *stolen* Oldsmobile, then drove to Queens and had the VIN numbers swapped. By afternoon, Maher had a "legitimate" automobile.

Prior to his parents' separation, it never occurred to Maher that bad things could happen to good people. Once he realized that emotional disaster loomed just ahead of every happy moment, Maher developed a sense of impending doom. And a feeling that he had to hurry his life to outrun the disappointment. Which is why he joined the Marines at fourteen. And why he couldn't resist speeding up the Major Deegan Expressway on this day. So he rammed the accelerator to the floorboard and urged the Oldsmobile past eighty miles per hour. At 230th Street Maher heard sirens. He checked the rearview mirror, and when he saw the flashing lights of a pursuing squad car, he was tempted to make a dash for the Catskills again. But this time everything was in order. Tags. Registration. He even had a forged driver's license with a brand-new name on it.

Maher pulled over and waited while the cop called in the plate number. It came back as being registered to Edward Maher. The cop stepped from his squad car and walked to the window of the Olds.

"License and registration, please."

Maher complied, chattering all the while that he didn't realize he was speeding.

A few minutes later, the cop returned with a ticket and handed it to Maher without a word. The cop started to walk away, then whipped around.

"I *know* you!"

Maher diverted his eyes.

"Wait a minute!" the cop shouted. "You're Kevin Maher!"

The cop was from the MCY, the police unit that patrols the snaking highways around the five boroughs of New York City. He had ticketed Maher several times, had heard about the now infamous Bronx-to-Catskills chase, and knew that Maher had a penchant for stealing cars. Which could explain why the cop drew his gun. He may have speculated that the Olds was stolen and, despite the DMV documents, Maher's reputation made the possibility that the car had been "tagged" worth checking. So Maher found himself looking into the barrel of a service revolver.

"Get out of the car," the cop ordered.

Maher eased the door open and stepped onto the asphalt.

"Turn around," the cop barked.

Maher did as he was told. Then he felt steel on his wrists and heard a metallic click. For the first time in his life, Maher was on his way to jail: the Rikers Island Adolescent Remand Shelter.

At fourteen, Maher had redefined the word "freedom," breaking away from parental supervision and eluding the educational system. Now that he was penned in, panic overtook him. And although he was exhausted from the ordeal of being arrested and booked, he didn't sleep.

The following morning, Maher was brought into court and charged in connection with the theft of the Hemi and the subsequent car chase: grand larceny, possession of stolen property, unauthorized use of a motor vehicle, reckless endangerment in the first degree, altered VIN number, and six counts of attempted assault on a police officer. A court date was scheduled for December 24, and bail was set at five hundred dollars *cash*. Unlike bail, which is set at five hundred dollars *bond*—in which case a suspect can find a bail bondsman and post 10 percent of the bail—a *cash* bail meant that the court would *not* accept a bond. And though the cash bail was only five hundred dollars, even that small amount was too much for Agnes and Edward Maher to raise. However, had the court been willing to release

Maher on a five-hundred-dollar bond, it still would not have made any difference. Bail bondsmen wanted assurances that the bond would be paid if the suspect fled and usually required real estate as collateral. Maher's parents owned no real estate.

That afternoon, things got worse. The Olds was taken to the Whitestone Impound Lot, and cops did what is called "a search for true VIN number." While thieves knew the standard location of a VIN number—under the windshield—they also knew that auto manufacturers hid the VIN number in several other locations on the vehicle. The redundancy scheme—which was a closely guarded secret shared by Detroit and law enforcement—enabled police to determine if the VIN number had been altered. The Olds came up bad. And Maher was charged with a second theft.

Six days later, on Christmas Eve, Maher was led into a courtroom. Represented by a public defender, Maher listened as the charges were read. Then the public defender pointed out that Maher had no previous record and asked for a bail reduction. After reflecting for a moment, the judge looked down from the bench and smiled.

"Merry Christmas, Kevin," the judge said as he released Maher on his own recognizance.

Maher spent Christmas week running between his mother's apartment and his father's. Both of his parents were relieved that he had been released from jail, and both pleaded with him to stay out of trouble.

On New Year's Eve, Maher prepared for the evening by buying a destroyed 1965 Chevrolet from a junk yard for twenty-five dollars and then snatching a pristine '65 Chevy off a Bronx Street. Following the usual drill of swapping license plates and VIN numbers, he picked up his girlfriend Kathy Salak, a beautiful Ukrainian teenager, and headed for Manhattan to party. At 11:00 P.M., the '65 Chevy shot onto the 59th Street Bridge at seventy miles per hour. And then came the familiar sound of sirens.

By now Maher's name and photo were plastered all over police blotters from the Bronx to Manhattan. He was arrested on the spot. The Chevy was sent to the Whitestone Impound Lot, where a search for true VIN number determined that it was stolen.

Maher appeared before a judge the next morning, and bail was set at $2,500. *Cash.* It might as well have been a million. And so it was that on the very first day of 1972, a seventeen-year-old Bronx kid found himself in quite a predicament.

MAHER'S MOTHER SCRAPED TOGETHER ENOUGH FOR A RETAINER AND hired an attorney named James Morihan. Morihan was a large man, six feet, two inches tall and weighing more than two hundred fifty pounds. He had bloodshot eyes, a ruddy complexion, and a drinker's nose. When Maher met Morihan it was the middle of the afternoon. Yet Morihan reeked of alcohol.

"Don't worry," Morihan said.

But Maher was more worried than before. *This drunk is my lawyer?*

On February 1, after spending a month at the Adolescent Remand Shelter on Rikers Island, Maher appeared in court for his arraignment, and Morihan was ready to plead his case for reduced bail. Youthful offender. No previous record. Morihan was confident that it would merely be a formality.

The court officer called Maher's case. Morihan and Maher stood. So did an assistant district attorney.

"Second call!" the ADA shouted toward the bench.

"What does that mean?" Maher whispered to Morihan.

"They want to postpone the hearing until the second roll call," Morihan answered.

"Why?" Maher asked. His gut told him whatever the reason, it couldn't be good.

Morihan shrugged.

"Your Honor," the ADA explained, "Burton Roberts has taken a special interest in this case and is on his way."

Morihan began to sweat, and his face flushed. Burton Roberts was the Bronx district attorney, and Morihan knew that as district attorneys went, Roberts was a judicial pit bull. *Why was Burton Roberts personally prosecuting a car thief?*

During second call, the double doors in the back of the courtroom burst open, and Burton Roberts—a small man with a full head of bright red hair—made a grand, theatrical entrance. A stack of folders was cradled in one arm, and he held what looked like a ream of paper in his hand.

"Your Honor," Roberts began, "Kevin Maher is a threat to himself and to society."

Maher shrunk into his seat, looking considerably younger than his seventeen years. The judge peered down at him. *Threat to society?*

Roberts shook his head and glanced at Maher for a moment. Then Roberts took a step toward the bench and stared intently at the judge.

"I couldn't keep my head on the pillow knowing Kevin Maher was on the street," Roberts insisted. He held up a ream of computer printouts. "Maher has stolen a number of cars, Your Honor, has dozens of unanswered traffic summonses, and has been linked to numerous bank robberies."

Maher jolted. *Bank robberies? How could they know about the bank robberies? They never caught me.*

Roberts's voice built to a crescendo. He recounted the car chase to the Catskills, pointing out that three State Police cars and one Highway Patrol car sustained $28,000 in damage. Roberts concluded with a flourish.

"The charges against Kevin Maher are hereby modified," he said as he placed a document in front of the judge. "The grand jury has returned an indictment charging Mr. Maher with six counts of attempted *murder* of a police officer."

Morihan finally reacted. "Objection!"

The judge called for a "sidebar," a private conference at the bench, and Maher watched as Morihan, Roberts, and the judge discussed his fate. After a few minutes, Morihan returned to his seat.

"What?" Maher pleaded. "What?"

Before Morihan could answer, the judge struck his gavel.

"Bail is revoked," the judge bellowed, "and defendant is remanded to Bellevue Hospital for thirty days' MO."

"Does that mean I get out?" Maher asked. All Maher had heard was the word "hospital." And he didn't know that "MO" stood for "mental observation." "Does that mean I have to go to a hospital for a month?"

Morihan didn't have time to answer. A bailiff quickly placed a *second* pair of handcuffs on Maher—the standard treatment for mental cases—and led him from the courtroom.

Chapter 2

BELLEVUE WAS A HORRENDOUS EXPERIENCE, ESPECIALLY THE FIRST week. Maher found himself in a cramped prison ward that was a honeycomb of small steel cells. Adding to the ambience was the fact that the entire ward smelled of urine. The stench was almost unbearable, and Maher spent much of his first hours there retching. His wardmates included an assortment of mentally disturbed patients. Muttering paranoids. Dead-eyed catatonics. Even a few homicidal manic types who ranted and raved as if they were possessed by demons. And then there was Johnson.

Johnson, it seemed, refused to sleep on his bed—a steel frame with a thin mattress—preferring to curl up on the floor underneath. When the nurse would make her late-night rounds with medication, she would stop at Maher's cell first. After she had handed Maher his pills, she would walk to the front of Johnson's cell.

"Johnson!" she would scream as loud as she could. "Medication!"

Johnson would wake with a start and raise up, cracking his head on the bottom of the bed frame. As Johnson crawled across the cell in obvious pain, the nurse would say, "Mr. Johnson, don't you think it would be better if you slept on *top* of your bed?"

A week after Maher arrived he was moved to the sixth floor, a setting more like a dormitory. For the next three weeks he

18

underwent all manner of tests and attended group therapy sessions. Finally it was determined that Maher was not insane, and he was returned to Rikers Island. This time Maher wasn't placed in the Adolescent Remand Shelter; he was tossed into Cell Block 2 amid the "general population."

Meanwhile, Morihan tried to console Maher's parents. Yet when Agnes asked how her teenage son could receive treatment usually reserved for monsters who had butchered their families or sociopathic career criminals, Morihan had no plausible explanation.

"I've never seen anything like it," Morihan admitted. "It's just a stolen car. And he's a minor, for God's sake!"

Maher's father was beside himself. He had heard about what happens in prison, the beatings, the rapes. And now his son was on Rikers Island. It was the worst nightmare a father could endure.

But Edward Maher need not have worried about his son. A couple of days after arriving at Rikers, Maher was approached by an inmate who was in for armed robbery.

"I want you to be my sweet boy," the man said. "I'll buy you things from the commissary and look out for you."

When Maher tried to ignore him, his prospective suitor became enraged. "Hey, you don't give it to me, I'll beat your fuckin' brains in and take that pussy!"

Maher walked over to the man and smiled. The man smiled back. Then Maher leaned in slightly, crouched a little, and bawled up his fist.

"Oh, yeah?" Maher said.

"Yeah," the man responded with a snarl.

Maher brought his fist up with all the force he could muster, landing a solid punch under the man's chin. The man staggered back and Maher set upon him like a wild animal, biting him on the face. It took four guards to peel Maher off. When it was over, the man was a bloody mess, and Maher—due to the bites he had so savagely inflicted—had acquired a prison nickname: "Dirty Red." From then on, nobody messed with the "crazy white boy."

Two mysteries were answered early in March as Maher settled in to prison life at Rikers: (1) how Maher came to be implicated in the bank robberies and (2) why Burton Roberts prosecuted Maher so zealously.

At first Maher had thought the Braccini brothers had given him up. But then a detective from Burton Roberts's office stopped by Rikers to see Maher.

"Who was with you on the Cross Bay bank jobs?" the detective asked.

Obviously the cops had *not* identified the Braccini brothers. And Maher refused to name them.

Day after day detectives would come to Rikers and badger Maher for hours. When the badgering didn't work, they would resort to offering a deal.

"Give us the Cross Bay bank robbers," they would say, "and we'll get you out of here."

It became increasingly clear that Bronx DA Burton Roberts had little interest in locking up a car thief; rather, he had been after the Cross Bay robbers all along.

As the interrogations continued, Maher was told he had been identified by a bank employee. It made sense. After all, Maher hung around Cross Bay Boulevard all the time, and everybody knew that baby face of his. Yet, when Maher asked when and where he was identified, the interrogators were vague. It occurred to Maher that he had not been *positively* identified by the employee. Otherwise the DA would have charged him with armed robbery.

More damning than the uncertain testimony of a bank employee was Maher's own propensity to boast about his exploits.

"Sources tell us you were bragging about the jobs," a detective told Maher one day.

Maher grimaced. He *had* told people about his daring getaways. *If the cops know I did the bank jobs, it's my own fucking fault.*

Various detectives filed in and out of Rikers to see Maher, each new face expressing optimism that *he* would be the one to get Maher to break down and name the Cross Bay gang. But Maher became inured to the drama after a few days. The characters were always the same: the "bad cop," the "good cop," and the prisoner. Maher had come to know the script so well that he sometimes played along as if he were an actor in an old prison movie.

BAD COP

Look, you little rat bastard, you give me the
fucking Cross Bay gang or I'll make sure you *never*
get the fuck out of here.

GOOD COP

(stepping in front of the bad cop)
Hold on. Hold on. He's just a kid. Why don't
you let me talk to him.
(turning to Maher; in a soothing voice)
You don't belong here, Kevin. You belong at home
with your parents.

MAHER

I *would* like to be home.

GOOD COP

Then let me help you.
(off Maher's hopeful expression)
All you have to do is give me the names of your
accomplices and we can work a deal.

After a long beat.

MAHER

Fuck you! I don't know nothin' about no Cross
Bay bank robberies.

No matter how hard the detectives pressed him or how much
his parents begged him or how dire Morihan painted the consequences, Maher refused to snitch on the Braccinis. *No way I'm
giving up Joey Braccini. Joey is my friend.*

As the daily interrogations continued, Maher was struck with
the thought that cops often were reduced to being little more
than information brokers, bartering small crimes for big crimes,
constantly negotiating deals. And district attorneys would do
almost anything to get an edge in that negotiation, even if it
meant sentencing a minor to four years in prison for a car theft.
Maher wasn't sure what he would do with that little pearl of
wisdom, but it stuck in his mind like a grain of sand in an
oyster.

*   *   *

DURING MAHER'S FIRST MONTH AT RIKERS—A HUGE INSTITUTION WITH eight thousand inmates—Maher's mother visited him. She had to go through several checkpoints, got frisked more than once, waited three hours, and finally got a thirty-minute visit in a small booth with thick glass separating her and her son.

"Ma," Maher said toward the end of the half hour, "I don't want you to come here anymore."

Agnes was insistent. "I miss you, Kevin. I worry about you."

But Maher didn't want his mother being hand-searched by male correction officers.

"I mean it," Maher asserted. "I won't see you if you come here again."

Agnes did come again and, as he had warned her, he refused to receive her.

Maher afforded the same treatment to his father and his sister, Susan. Edward Maher came once and from then on his son would not receive him. Nor would he allow Susan to enter the gates of Rikers. Maher just didn't want his family to go through the agony of the visit.

After the horror of seeing their son at Rikers, both Agnes and Edward pushed Morihan for some kind of resolution.

"Why doesn't my son have bail?" Edward Maher wailed. "Every day, I see murderers getting out."

"It's because he's still under an MO order," Morihan explained. "But I'll see what I can do. I'll try."

Morihan frequently contacted Burton Roberts's office and was always rebuffed. It soon became obvious that the Bronx DA's office had a plan: Keep Maher locked up until he gave up the Cross Bay bank gang. March turned to April, and April turned to May. June. July. August. September. Maher remained entrenched, and the DA's office continued to file motions and postponements. In fact, Morihan cracked before Maher. He was arrested for selling forged green cards to illegal aliens. Consequently, another lawyer was hired by Maher's father: Nathan Gottosman. Gottosman made a determination: "The only way out of this is to plead it down."

The deal was simple: In place of the myriad charges against him, Maher would plead guilty to a single count of reckless endangerment in the first degree, which was a "D" felony carrying a maximum sentence of seven years.

Maher balked. "Seven years?"

Gottosman soothed him. "Don't worry. I can tell you right now, if anybody deserves probation, it's you. No record. Youthful offender. And you've already served fourteen months. You should get time served or probation."

"Okay," Maher said with a sigh. "I'll do it."

JUDGE GEORGE STARK HAD A REPUTATION FOR BEING TOUGH, AND STORIES about him abounded. The tales may have been apocryphal, but they frightened criminals nonetheless. One anecdote went like this: Judge Stark peered at a defendant and asked him how many buttons he had. When the defendant looked down at his shirt and answered "six," Judge Stark pronounced sentence: "Six years!" Another story had Judge Stark pointing out a window and asking a defendant what he thought of the tree. When the defendant told the judge that there was no tree outside the window, the judge responded by saying, "That's right. There is no tree. But by the time you get out of jail, there will be."

While Gottosman was not pleased with the fact that Judge Stark would be passing sentence, he had a more personal reason to be unhappy. The protracted maneuvers by the Bronx DA's office had caused Gottosman to spend a great deal of billable time on the case, resulting in a fee that outstripped Edward Maher's ability to pay. Gottosman had not received a check in some time.

"I want to withdraw," Gottosman told Judge Stark, "because I haven't gotten paid."

"You are the attorney of record," Judge Stark declared, "and you may not withdraw. If you have a problem, you can take it up in civil court at a later time." Judge Stark stared at Gottosman. "So, counselor, do you have anything to say before I pass sentence?"

Gottosman stood and collected his thoughts. Finally, he drew in his breath and spoke. "He's a good kid, Your Honor, he served in the Marine Corps. He's good with his hands. He knows how to work on cars."

Maher almost fell off the court bench. *Knows how to work on cars? Is this fuckin' idiot crazy?*

Judge Stark wasted no time in reading the sentence: "Kevin

Maher, you are to serve an indeterminate sentence of not less than one day nor more than four years." He banged his gavel, and a bailiff started to lead Maher away.

"Four years?" Maher gasped. "I can't do *four years*."

Judge Stark waved at the bailiff to stop. He looked at Maher. "You can't? Okay. Do what you can. And then all the rest." Judge Stark waved his hand again, this time in a dismissive manner, and Maher was led out of the courtroom amid the hysterical cries of his mother.

A SHORT TIME AFTER SENTENCING, MAHER WAS PICKED UP AT RIKERS Island by three corrections officers who would transfer him to Elmira Prison in upstate New York. They loaded Maher into the third seat of a 1968 Plymouth station wagon, then headed to the Bronx House of Detention to sign out two additional prisoners scheduled for transfer.

On the way to the Bronx, Maher chattered and joked with the officers. Among other things, he told them he had a cousin named Eddie Lacey, who was a corrections officer.

"Yeah," one of the officers reacted in recognition. "I know Eddie."

Maher told them about his car chase and subsequent four-year sentence. The officers were sympathetic.

"You don't belong in prison," one of them said.

"You steal three cars and get four years?" another chimed in, shaking his head in disbelief. "Kid, you'll be out in six months."

The Bronx prisoners, who were black, appeared to have nasty dispositions, so one of the officers pulled Maher from the back of the station wagon.

"Come on up with me, kid," the officer said. "You'll be more comfortable."

About an hour and a half into the trip, the station wagon started to shimmy, and the driver pulled to the side of the road.

One of the officers nodded toward Maher. "This kid knows about cars. Let him fix it."

Maher stepped outside and started to crawl under the car.

"Hold it," an officer shouted.

Maher turned around. The officer had a handcuff key. "Let me take those cuffs off."

By then everyone—the three officers and the two other prisoners—had gotten out of the station wagon. Maher glanced at the ignition and saw that the key had been removed. *If that key was in there*, Maher thought. But it wasn't, so Maher knelt down and stuck his head under the car.

"Here's your problem. You've got a bubble in the left rear tire. It's got to be changed."

An officer knelt down to take a look, his gun suddenly positioned right in Maher's face. *I could take the gun*, Maher thought. But he didn't.

Maher changed the tire, and in a few minutes the station wagon was back on the road.

In Ithaca, which was thirty miles from Elmira, they stopped for gas.

"I have to go to the bathroom," Maher said.

"I do, too," one of the officers said.

Maher started to get out of the car.

The officer stopped him. "Sit back down." He unlocked Maher's cuffs.

Maher and the officer walked toward the bathroom. Once inside, the officer went to a urinal and Maher went into a stall. The stall had an *open* window.

Maher sat on the toilet and waited until he heard the flush of the urinal.

"Okay," the officer yelled, "I'll wait for you outside in the car."

The moment Maher heard the bathroom door shut, he dove out the window, landing in a thicket of rose bushes. Bloody but free, Maher sprinted away.

The officers became concerned when Maher hadn't emerged after five full minutes, so they ran to check the bathroom. Maher was gone.

Cruising the area in the station wagon, the officers spotted Maher running down a side street. One of the officers jumped from the station wagon and fired off three shots. The first splatted into the brick wall. The second whizzed by Maher's head, sucking air away from his ear. The third also missed, but Maher pretended to be hit. As Maher knew it would, it caused the officer to stop firing and put his gun away. Maher took off again, disappearing around a building. As he ran, he lost a shoe.

A car, Maher thought, *I need a car.* Maher scanned the ground for a piece of metal, anything he might use to pop an ignition. But Ithaca wasn't like the Bronx. The streets were spotless.

Within minutes, a cacophony of sirens shattered the quiet night, and helicopters filled the sky. Even the media were alerted. Suddenly the town of Ithaca was buzzing. Cops. Fire trucks. Reporters. All hunting for a redheaded teenager.

Maher's escape attempt finally ended in the concrete stairwell of a record store. When the officers found him huddled against a locked steel door at the bottom of the steps, they began beating him unmercifully.

"I talked to you like a brother," one of them said as he kicked Maher in the face.

"You fucking scumbag," another said as he slammed his fist into Maher's stomach.

"You little bastard," the third officer screamed as he punched Maher in the face. "We've got seventy-six years of service among the three of us."

As the officers were pounding Maher, an Ithaca cop arrived and pulled them off.

"I don't know how you guys do it in New York City," the cop said, "but this is Ithaca."

When the television cameras arrived, the bloody and bruised Maher grabbed the Ithaca cop. "Please! Take me with you! They're going to kill me!"

The Ithaca cop explained that he couldn't do anything. "You're the property of the state," he said.

The corrections officers handcuffed and shackled Maher, then threw him face down into the back of the station wagon.

"We've got thirty miles to go," an officer said. "You try anything else and I'll blow your brains out."

A few miles outside of Ithaca, Maher looked out the back window and saw an Ithaca cop car following at a discreet distance. It made Maher feel better. At least he would make it to prison alive.

ELMIRA STATE PRISON WAS NOT ALWAYS A FINAL DESTINATION. TWO cellblocks were designated as Elmira Reception Center, a place where prisoners were evaluated to determine which type of institution would best serve them. In July 1973 it was resolved that Maher should serve his sentence at Coxsackie Correctional Facility, a medium-security institution near Albany.

At this point, Maher had served a month at the Rikers Island Adolescent Remand Center, a month in Bellevue, fourteen months in the Rikers main prison, and two months at Elmira, a total of eighteen months. Since New York State only required prisoners to serve eight months out of each year—four months off for "good time"—Maher's four-year sentence translated to thirty-two months. He was more than halfway home when he arrived at Coxsackie.

The conditions at Coxsackie made serving time there relatively easy. It was clean. There was a television room, a gym, and good food. A month after arriving there, Maher was chosen for a program called DVR—Division of Vocational Rehabilitation —and was given a job as a clerk at the prison hospital. The job was a hard one to get, although there were only two requirements: (1) that the inmate have no prior record of drug abuse, and (2) that the inmate be white, because the nurses were white and they were afraid of black prisoners. The color specification was not official.

When he wasn't working in the hospital, Maher exercised in the gym and played cards with the other inmates. Except for the bars and barbed wire, it was almost a normal life. In fact, the most difficult aspects of his incarceration was his internal rage about being given such a harsh sentence and his constant worry about how his father was taking the fact that his son was locked up. Maher realized he had let his father down. And it gnawed at him. It was understandable then, that in May 1974, Maher fell apart when he called his father and his father said:

"I'm going in the hospital, Kevin. I need to have a heart operation."

Edward Maher explained that he had a faulty heart valve and doctors were going to remedy the situation by implanting a recently developed mechanical micro valve.

Maher hung up and ran to see Father Dirken, the prison chaplain.

"I killed him," Maher said, sobbing. "I broke my father's heart."

Maher immediately applied for a furlough to be with his father, but he was told he was ineligible because of the escape attempt. Upon hearing that, Maher grew despondent, even suicidal. So Father Dirken interceded and approached Coxsackie's warden, Harry Fritz.

"Harry," Father Dirken said, "I think we have to find a way that this boy can see his father before the operation." Dirken had called Lenox Hill Hospital in New York and verified the serious nature of Edward Maher's condition.

"Bring him into my office," Fritz responded.

Maher met with Dirken and Fritz.

"I can't grant you a furlough," Fritz said. "But I'll tell you what I can do. I can take you off the count."

Taking a prisoner off the count was a dangerous thing for a warden. Essentially, it meant looking the other way while a prisoner took an unauthorized leave.

Fritz pointed at the name on his door. "Kevin, if you don't come back, that name won't be on the door anymore. My career will be over."

Maher broke down and cried like a baby. "I'll come back, Mr. Fritz. I *swear* I'll come back."

MAHER WAS SHOCKED BY HIS FATHER'S APPEARANCE. THE STRONG, VITAL man he had left behind was now weak, almost fragile. In fact, the operation had been postponed because Edward Maher's blood count was too low.

"I love you, Kevin," Edward Maher told his son. "No matter what you did, you're still my boy."

After three days, during which they were closer than they had ever been, Edward Maher drove Kevin to the bus station.

"Please," Edward said as he hugged Kevin tightly. "Please go back."

"I will, Dad. Don't worry. I will."

And he did. Maher returned to Coxsackie to finish the last three months of his sentence, three months that were far more difficult for Maher to serve than all the previous time he had spent behind bars. Besides dealing with his father's illness, Maher's mother—*the woman who had left his father for a drunken bum*—married for a third time.

Every day Maher called to see if the operation had been rescheduled. Finally Maher was informed that the procedure would take place August 9, 1974, which also happened to be the same day Maher was to be released from Coxsackie.

On the morning of August 9, Maher walked out of Coxsackie and boarded a Greyhound bus for New York. The entire trip, he rocked back and forth, holding his stomach.

At 3:00 P.M., Maher ran into Lenox Hill Hospital and jogged to the cardiac ward.

"I want to check"—Maher was out of breath—"on the condition of Edward Maher."

The nurse looked at Maher and then quickly looked away. Edward Maher was dead.

MAHER MOVED INTO HIS FATHER'S APARTMENT AT 1609 AQUEDUCT Avenue. The grief was overwhelming, the guilt suffocating. Maher had planned to make it all up to his father, spend more time with him, look after him. He was going to be a good son for a change. Stay out of trouble. Hold a job. Maher wanted desperately to make his father proud. But now it was too late.

After nearly three years behind bars, Maher realized that the adjustment to life on the outside would be difficult, but he hadn't expected that even the most ordinary things would seem strange. The front door of his apartment closing with a thud instead of a clank. Eating whenever he was hungry. And children. The first time he saw a group of children, they appeared to be surreal little beings. Munchkins from *The Wizard of Oz*.

A week after he was released, Maher began working as a bartender at a Blarney Stone in Manhattan, located on 59th Street between Second and Third avenues. It was a job his father had arranged nearly a year ago.

"I want you to have a place to work when you get out," Edward Maher had told his son during one of their weekly phone calls.

After three days on the job, Maher had his first meeting with his parole officer, Jerry Israel, and dutifully reported that he was employed. Israel was upset.

"You can't work in an establishment that serves alcohol," Israel almost shouted. "Didn't you know that?"

Maher shook his head.

"I could report you for a parole violation!" Israel grumbled.

Maher quit his job at the Blarney Stone and tried to find other employment. Of course, nobody would hire an ex-con. This left Maher with no money and no legitimate way to make money. The "system" had done it again. So when one of Maher's friends, a man named Brian O'Neal, suggested a way to make a quick buck, Maher went along with the plan.

"It's easy," O'Neal said. "You go over to one of these places where they have the opera and shit like that. And you go up to one of these old ladies wearing a mink and rip the fuckin' coat right off her back."

O'Neal added that he had a fence who bought the coats.

Maher and O'Neal decided upon Lincoln Center. Naturally, Maher was the "wheel man."

A few minutes after they parked in the Lincoln Center service road, O'Neal spotted a mark. He jumped from the car, ran to an old woman, and hit her so hard she actually lifted off the sidewalk. He then bent over her crumpled body and tore off her mink.

"What the fuck did you hit her for?" Maher screamed as O'Neal climbed into the car.

"She was a Jew," O'Neal sneered. "Jews don't give it up so easy."

Maher punched O'Neal in the face. "You motherfucker!"

What the hell am I doing? Maher wondered. *Mugging old ladies?* Maher was disgusted with himself. And then, as he jammed his foot onto the accelerator and sent the car speeding up Broadway, it occurred to him that there was one thing he was very good at: stealing cars.

After stealing and selling several cars, Maher was pulled over for speeding in a stolen 1974 Plymouth. The familiar scenario then played out: Whitestone Impound Lot. A search for true VIN number. And then a charge of grand theft auto. By now, however, Maher had accumulated quite a stash and bailed himself out.

Jerry Israel, his parole officer, was not pleased. But Israel could do nothing because of a New York State law that did not allow him to file a parole violation upon an *arrest*, only after a *conviction*.

Maher was caught a second time. And a third. Still there was nothing the parole board could do. But then Maher helped a few friends break into a speed shop and was charged with burglary, a much more serious crime. This time he couldn't make bail—which was set at three thousand, five hundred *cash*—and he was incarcerated at the Bronx House of Detention. Within three months of his release from Coxsackie, Maher was back behind bars.

After spending Christmas at the Bronx House of Detention, Maher was warehoused for a while at Sing Sing, then was shuttled to the Queens House of Detention to await a parole hearing, which was scheduled at Green Haven State Prison. The vicious circle that had begun one winter night on the Bronx River Parkway was now complete. Kevin Maher had become a repeat offender, an incorrigible felon. Except for a month or two here and there, he would probably spend the rest of his life languishing away in one penal institution or another.

Chapter 3

JUST AS NATURE ENDOWS CERTAIN SPECIES OF POISONOUS SNAKES WITH bright colors, some inmates bear colorful nicknames, monikers such as "The Greek" or "Hammerhead" or "The Weasel." But the most feared resident of the New York penal system had no such label. He was known simply as Mr. Weiss. Morris Weiss. A charter member of Murder, Inc., the infamous 1940s crime organization.

Murder, Inc., got its name from its detached, almost corporate approach to contract killings. Essentially, a "retainer" was paid and a hit man from, say, Chicago would fly into New York, make the hit, and then fly back to Chicago. Since the killer had absolutely no connection to the victim except an untraceable monetary one, the murders were virtually impossible to solve. But Murder, Inc., was visited upon by its own form of justice: Most of the membership was terminated by other segments of the membership. Not Morris Weiss. Morris Weiss was considered untouchable. And if it weren't for the same catchall charge that got Al Capone—tax evasion—and if it weren't for the turncoats who panicked and took the state's evidence route, Weiss most likely would still be trading in death. As it stood, he was serving a life sentence.

Despite his advanced years, the Mafia moneyman was intimidating. Although his body had grown frail from age and his skin had waxed pasty white from lack of sunlight, his power had grown stronger and more far reaching, even from the confines of a prison cell. Nobody fucked with Morris Weiss. *Nobody.*

In early 1975, the NYPD was able to link Weiss to a decade-old unsolved murder. To facilitate his availability for court appearances in New York City, Weiss was temporarily transferred from an upstate maximum security facility to the Queens House of Detention.

Although Weiss kept a distance from the prison population at the QHD, he took a liking to Maher. And likewise, Maher found Weiss a good ally to have in a place like the Queens House of Detention. They were an odd pair indeed but they got along famously, neither asking much of the other. In fact, their friendship consisted of but one exchange of favors. Weiss, who always seemed to have wads of cash, would buy whatever Maher wanted from the commissary. Food. Clothing. A television. Whatever. And Maher, who knew plenty of girls, would invite a pretty one over to the QHD once in a while and arrange for her to be alone in the visiting room with Weiss. Weiss never touched the girls, he just had them strip and dance in front of him while he masturbated. Then he'd hand the girl a hundred-dollar bill and shuffle back to his cell.

In May 1975, Maher was informed that two detectives from the Manhattan district attorney's office wanted to see him. Maher shrugged his approval and was led to a holding area to wait for yet another detective duo, bracing himself for the inevitable tag team as each of the cops took turns hammering at him for information regarding past crimes, specifically the Cross Bay bank robberies. But Maher was no rat. Hadn't the cops learned at least that after five years?

As Maher waited in the small room, *The Hustle* by Van McCoy echoed in the cell block. The perky melody of the disco anthem irritated the hell out of Maher. Stealing cars was a hustle. Prison was a hustle. His whole life had been just one big hustle. And it sure as hell didn't feel like violins.

The door swung open. Detective Sergeant Jim Doherty and Detective Josh Wainright walked in. Maher had met Wainright a couple of weeks before. The six-foot, four-inch detective, who was black, had interviewed Maher while investigating a robbery on Manhattan's Upper East Side. Although the suspect was someone with whom Maher was acquainted, Maher was unable to tell Wainright anything about the robbery, and nothing ever came of the investigation. However, Wainright felt Maher might have some other useful information, and, with a long prison term looming ahead of him, might be willing to make some kind of deal. To that end, Wainright brought his sergeant along this time. Maher certainly was in a vulnerable position. And Sergeant Jim Doherty had the power to initiate deals with the district attorney.

Doherty had a benevolent, almost fatherly demeanor, an Irish smile in his clear blue eyes. His ruffled red hair, now specked with gray, added to the illusion that an overgrown leprechaun had arrived. Indeed, Doherty exhibited none of the oozing cynicism Maher had come to expect from a seemingly endless parade of jaded investigators. To Maher, that meant one thing: Here was a soft touch. *Maybe*, Maher's instincts told him, *I can get something out of this guy. Maybe I've finally found the end of the rainbow.*

Born in New York City in 1931, Doherty enlisted in the Marine Corps at age twenty and fought with the 1st Marine Air Wing K-6 during the Korean War. Upon discharge, he went to work for Merrill, Lynch as a "troubleshooter" who investigated problem accounts and then, in 1956, became a cop. After a year in Harlem's 25th Precinct, he was assigned to an elite group of traffic cops chosen to work in unmarked cars at accident-prone locations. Doherty saw the assignment as an opportunity. Knowing that no one paid much attention to traffic cops, he kept his eyes and ears open. As a result, he issued more than traffic tickets: He quietly tracked down four car thieves and an armed robber.

When he heard of an opening for a detective in the Central Investigation Bureau—an instant shield—he applied. However, there were forty other applicants. And, of course, only one job. But then Doherty learned of a clerical position at the bureau, a desk job no one wanted.

"I can type," Doherty announced. "I'll take that job."

Doherty didn't think of it as becoming a clerk, rather as an opportunity, reasoning that once inside the bureau, anything could happen.

In March 1958 Doherty met an auburn-haired beauty named Elizabeth Riley. They were married in May 1959.

Although deskbound in his job at CIB, Doherty carefully observed everything and everyone around him. In 1964, after six years as a clerk, he started accompanying a lieutenant on investigations. Two years later Doherty was promoted to detective. In 1969 he made detective second grade and then, in 1972, detective sergeant. As a result of his rise, Doherty was often asked: "How the hell did you do it?" In response, he always smiled and said: "I can type."

(Doherty could also father children. He and Elizabeth now had *six* kids: Pat, Pam, Betsy, Gerri, Jimmy, and John.)

In 1973 Doherty was tapped by Deputy Inspector Joe Comperiati as one of six investigators in the theft of the French Connection heroin. (The other investigators were Jack Vobis, William Grimes, Tom McCabe, Ed Killeen, and Harry Fagan.)

The French Connection heroin—a hundred pounds of dope packed into a suitcase—had been stored at the property clerk's office since 1969. At the end of 1972, someone opened the suitcase to find roaches devouring the stuff. Yet the little bugs were still alive. A test revealed that the white powder was not heroin, it was flour.

No one was certain precisely when the switch occurred, but it was clear *how* it might have been carried out. And it sounded like a Keystone comedy.

Following the media hoopla surrounding the French Connection bust, the feds wanted to show off what was then the largest cache of illegal drugs ever seized. Accommodating Washington, New York cops escorted the contraband to Capitol Hill, where it was carted from one location to another, like a circus sideshow. When the bloom of publicity began to fade—and thus the political benefit of displaying the heroin—the feds decided to give the suitcase back to the NYPD. They didn't deliver it, however; they *shipped* it. Railway Express. Along the route, someone could have penetrated the "formidable" security of Amtrak and exchanged crushed wheat for crushed poppies on the train. But evidence seemed to indicate that the suitcase had made it back to the property clerk's office intact, so Comperiati, Doherty, and the team of investigators zeroed in on what they considered to be a more likely scenario.

Since the property clerk's office was not a desirable assignment, the station was manned by cops who were designated as "light-duty police officers," predominantly those who had lost their right to carry a gun due to mental instability or alcoholism.

Detectives had two nicknames for them: "The Rubber Gun Gang" and "The Bow and Arrow Squad." If the heroin had been taken from the property clerk's office, these misfits had to have been involved, either inadvertently or conspiratorially.

The subsequent investigation not only uncovered gross incompetence by property clerk officers but also netted a number of indictments, including corrupt narcotics cops and organized crime figures. Case closed, the French Connection saga dissolved into a historic footnote, and Doherty was transferred to the office of Robert Morgenthau, Manhattan district attorney.

And so it was that Doherty found his way to the Queens House of Detention on this day to meet a potential source of information named Kevin Maher. Most cops wouldn't have bothered. But Doherty always bothered. If he got a good lead on some difficult case, great. If not, he would only be wasting a few minutes. So when Wainright had told Doherty about "this kid over in the QHD who may have driven the getaway car in a series of bank robberies," Doherty shrugged and said: "Let's go talk to him."

Doherty looked Maher over. This couldn't be the notorious South Bronx wheel man he had heard about, the Billy the Kid of grand theft auto. Hell, the inmate sitting there was just a freckled-faced Irish boy with a smile that could melt a nun's heart.

"You Kevin Maher?" Doherty asked.

"Yeah. I'm Kevin Maher."

Maher and Doherty studied each other like two chess players sitting across a board, one used to playing the white pieces, the other always playing black.

"You gotta get me outta here," Maher said in his best "little boy lost" voice.

"Sure, Kevin, I'll get you out of here," Doherty responded with conviction. "But you've got to give me something first."

Two pawns thrust forward, and now it was Maher's move again. Maher eyed Doherty for a moment, then looked at Wainright. Wainright smiled and stepped back, signaling that this was Doherty's game. So Maher turned and stared at Doherty.

"Like what?" Maher asked.

"Like what have you got?" Doherty countered.

Maher frowned. "I don't know nothin' about the Cross Bay bank robberies."

"I didn't ask you about any bank robberies," Doherty said quietly. "And I'm not going to. The Cross Bay bank robberies are four years old and the case is as cold as a block of ice."

Maher racked his brain. What *could* he give Doherty? Maher realized he better come up with *something* because he was a two-time loser and, considering the fact that he had been charged with burglary and grand theft auto, he had *really* screwed himself to the cell block wall this time. Suddenly it struck him. *The rug guy. Nobody likes him anyway, always whining about how cold it was on the cell block. I'll give up the rug guy. And Doherty will think he's got the bust of the century.*

Maher looked directly into Doherty's eyes. Doherty stared back with equal intensity. Finally Maher spoke: "How about a rug?"

Doherty rolled the concept over in his mind for a moment.

"A rug? What kind of rug?"

"Persian. Supposed to be worth seventy-five hundred dollars."

The corrections officer standing nearby was surprised. He had seen a hundred cops try to pull information out of Maher with no success. Now this guy Doherty waltzes in and gets something right away, even if it was just a rug.

"Okay," Doherty said after an appropriate pause. "Let's talk about this rug."

Actually, there were many levels of interplay between Maher and Doherty, and none of them had anything to do with a rug. On Maher's part, he still believed he had found an easy mark and could parlay almost any crumb of information into some kind of concession. On Doherty's part, he felt that the baby-faced Maher just didn't belong in jail, and if the conversation yielded anything, *anything* at all he could use, then he would see what he could do for the kid. But underlying that noble thought, there was a motive. Doherty was a methodical investigator who was used to building cases one piece at a time, and he speculated that Maher's jailhouse contacts might reap a bumper crop of leads on unsolved crimes. The trick was to lure Maher into the game.

Beyond the objectives, however, there was the immediate

bond between the two, a spontaneous connection that transcended logical explanation. Something they saw in each other fit together. The underdog and the hero, happening upon each other in a concrete room.

"A guy asked me if I knew a rug dealer," Maher told Doherty. "Said he wants to sell this Oriental carpet."

"Maybe he owns it," Doherty said matter-of-factly.

"No," Maher insisted, jumping from his chair. "He stole it from Sloane's furniture store. And he's been hiding it in the Bronx."

Doherty sat silently for a long moment as Maher squirmed.

"And what do you want for this rug?" Doherty asked.

"I want to get out of here until my trial. I want my bail reduced."

Doherty looked away for a beat then stared back at Maher. "What are you in for?"

"Auto theft. Three counts."

That was no problem. In New York, everybody walks on stolen car raps.

"And then I've got one count of burglary."

Now, *that* was a problem. Not only did the courts look at burglary as a serious felony, Maher already was a convicted felon, which exacerbated the situation because of a statute called the Rockefeller Law. Simply put, the Rockefeller Law— also known as the Predicate Felony Offender Law—stated that anyone who had been convicted of a felony during the previous ten years *must* serve half the maximum jail time on any new felony conviction. In Maher's case that would be one and a half years of a three-year sentence for burglary. Doherty knew that the only way to get around that provision was to plead the charge down to a misdemeanor. But this was no simple task. Once a suspect had been indicted, as Maher had been, the law *prohibited* any plea arrangement that reduced a felony to a misdemeanor.

Doherty was suddenly troubled. Maybe he was wrong about Maher. Maybe Maher was just a punk after all. Snatching hot rods was one thing, but burglary?

"It was an auto supply house," Maher elaborated. "I needed parts."

"Sure," Doherty said, "that explains it."

Maher smiled. Doherty appeared deep in thought.

"I'll see what I can do," Doherty said, knowing full well that the chances of extricating Maher from the mess were almost nonexistent. "All right, give me a name."

Maher hesitated. "There's something else."

Doherty rolled his eyes. *Something else? Weren't three counts grand theft and one count burglary enough?*

Maher explained to Doherty that he had served thirty-two months of a four-year sentence, the last sixteen months being suspended via good behavior. But now, after three more car thefts and a burglary, he had been notified by the parole board that, despite the absence of a conviction, they were deeming him in violation of the conditions of his release for "failure to lead a law-abiding life."

"I'm not surprised," Doherty said, laughing.

Maher laughed, too. "So I need you to go to the parole hearing with me and put in a good word."

Doherty stopped laughing. *All this for a rug?*

"Where?" Doherty wanted to know.

"Green Haven."

"Green Haven?! That's in Stormville! Four hours upstate!"

"Yeah," Maher acknowledged.

"When?"

Maher took a deep breath. "Friday."

"Which Friday?" Doherty was incredulous. "Not *this* Friday?"

Maher nodded.

"It's Memorial Day weekend," Doherty bellowed.

"I know," Maher said with a sigh, "but if my parole is revoked I'll have to go back and serve the sixteen months I owe them."

Maher sounded desperate, even pathetic, and Doherty felt queasy. As much as Doherty had wanted to lure Maher into *his* game, the opposite had occurred. Indeed, Doherty was suddenly fretting over Maher's well-being.

"Will you come with me, Sergeant Doherty?" Maher asked.

Doherty could, of course, turn and walk out of the room. But he saw too much of himself in Maher. The patter, the nervous energy, the smile, all reminded Doherty of his younger self.

"Okay, Kevin," Doherty said softly.

Maher broke into a broad grin. "Thanks, Sergeant Doherty. Thanks!"

Doherty didn't know whether to feel warm and fuzzy or like a complete sap. After all his years on the force, what was he doing in a Norman Rockwell painting?

Something suddenly occurred to Maher.

"Oh, yeah," Maher said, "I almost forgot. I have a few speeding tickets. Can you take care of them, too?"

Doherty held his hands to the sky. "Why not?"

"Thanks, Detective."

Doherty had to ask. "How many tickets we talking about?"

Maher stared away, thinking, then looked back at Doherty. "Seventy-one. I think."

Doherty couldn't help but smile. "Seventy-one?"

Maher nodded.

Doherty shook his head then stood to leave. Maher seemed surprised.

"Don't you want the name of the rug guy?" Maher asked.

Doherty frowned. *Rug? Jesus, that's right. This whole thing was about a goddamn rug!*

WHEN DOHERTY ARRIVED HOME THAT NIGHT HE TOLD HIS WIFE, ELIZA-beth, about Maher.

"What kind of guy is he?" Elizabeth asked.

Doherty regarded her silently for a moment. She generally didn't ask him about his workday. Then again, he rarely talked about the felons he encountered. But Maher was different.

"If you saw him," Doherty said of Maher, "you'd think he was one of your kids in home study."

Elizabeth taught a Confraternity class (Catholic religious studies) after school. She pictured her students for a moment.

"They're just young kids," Elizabeth noted.

"Exactly," Doherty sighed. "Kevin is just a kid. He doesn't belong in the QHD."

The following morning, Doherty set about fulfilling his promise to Maher. As always, Doherty looked at the problem in a series of incremental steps. First order of business was to get Maher to Green Haven for his parole hearing. Then he would work on reducing bail for the grand theft auto and burglary charges. Beyond that, he just didn't know.

Getting Maher to Green Haven was supposed to be the easy part, and—except for the snarling bureaucracy of the criminal justice system—it would have been a cinch. Unfortunately, the documents that were intended to effect Maher's transfer from the Queens House of Detention to Green Haven were written in such a way that they *precluded* such a transfer. Something about a phrase that said in part: ". . . to be returned whence he came." It was nothing more than semantics, a legal paradox created by an obscure reading of the law pertaining to relocation of prisoners. Nonetheless, if the paperwork could not be amended by the weekend, Maher could not be released from the QHD for his parole hearing in Stormville. Since the penalty for missing a parole hearing was automatic revocation, he would be turned over to the state to begin serving the balance of his previous sentence.

Doherty was outraged at the legal quagmire. And he grew more and more outraged as the hours ticked by and he was unable to find the "right" person to speak with regarding Maher's release forms. On the eve of the parole hearing, Doherty called the Queens House of Detention and asked for the warden. Not in. Doherty asked to speak to the assistant warden.

"You guys got about as much chance of gettin' him out of here," the assistant warden said, "as a snowball's chance in hell."

"You don't know us guys," Doherty said with a growl. "Give me the warden's home phone number."

Doherty reached the warden at home and presented his case.

"All right, Doherty," the warden said, "I'll call up there. You can take Maher out. No paperwork. But if he gets away, I don't want to know you."

Doherty laughed. "If I can't transport a kid to Green Haven and back, then I—"

"Watch yourself," the warden interrupted. "He's an escape risk."

A few minutes later, Maher called from Rikers.

"You escaped?" Doherty asked, his voice not overly warm.

"Yeah," Maher said. "But only *once*."

"Well, let me tell you something, Kevin. You try to escape on me and I'll blow the back of your head off. I've got more than twenty years in this job, and you're not going to jeopardize that."

Maher chuckled. Somehow he couldn't picture Doherty pulling the trigger.

"Don't worry, Sergeant Doherty," Maher assured him. "I won't try to escape."

Doherty next called Paul Renaldo, Maher's Legal Aid lawyer and was told that Renaldo had left for the weekend.

"What's his home number?" Doherty shouted into the receiver.

After several rings, Renaldo answered, sounding out of breath. Doherty recounted how he had arranged to get Maher out of the QHD for the day and asked Renaldo if he wanted a ride to Stormville the following day.

"I can't go to Stormville tomorrow," Renaldo countered. "In fact, I was just on my way out the door to the country. I'm getting a jump on the long weekend."

Doherty was not pleased. "Wait a minute! You have a client with a parole hearing."

"I understand that," Renaldo said, "but I was told that he wouldn't be released. So I made plans. I'm sorry."

"No," Doherty roared, *I'm sorry.* You *are* going to Stormville even if I have to hold a gun to your head."

The next morning, Doherty and Detective Josh Wainright arrived at the QHD to pick up Maher. Two corrections officers led Maher to the front gate in handcuffs.

"Here's your prisoner," one of the guards said as he unlocked the cuffs.

Maher stepped up to Doherty and held out his hands, waiting to be cuffed. Doherty just turned and started for the car.

"Aren't you going to cuff me?" Maher asked.

"Nah," Doherty said. "You ain't going anywhere."

Maher looked at Doherty and then at Wainright. Wainright was an imposing figure.

"That's right," Wainright chimed in. "You ain't going *any-where.*"

Doherty stopped and picked up Renaldo, then headed to Stormville. They arrived a half hour before the hearing and took a seat next to a long line of inmates who also were waiting for their chance to be heard. Both Doherty and Wainright, bleary-eyed from the early wake-up call, fit right in. Dressed in plainclothes, the two detectives were indistinguishable from the prisoners. A particularly psychotic-looking man fidgeted nearby, then leaned over to the man next to him.

"If I get denied," the man said with a growl, "I'm going to kill me a cop."

Doherty looked at Wainright. Neither of them wanted to grapple with this crazo. They stared straight ahead and listened to the man rant and rave, happy that he was unaware he was sitting next to two detectives. But then a corrections officer approached with a clipboard.

"Who are you?" the officer asked, alternately sizing up Doherty and Wainright.

Doherty leaned close to the officer. "We're cops," Doherty whispered.

"What?" the officer asked.

"We're the good guys," Doherty whispered more insistently.

The officer shrugged and looked down at the clipboard. "Maher! Kevin!"

Maher and Renaldo entered the hearing room. During the next fifteen minutes, Doherty must have glanced at his watch a hundred times.

"What the hell's taking so long?" he asked rhetorically.

Finally Maher emerged.

"They don't need to see you," Maher told Doherty.

Doherty slumped in his chair. After everything he had gone through, after driving four hours, it was all for naught.

But then Maher smiled broadly. "They upheld my parole."

Indeed, the mere presence of two high-level detectives from Morganthau's office had swayed the board.

"The luck of the Irish," Doherty said with a chuckle as he put his arm around Maher.

WHEN A PRISONER IS ABOUT TO LEAVE A PRISON, EVERYONE ON THE CELL block hears about it. So, on the night Maher returned to the Queens House of Detention from Green Haven, Morris Weiss summoned him to his cell.

"You're a good kid," Weiss said as he hugged Maher. "I'm going to miss you."

"Me, too," Maher said, returning Weiss's embrace.

"You think you can still send me a girl over here once in a while?"

Maher laughed. "Sure, Morris."

Weiss paced for a moment and then looked at Maher with a piercing gaze. "Kevin, I got a couple of jobs. You interested?"

Maher weighed the question for a moment. And then he recalled what Doherty had done, how Doherty had taken his side like a father. *Sergeant Doherty is a good man*, Maher thought. Suddenly, it was as if a curtain had been drawn. *Morris Weiss is nothing more than an old, weak, pitiful, evil man*. Maher wanted to retch.

"Sure, Morris." Maher said with a smile. "I'm interested."

Weiss paced again, then stopped.

"You know 'Fat Boy' Parlati?"

Maher thought for a minute. "Sure. I've heard of him."

"Needs a wheel man. Next week."

Maher beamed. "No one's better than me, Morris. If I told you that once, I told you that a hundred times."

Weiss rolled his eyes. "Another guy I know is lookin' for a wheel man," Weiss continued. "Guy named Joe Jeffries."

Maher looked at Weiss and thought: *Keep talkin', you fuckin', shriveled-up old bastard. Just keep talkin'*.

"And then I got this friend," Weiss continued. "Henry Bohle. Owns Flushing Car Service."

"What, he need a chauffeur?" Maher laughed at his own joke.

Weiss frowned. "He's got a partner. Louis Izzo. Lou's fuckin' up. So Henry don't want Louis as a partner no more."

Maher mulled over what Weiss was saying. "You want me to whack him?"

Weiss smiled.

"Hey," Maher said, growing animated, playing the part of a hit man, "I'll whack this guy. I'll *whack* this fuckin' guy."

As he watched Weiss shuffle to a chair and fall into it like a half-empty sack of flour, Maher had just one thought: *My friend Sergeant Doherty's gonna put you out of business, you old fuck*.

The following week, Doherty arranged for Maher's bail to be

reduced to one dollar per count, paid the four dollars, and bailed Maher out of the Queens House of Detention. But Maher wasn't free yet. He was handed over to state authorities for transport back to Green Haven, where he would stay until he met the ongoing conditions of his parole: a certified address and a certified job. And then there was the paperwork, of course, which was requisite to any ruling by the parole board. Basically it looked as if Maher would be spending about six weeks in Green Haven.

The certified job was easy. Maher called his uncle, Chick Maher, who was an elder statesman in Local 32B—the union that controlled doormen and concierge desks in luxury high-rise apartment buildings. Uncle Chick's influence and a good word from doorman Buddy Hample—the family friend who took Maher in after the Catskill car chase—led to Maher being hired as a part-time doorman and handyman at 200 East 58th Street.

As for the certified address, Maher listed 1609 Aqueduct Avenue, the Bronx, where he had last lived with his father. The apartment held special meaning for Maher, given the fact that his father had moved into the two-bedroom residence just so his son would have his own room when he was released from prison. Recently his mother had fled to the place, having divorced her third husband.

Compared to the Queens House of Detention, Green Haven Prison was a country club. Situated about two hundred fifty miles north of Manhattan in the forests of Stormville, New York, it was surrounded by towering pine trees instead of crumbling tenements, greenery instead of concrete. Even the name sounded inviting if you rolled it around on your tongue: Green-haven.

One acquaintance Maher made while at Green Haven was Brian Molese, a thirty-six-year-old man with movie star looks and a dancer's body. One might expect a pretty boy like that would have a hard time in prison, what with sex-starved inmates roaming the cell block. But that sort of thing didn't seem to worry Molese. He was friendly and open. Almost *too* friendly, Maher thought.

One day in the cafeteria Maher and Molese were sharing a table and talking about life behind bars. As the conversation continued, Molese admitted to having an arrest record that went back to 1959. As far as how he wound up in prison this time, Molese had essentially *three* stories: his version, the version he related to police, and the prosecutor's version. All three stories had one thing in common: On the night of February 23, 1970, a bar in Greenwich Village called Danny's burned to the ground.

According to Molese, he set fire to Danny's, one of his favorite haunts, because he was helping a friend collect insurance on a failing business. Naturally, Molese had not told police he had anything to do with the blaze that gutted the place. When cops discovered him unconscious in the basement, Molese explained that he happened to be passing by Danny's when a fire "broke out." Since he was a friend of the owner, he ran to the basement in an attempt to save the night's receipts, some twenty-three hundred dollars. He was overcome by smoke and passed out.

The prosecutor, however, had a different theory. He charged that Molese had stolen the money and then set fire to the bar to cover up the theft. The prosecutor speculated that the reason Molese was unconscious was because he was so drunk.

Notwithstanding which story was true (arson to defraud an insurance company or arson to cover up a burglary), Molese entered a plea bargain and was given a ten-year sentence.

After Molese finished telling Maher about the fire, he mentioned that he had a wife named Alice. According to Molese, he had held several jobs in the "financial community," and it was at one of those jobs that he met Alice, who worked for American Express. After he was sent to prison in 1970, the only person to visit him was Alice. They were married in a jailhouse ceremony in 1971.

"I married the fat bitch for her money," Molese said with a sneer. "And to build a case for my parole."

Molese shoved a forkful of mashed potatoes into his mouth.

"She's a fat, fat, *fat* pig," Molese ranted, mashed potatoes oozing from his contorted lips.

Maher was startled by Molese's sudden rage.

Molese wouldn't let up on Alice. He laughed derisively. "Fat Alice. That's what she is. *Fat* fucking Alice. You'll see. She's coming up here later."

Later that afternoon, Alice showed up with her usual care package full of cakes and cookies. Poor Alice was indeed fat—obese, really—but as is so often said of the overweight, she had a pretty face.

Maher watched as Alice fawned over the handsome Molese, and he did little to hide his contempt.

"You lose fifty pounds," Molese said, snarling. "You lose fifty pounds or you don't come up here anymore."

It was pathetic, and Maher felt sorry for her. She quivered like a rabbit. Helpless. Terrified.

"I brought you some cookies," Alice said.

"You got any money?" Molese snapped.

Alice began to stammer. Molese grabbed her by the shoulders. "I *said*, you got any money?"

Maher couldn't bear to watch anymore and left the visitors' room. A little while later, Molese stopped by the cell. He was livid, red in the face.

"That fat slob," Molese bellowed.

In between Molese's ravings, Maher made out that Alice hadn't brought the normal couple of hundred dollars for Molese, and Molese had promised one of his cell block buddies some commissary money.

"I want her killed," Molese roared.

Molese was hyperventilating. "You'll be out before I am. And I want you to kill her for me."

Maher looked in Molese's eyes. He was dead serious.

"I'll have her heavily insured," Molese said, his voice coming down from its fever pitch. "We can make a lot of money out of that fat whore. A *lot* of money."

Maher stared at the floor.

"Don't worry about it," Molese went on. "We'll make it look like a burglary."

"I ain't no killer, Brian," Maher said.

Molese's eyes burned with rage. But Maher felt certain that Molese's words were not just borne out of anger. Brian Molese really was going to kill his wife.

As the days fell away, Maher had a great deal of time to contemplate. He often thought of Doherty, and each time he cringed. Sergeant James Doherty. Who *was* he, really? Maher prided himself on categorizing people, figuring them out, filing them away. But Doherty was different. He had gone to all kinds of trouble for what? A rug? And even though Maher was an escape risk, Doherty hadn't even handcuffed him on the way to Green Haven. Did that make Doherty a sucker? At first Maher thought it did, but now he was beginning to wonder. After all, Maher was starting to feel guilty about Doherty, and Maher *never* felt guilty. Even when Maher was caught in the euphoria of his parole reinstatement and he asked Doherty what he could do to repay him, all Doherty said was: "Do the right thing." *Do the right thing? What the fuck did that mean?* Maher wished Doherty had leaned on him like other cops and demanded that he give somebody up. But Doherty had simply said: "Do the right thing." Maher pounded on the cot in his cell and cursed Doherty. *That sneaky son of a bitch, using my fuckin' conscience like that. Fuck him. Fuck him!*

Maher fell back on his cot and stared at the ceiling. Doherty had trusted him. Shown faith in him. *Nobody* had ever done that before.

MAHER HAD JUST FINISHED BREAKFAST ON THE MORNING OF JUNE 12, 1975, when he looked up to see a corrections officer peering into his cell. The CO—or "hack," as the prisoners referred to them—eyeballed Green Haven inmate number 21628 and then said the three words Maher had been longing to hear for six weeks.

"Pack it up."

"I'm packed," Maher said as the hack shoved a key into the lock and pulled open the cell door.

Maher swung the duffel bag over his shoulder and followed the guard down a corridor toward a metal gate where a camera kept constant vigil. After a moment, the gate slid to the side and Maher stepped forward a few feet to a second gate. By now he knew the drill: The second gate would not open until the first gate had been secured. Maher waited, staring straight ahead until the clank of the gate closing behind him caused him to glance over his shoulder. The hack was gone, and the corridor was empty. Maher was alone, without escort. He was a free man.

Maher proceeded to the property clerk's office to collect his wallet, watch, keys, and whatever money he had in his commissary account. He also was given the customary seventy-five dollars from the state of New York.

"Good luck," the clerk said, his voice flat. He had said those words often before.

"Yeah," Maher said with a laugh, "I guess I'll need it."

As Maher continued his short walk to freedom he passed the visitors' room, its doors wide open, and spotted Brian Molese.

"Hey, Kevin!" Molese shouted.

Maher started toward the visitors' room when he noticed Detective Josh Wainright standing beyond the last gate. Next to Wainright was Detective Greg Demetriou, another of Doherty's charges. *What are* they *doing here?* Maher wondered.

"Hey, Kevin," Molese said again. "Come over here. I want you to meet Beth."

Maher looked across the room and saw a petite brunette standing near Molese. She was cute. Sexy, even. Molese had mentioned her before. Elizabeth Eschert and her son were staying with Alice for the time being while her husband, Robert, was awaiting trial on a couple of contract killings. *So that's the kind of woman who marries a hit man*, Maher mused.

"You need a ride?" Molese yelled. "Beth here will take you back to the city."

Beth smiled sweetly and made eye contact with Maher. After a moment, Maher broke the gaze and looked at Wainright. The look in Wainright's eyes seemed more to the point: *Get your ass over here or there won't be enough of you left to fit in a lunchbox.*

"I got these guys waiting for me," Maher shouted back, then nodded toward Wainright and Demetriou.

Maher cleared the last gate and walked up to Wainright.

"I didn't know I rated a police escort," Maher said. "I was planning to take the bus."

Wainright looked down at Maher. "Doherty thought someone should meet you when you got out."

AT FOUR O'CLOCK IN THE AFTERNOON, MAHER ENTERED THE LOBBY OF 1 Hogan Place in lower Manhattan and took the elevator to the ninth floor to the district attorney's office. Even from way across the bullpen of desks that made up the squad room, Maher could see Doherty's face. Doherty was smiling. Maher couldn't help himself; he ran to Doherty's desk and hugged Doherty like a father.

"I really appreciate everything you did," Maher said softly.

Doherty laughed. "Hey, Kevin, I didn't do anything."

Maher looked at Doherty and searched his eyes. This truly was a good man. "Sergeant Doherty. I got something for you."

Doherty studied Maher for a long moment. "Another rug?"

They both laughed.

"Morris Weiss," Maher said.

Doherty and Wainright exchanged glances. Another of Doherty's investigators, Detective Tom Harkins, walked over to Doherty's desk.

"What about Morris Weiss?" Wainright asked.

"He wants me to kill a guy. A guy in Queens."

Doherty digested what he had just heard.

"And that's not all," Maher continued. "Morris told me 'Fat Boy' Parlati needs a wheel man."

Doherty visibly reacted. Tony "Fat Boy" Parlati was a Mafia soldier. The cops knew whom he had killed, where he had killed them, and what his motive was, but they could never pin Parlati for even as much as spitting on the sidewalk. (Parlati is not his real name. His identity has been changed at the request of the detectives involved in the case.)

"Morris gave me a phone number," Maher said.

Doherty picked up a phone receiver and dialed an extension. "Peter, I think you better come in here."

A few seconds later, Assistant District Attorney Peter Benetiz entered. Benetiz, in his late twenties, was working on a case that could make his career: "Fat Boy" Parlati.

"Kevin here is about to make a phone call to 'Fat Boy' Parlati," Doherty said.

Doherty slid the phone toward Maher. Everyone in the room stared at the phone for a long time. Finally Maher picked up the receiver and dialed the number Weiss had given him. After a moment . . .

"Hello? Mr. Parlati? Yeah. This is Kevin Maher. Morris Weiss told me to give you a call."

To everyone's surprise, Parlati told Maher he wanted to meet him that night.

Doherty had succeeded. He had a new informant. So why didn't he feel like he had won the game?

"How'd I do?" Maher asked as he hung up the receiver.

"You did great, kid," Doherty assured him.

Doherty looked at Benetiz. "Can you get me a Nagra?"

Maher was suddenly uncomfortable. He had spent enough time around crooks and cops to pick up the vocabulary, and he knew what a Nagra was. "You mean a tape recorder?"

Doherty nodded.

Maher tapped his foot nervously. "Parlati won't be able to tell I'm wearing a recorder, will he?"

"No," Wainright said.

"The Nagra goes in your pants and the mike is taped right here," Doherty said, touching Maher's sternum.

Maher looked at Doherty with pleading eyes. "What happens if Parlati catches me with a fuckin' tape recorder?"

"He won't," Doherty said with emphasis. At least he prayed to God that Parlati didn't discover Maher was wired. For Doherty knew that if Parlati *did* find a Nagra on Maher, Maher would be dead before the microphone was ripped from his chest.

Chapter 4

MAHER FIDGETED AS DOHERTY AND WAINRIGHT ATTACHED THE TAPE RE-
corder and microphone.

"You'll be able to hear me," Maher said. "Right?"

"Not with this," Doherty responded.

Maher frowned. "This thing doesn't transmit?"

"No," Doherty responded, holding up a Kell, which was a
small transmitter. "But *this* does."

Doherty finished fastening the microphone to Maher's chest
with heavy-duty tape and then added the tiny transmitter that
would essentially be the lifeline between Maher and Doherty.
Even then, Doherty remained a breath away from calling the
whole thing off. Not only was he dubious about Maher being
able to con a con, Doherty also had grown attached to Maher.
The long day the two had spent together on the trip to Green
Haven had bonded them somehow, and now Maher was more
than just a source of information to Doherty. In fact, if Doherty
had taken a free association test that night and been given the
word "Kevin," he probably would have answered, "Son."

"You sure you want to do this?" Doherty asked.

"Hey," Maher countered, "what's with you? You're the one
who talked me into this in the first place."

They sat in silence for a moment and Doherty contemplated
the responsibility he had to Maher. If anything went wrong,
how would he feel?

Maher patted his shirt where the microphone was attached to
his chest and looked at Doherty.

"Parlati won't spot this thing," Maher said nervously. "Right?"

"No," Doherty snapped, sounding vaguely annoyed at the question. The inference was clear. Doherty was worried about Parlati finding the recorder.

"Try to keep Parlati in the parking lot," Doherty said. "Where I can see you. And, if you can, get Parlati to sit in your car."

"My *car?*"

"Yeah. The car we gave you is wired, too."

Maher howled. "You guys are something else."

"Pay attention," Doherty scolded. "Now—don't ask too many questions. Let Parlati tell *you* what's going on."

Doherty looked at Maher. *Jesus*, Doherty thought, *what the fuck am I asking this kid to do?*

Maher drove to the meeting place, the parking lot of an Italian restaurant on Long Island. Doherty and Detective Tom Harkins followed closely—but not too closely—behind.

Maher parked his car, stepped onto the asphalt, and looked toward the street. Doherty's car drifted past and stopped a block away.

The small lot was deserted except for a Cadillac, which was parked next to the building. After a moment, "Fat Boy" Parlati and two henchmen emerged and ambled slowly toward Maher.

"Who are you?" Parlati demanded. Antarctica was warmer than his eyes.

"Kevin Maher."

Parlati looked at Maher and squinted. "You ain't wearing a wire, are you?"

Maher jolted at the question, visibly shaken.

"Hold your arms out," Parlati ordered.

Maher's heart began to pound. *This is it. I'm going to die right here in the parking lot of a two-bit pasta joint.*

"I *said*, hold your arms out." Parlati was not particularly patient.

Maher stuck his arms straight out.

Doherty and Harkins were listening from a discreet distance. Since they didn't want their sedan to be conspicuously parked, they did not have a line of sight on the meeting, which rendered the audio-only surveillance even more ominous than if they had been watching the action as well.

"Oh, shit!" Doherty exclaimed. "The bastard's going to frisk him." Doherty slid a hand onto his gun and reached for the door handle.

Parlati smiled and began patting Maher down.

Doherty and Harkins heard the pat, pat, pat of Parlati's hands making contact with Maher's body. And they heard a rubbing sound as Parlati reached around Maher's waist and ran his hands up and down Maher's back.

"I've been burned by a wire before," Parlati said with a growl. "It ain't gonna happen again."

Parlati patted Maher in the chest. Maher held his breath. *No way Parlati didn't feel the fucking microphone. I'm dead.*

Meanwhile, in Doherty's car, the last thing Doherty and Harkins heard was Parlati saying "It ain't gonna happen again," followed by a loud thud. After that, dead silence.

"We lost the wire," Harkins reacted.

"Let's go," Doherty said, climbing out of the car.

Doherty and Harkins eased down the sidewalk until they could see what was going on in the parking lot. From what they could tell, all was well.

In fact, all *was* well. Although Parlati's heavy-handed frisking had disabled the transmitter, he had not felt the presence of electronic equipment.

"Morris says you're good with cars," Parlati said with a smile. "That so?"

"Good with cars?" Nervous energy arced out of Maher like electricity. "Let me tell you something, Mr. Parlati, when I was seventeen I took the fuckin' cops on a chase from the Bronx to the Catskills and then . . ."

Maher chattered away. Every time Parlati said something, it triggered another burst from Maher.

"You know Long Island?" Parlati asked.

"Long Island? Hey, I know Long Island like the back of my hand. One time, I was heading out to Hempstead and . . ."

SAFELY BACK AT HOGAN PLACE, DOHERTY TOOK THE NAGRA FROM Maher and played the tape. Doherty, Maher and Harkins listened as Parlati patted Maher down. There was a loud thud.

"You hear that?" Maher exclaimed. "He hit the fucking mike."

"The mike is working fine," Harkins deadpanned as the recording continued. "But Parlati knocked out the Kell."

"We lost the transmission," Doherty added.

Maher stopped laughing. "You lost the transmission?"

"Yeah," Doherty said. "Now be quiet so we can listen to the tape."

On the tape, Parlati related how he intended to rob the home of a wealthy Long Island art collector, speculating that, in addition to the paintings, there would be a great deal of jewelry and cash. Parlati and his gang would impersonate police officers to gain access to the house. A man of few words, Parlati summarized it this way: "It's a house on Long Island. Art. Jewelry. Cash. We go in as cops." However, because of Maher's frequent diatribes, it took Parlati ten minutes to get that out.

Doherty snapped off the tape recorder and looked at Maher. "When do you shut up?"

"See, I was just trying to make Parlati feel at ease, you know, and so I told him about—"

Doherty snapped on the tape recorder again. Parlati wrapped up the conversation and dismissed Maher.

Doherty clicked off the recorder and leaned back in his chair. "I think we can get a wiretap order with that, don't you, Tom?"

Harkins nodded.

"I did good, huh?" Maher said, fishing for a compliment.

"Hell, no," Doherty said with a laugh. "You wouldn't let him talk." Doherty looked at the suddenly crestfallen Maher. "Yeah, Kevin. You did great."

For whatever reason, Parlati never called Maher again. However, the wiretap reaped instant rewards, specifically a phone conversation two weeks later between Parlati and an unidentified accomplice.

ACCOMPLICE: So we go in as cops?
PARLATI: Yeah.
ACCOMPLICE: What about masks? We wearin' masks?
PARLATI: No masks. I told you. We're cops, see?
ACCOMPLICE: Yeah. But our faces. They see our faces?

PARLATI: Don't worry about it. We're whackin' everybody in the house.

MAHER REPORTED TO HIS JOB AS DOORMAN AT 200 EAST 58TH STREET. The place advertised "white glove" service, and Maher found it funny that it was his ex-con hand under the white glove. But then again, it didn't take him long to find out that not everyone in the building would have been appalled by his background. Indeed, living among the well-heeled tenants were more than a few high-heeled hookers.

On his second shift as all-night doorman, a petite brunette approached Maher and introduced herself as Lisa. Dressed in a designer silk dress, her hair perfectly coifed, her manner decidedly sophisticated, Lisa could have been a corporate wife. But she wasn't.

"Listen, Kevin," Lisa said, "I just want you to know I usually have frequent visitors, especially late at night." She rubbed Maher's arm. "I don't want any trouble."

Lisa stared seductively into Maher's eyes. "The other guy took care of me and I took care of him. You know what I mean?"

Although his job was gratifying enough, his home life was not. When Maher moved back into 1609 Aqueduct Avenue, he expected it to feel familiar. But with his mother now living there, it was as if his father's hallowed territory was being desecrated. After all, didn't his mother leave his father for a drunken bum? What right did she have occupying his father's home? And so the place seemed haunted by his father instead of filled with his memories.

During the first week following his release, Maher made two additional calls at Doherty's request, one to Henry Bohle— whom Morris Weiss had said wanted to kill his business partner —and another to Joe Jeffries, who had asked Weiss for the name of a "wheel man."

"Morris says you don't want to be partners with Louis Izzo anymore," Maher began his telephone conversation with Bohle. "Morris says you're looking for someone to take care of the situation."

A meeting was set for that evening at a diner on Long Island.

Maher didn't expect Bohle to be so old. His eyes were sunken in wrinkled sockets, and his gray, leathery skin hung off his bones like half-dry cement. He looked more like an ancient Ichabod Crane to Maher than a man about to hire a contract killer.

"Morris says I can trust you," Bohle said several times during the conversation.

"You better hope so," Maher replied each time, playing the part coolly.

"What do you need?" Bohle finally asked.

Maher, who was wearing a wire, leaned over the table. "I need money to buy a gun. And a picture of Izzo."

Those were the two items Doherty had instructed Maher to request: money and a photo. Doherty knew that merely having Bohle on tape was not enough to get an indictment. Intent, rather than anger, had to be demonstrated.

"How much money?" Bohle wanted to know.

"Five hundred," Maher shot back.

Bohle hesitated. "How do I know you won't take the money and disappear?"

Maher acted insulted. He pointed in Bohle's face. "Hey. I ain't no fuckin' thief."

Despite Maher's performance as a tough guy, Bohle wasn't entirely convinced.

"I've got to think about it," Bohle said.

"Let me give you my phone number," Maher said, then wrote down the number for the UC, or undercover, line at 1 Hogan Place.

When Doherty heard about Bohle's reaction, he told Maher: "Okay, let's put that one on the back burner."

Bohle was a little spooked, that's all. Doherty was certain that after Bohle checked in with Weiss, he'd resurface.

Joe Jeffries was more trusting.

"There's this old Greek couple out in Kew Gardens," Jeffries explained, "and they hold this weekly dance at a nightclub. Charge admission. They take in a bundle of cash at the door."

The way Jeffries planned it, he would arrive at the club late, pull a gun, and rob the old Greek couple. Maher would come along and supply the getaway car.

A couple of nights later, Maher and Jeffries parked in front of the club, on Queens Boulevard. Jeffries opened the glove compartment and removed two pistols, handing one to Maher.

"Listen, Joe," Maher said, shaking his head, "don't you think we ought to case the place first?"

Jeffries thought about it. "Yeah. Maybe you're right." He stuffed the gun in his waistband.

"I mean *without* the guns," Maher insisted. "All we're gonna do right now is take a look." Maher held up his gun. "We don't want to be caught with these things."

Jeffries thought about that. "Yeah," he said again, "maybe you're right."

Maher and Jeffries put the guns back into the glove compartment and climbed from the car. The duo walked to the front door and disappeared into the club. Once inside, they were immediately confronted by an old Greek woman.

"Five dollars," she barked.

"We just wanted to look around," Jeffries said.

Maher frowned at Jeffries and dug into his pocket for a ten.

"Here you are," Maher said as he shot Jeffries a glance and then handed the money to the old woman.

The old woman grabbed the bill, then shuffled to a cash box that was set up on a table near the coat check.

"Look," Maher whispered in Jeffries' ear, nodding toward the old woman, "for ten bucks we get to see where she keeps the cash."

"Yeah," Jeffries whispered back. "Good idea, Kevin."

Maher shook his head in mock disgust. Jeffries turned and watched as the old woman opened the metal lid of the cash box and stuffed the ten-dollar bill into a stash of green.

Maher and Jeffries walked through the club and then back toward the front door. Suddenly a look of horror washed over Jeffries's face as his head snapped toward the window of the bar. Through the window, Jeffries could see the car being towed.

"You dumb shit," Maher chastised him. "Look what you did. You made me park in a towaway zone."

"I *borrowed* those guns," Jeffries wailed.

Jeffries was panicked, certain he was about to be arrested.

But Doherty had no intention of arresting Jeffries at that time. He would follow his usual MO and get a wiretap order based on the attempted robbery. He would build a stronger case on Jeffries. Get an arrest warrant for multiple crimes. Then—when Jeffries was surrounded by evidence and had no legal loophole from which to escape—*then* Doherty would pull the string.

In fact, the aborted robbery enabled Doherty to obtain a court order to tap Jeffries's phone. Often Doherty and Harkins would listen in on Jeffries as he planned his crimes with an accomplice. Most of the conversations went like this:

JEFFRIES: You wanna do a thing?
ACCOMPLICE: Yeah, I'll do a thing with you.
JEFFRIES: You got a thing?
ACCOMPLICE: Yeah. I borrowed a thing from Danny.
JEFFRIES: Okay. 'Cause if you didn't have a thing I was gonna say I could get you a thing.

Jeffries thought he was talking in indecipherable code and that the cops, if they happened to be listening in on his phone calls, would never figure out what a "thing" was. Jeffries's dialogue earned him a nickname around the Manhattan DA's office: "Joey the Brain Surgeon."

MAHER WALKED INTO HIS APARTMENT ONE EVENING TO THE SOUND OF A ringing phone.

"Hey, Kevin, how's life outside?"

It was Brian Molese.

"Great," Maher responded.

After Molese related a few funny anecdotes from Green Haven, he grew serious.

"I'm worried about that fat bitch wife of mine."

"What happened?"

"I think she spent all the goddamn money."

Maher had heard Molese boast about "Alice's money" before, but Maher was never sure where she got it. Molese explained that Alice had inherited a Brooklyn brownstone from her two spinster aunts and had sold the place for a profit of $100,000. In addition, the aunts left Alice a valuable collection of jewels, silverware, and antiques.

"You gotta do me a favor, Kevin."

"Sure. What is it?"

"Go over there," Molese pleaded. "Check it out."

Molese gave Maher the address: 24 Sanford Road in Fair Lawn, New Jersey, a quiet bedroom community that served Manhattan.

When Maher arrived at the house the next day, he was shocked to see that the comfortable two-story brick home was in a state of disrepair. The grass on the large corner lot hadn't been mowed in months, and the bricks, which had been painted white, were peeling.

Alice answered the door and shrieked with delight when she saw Maher. She hugged him so hard he was embarrassed.

"Brian says you're going to give me a hand," Alice said, "and boy, do I need a hand."

When the conversation turned to Molese, Alice spoke of him like he was some kind of god. It made Maher uncomfortable, especially when he recalled the way Molese had talked about "Fat Alice." Maher felt like grabbing Alice by the shoulders and saying: *Alice. The fuck talked about killing you for insurance money.*

"Alice," Maher said instead, "I think the grass needs cutting."

Alice giggled. "Oh, dear. You're right. The town is suing me because the yard is so sloppy."

Maher spent the morning mowing the lawn and cleaning up the yard. During several breaks, he sat in the kitchen and chatted with Alice, learning a great deal about her. She sat there peering through her wire-rimmed glasses, holding her ever-present cigarette, and related a childhood devoid of affection. Her parents died when she was young, and she was raised by two spinster aunts whose emotional range, at least the way Alice told it, went from disapproval to distrust. The recollection of those years was painful. Her eyes misted over several times during the account. But she brightened when she recalled how her aunts left everything to her. And she smiled as she turned to talk of furs, diamonds, and designer clothes. She *was* a spend-thrift. From what Maher could tell, she probably had spent all of her inheritance, just as Molese had suspected. And as far as Maher was concerned, it served Molese right.

As Maher was standing on the front porch saying good-bye to Alice, a car pulled into the driveway. First a little boy about four

years old jumped from the car and then a young woman. It was
Elizabeth Eschert.

"Oh, my," Elizabeth remarked as she looked at the freshly
cut lawn, "doesn't this look wonderful."

"Kevin did it," Alice announced.

The little boy stared up at Maher. "You Kevin, mister?"

Maher knelt down to the boy's level. "Yes. I'm Kevin. Who
are you?"

"My name's Bobby. Bobby Eschert." He smiled proudly.
"Bobby Eschert, *Junior.*"

Maher looked at Elizabeth. "Weren't you at Green Haven?"

"I thought I recognized you," Elizabeth said.

"Yeah," Maher said, pointing his finger. "You had on a blue
bandanna."

Elizabeth laughed. "Bandanna? That makes me sound like a
pirate. It was a blue scarf."

For the second time their eyes met. And for the second time
Maher felt a little twinge in his stomach.

OVER THE NEXT MONTH, MAHER SPENT WEEKENDS IN FAIR LAWN
working on the house. Alice—with a permanent cigarette dangling from her permanent smile—was happy to have a handyman around. Maher found Alice to be warm, friendly, funny.
But the more Maher got to know her, the more he realized how
ditzy she was.

Elizabeth, too, found Maher's weekly presence to be comforting. She loved to engage Maher in philosophical discussions
about the human condition, and she came across as well-read
and intelligent. Once in a while she would bring up her husband, Robert, whom she said she deeply loved. When she
would insist that her husband had been wrongly accused,
Maher would just nod in agreement. Yet Maher couldn't help
but wonder how Beth could be two distinct people—the erudite
woman who engaged him in scintillating conversation and, at
the same time, the wife of a ruthless Mafia contract killer.
When he asked her about the circumstances under which she
met and married Robert Eschert, the answer deepened the mys-
tery about the two Beths.

"I was a flight attendant," Beth told Maher, "flying for United Airlines."

Beth recalled how she and a group of friends wandered into an East Side bar called Paddy Quinn's, which was at 77th Street and First Avenue. Eschert, according to Beth, was dashing and worldly, mysterious and manly. As Beth went on and on about "Robert," Maher cringed. He didn't want to hear how great Robert Eschert was.

"What did he say he did for a living?" Maher asked rather pointedly.

"He said he was in the insurance business," Beth replied.

Maher was astonished at how little Beth actually knew about Eschert. The more he pressed her for details the more he realized that the woman sitting across from him had entered into a marriage willfully ignorant of her husband's history. Fantasy, delusion, whatever it was, it became clear that Beth had allowed a stranger into her heart. Even now—with Eschert charged with murder—Beth chose to believe he was innocent or, conversely, refused to believe he was guilty. There was a subtle distinction between the two ways of looking at the situation, and Maher struggled to figure out exactly what it was that Beth really believed. She was either naive or in denial. Which one was worse?

Little Bobby claimed a piece of Maher as well. When Maher would work in the yard, Bobby followed him around like a pint-sized shadow. The boy seemed hungry for attention, and Maher was glad to oblige.

One weekend, Maher was in the yard when the mailman delivered a certified letter. It sent Alice into a fit.

"What is it?" Maher asked.

Alice handed Maher the letter. It was from the town of Fair Lawn. According to the letter, Alice hadn't paid her property taxes for three years, and the town was about to foreclose—Unless she came up with $7,500.

"Alice," Maher said after he read the letter twice, "this is serious."

When Molese called from the Taconic Correctional Facility, where he had been transferred as he neared release, Maher told him of the tax problem. Molese howled like a wounded animal.

"Kevin! Please! Whatever you have to sell—the fat pig's furs, her jewelry, her furniture—just do it. Just save the fuckin' house. It's worth a quarter of a mil."

Following his phone call from Molese, Maher sat Alice down and explained the seriousness of the situation. Clearly, she didn't have the money for the taxes.

"Oh, dear!" She kept saying it over and over. Then she broke down in tears, her rolls of fat shaking like Jell-O as she sobbed. "Is Brian upset? I don't want to upset Brian."

With Alice's permission, Maher carted boxes of jewelry to 47th Street in Manhattan, the heart of the diamond district. It wasn't easy, raising the $7,500. First of all, many places were leery of anyone with fistfuls of bracelets. And when they did agree to buy the stuff, they offered well below value. Maher persisted, however, and by the end of the day he had the money Alice needed.

Molese was ecstatic that Maher had saved the house.

"Why don't you move in?" Molese suggested. "You'd be doing me a favor."

The offer was tempting. For Maher, living with his mother at his father's old apartment had become unbearable.

"I wish you would," Molese pressed. "At least till I get out and I can deal with fat Alice myself."

Maher's mind reeled back to that day in Green Haven Prison when Molese, his eyes full of fire, said he wanted Alice dead.

"Let me think about it," Maher said.

As far as Maher was concerned, he had shown good faith by calling Parlati, Bohle, and Jeffries. Now it was time for Doherty to deal with his outstanding charges.

Doherty had already been working on it and, with indictments in three different counties, it wasn't easy. But he had succeeded.

Doherty spread some papers across the desk.

"All charges will be dropped. I got you an unconditional discharge."

Maher smiled. "Really?"

Doherty shook his head. "You better stay out of trouble. Don't make me come after you."

Maher laughed. "Thanks, Sergeant Doherty."

Doherty didn't need thanks, he was happy to do it. And it wasn't just because he liked Maher or because Maher had been willing to help him. In fact, there was an even more compelling reason. The more Doherty looked into Maher's convictions of five years ago, the more it disgusted him. Seventeen-year-old kid with a stolen car gets four years? It was appalling. Sure, Maher had led police on a dangerous chase, but *four years?* For a *minor?* In any other court in the state at any other time, Maher would have been given youthful-offender status and would have received probation.

As Doherty researched the case he discovered that James Morihan, Maher's lawyer, was an alcoholic who had been charged with obtaining illegal green cards for ineligible aliens. And the man who prosecuted Maher—Bronx DA Burton Roberts—seemingly had had his own political agenda, which could explain why he treated every case as if he were dealing with Public Enemy Number One. Since sending Maher away, Roberts had received an appointment as a New York State Supreme Court justice. *Those* were the reasons Doherty had worked so hard to make sure Maher didn't go back to prison. He had already been screwed by the system once.

"What about the tickets?" Maher asked.

"You got *some* balls," Doherty said with a growl. "You'll have to pay them. Sorry."

There was a certain element of irony in the fact that it was easier to deal with a felony than a moving violation.

"Oh, by the way," Doherty said, "we got Parlati."

"You did? When?"

"A couple of days ago," Doherty answered. "He hit the house on Long Island. We had pulled the family out and filled the house with cops. So when Parlati and his gang showed up, they got a helluva surprise."

"You knew because of the wiretap," Maher stated.

"Right. We caught Parlati saying: 'We're whackin' everybody in the house.' So you saved a couple of lives, Kevin."

Doherty shook his head. "Bohle. Parlati. And now Eschert. You're batting three for three."

Doherty handed Maher a New York *Daily News.* "Actually, you're four for four."

Maher looked at a picture of District Attorney Morgenthau

standing on a huge Oriental rug. It took Maher a minute, but he finally got it.

"That's the rug?!" Maher screamed.

Doherty nodded, a smile breaking across his face.

Based on Maher's lead, Doherty had sent Detective Greg Demetriou to the Bronx to pose as an Oriental-carpet dealer. Apparently Demetriou's act had been convincing because a man in the house just handed over the rug.

"We brought it back here and spread it out in Morganthau's office," Doherty explained. "He came in the next morning and said: 'What the hell is this?' So I said: 'It's a rug.' "

Doherty told Maher that the carpet—depicting four biblical scenes on its sixteen-by-twenty-foot tapestry—had been woven by small Persian children at the turn of the century. It was worth $50,000.

"I told you that rug was something," Maher crowed.

"The company that insured the rug is offering a reward," Doherty continued. "Fifteen hundred."

Doherty wrote something on a piece of paper. "Here's the name of the guy at the Insurance Company of North America."

Maher took the piece of paper. "Thanks, Sergeant Doherty."

Maher and Doherty shook hands firmly, then spontaneously hugged.

"Take care of yourself," Doherty said.

"Nobody else will," Maher laughed. "Except you."

THE BROKEN-DOWN PLYMOUTH MAHER HAD *ACTUALLY* OWNED—THE ONE that prompted him to steal the Roadrunner—had long since been sold by his father. So Maher used most of the $1,500 reward to buy some transportation: a 1966 Buick LeSabre. It wasn't fast and it wasn't slick, but at least it would get him around town. Maher drove directly from the used-car lot to see Doherty.

"I stopped by to tell you I might be moving," Maher said.

"Where to?"

"Jersey. Molese has a house in Fair Lawn."

Maher and Doherty had previously discussed Molese.

"Nice guy, you're friend Molese," Doherty said, snickering. "He kill his wife yet?"

"He asked me to look out for her."

"Better not look out too good."

Maher laughed. "She's five hundred pounds."

Doherty laughed, too.

"But there *is* a nice little number living there with her," Maher said. "Elizabeth. She has a cute little kid named Bobby."

"Where's her husband?"

"In jail," Maher answered. "For murder one."

"What's his name?"

"Eschert," Maher said. "Robert Eschert."

Doherty motioned to a chair. "Sit back down."

"Why?" Maher wanted to know. "What is it?"

"An ADA in the office here, Alan Sullivan, is working on one of the Eschert homicides. You mind talking with him?"

Maher sighed. "Sure. Why not?"

Doherty picked up the phone receiver and buzzed Sullivan.

A moment later Assistant District Attorney Alan Sullivan entered. Although he was just thirty-five, Sullivan was graying. Since he was also very tall and very thin, he looked older than his years.

Doherty introduced Sullivan to Maher and explained that Maher had performed well undercover in a couple of tense situations. Then Doherty dropped a bombshell as far as Sullivan was concerned.

"Kevin's about ready to move into a house with Elizabeth Eschert," Doherty said.

Sullivan's jaw dropped. "Robert Eschert's wife?"

After an intense nationwide manhunt, Eschert had been arrested in Lee, Massachusetts, on May 4, 1974, and charged with a double homicide in Queens. In addition, Sullivan was prosecuting Eschert for the murder of a well-known Manhattan musician named George Hodge.

"But we know he's responsible for at least fifteen contract killings," Sullivan added.

"Fifteen?" Maher's voice went up an octave.

Sullivan left Doherty's office and retrieved a New York *Daily News* dated October 14, 1973. The headline cried out, "Burglars Kill Musician, Attack Wife," and the subhead added another lurid detail: "Rape Attempt Fails in W. Side Flat."

Sullivan explained that Robert Eschert, an accomplice named

John Hemmers, and Beverly Donna Hodge, the victim's wife, had been indicted for the murder of George Howard Hodge. Then Sullivan related his theory regarding the brutal homicide. Essentially, Sullivan believed Beverly Hodge had contracted Eschert to kill her husband and stage a rape attempt that would make it seem as if she were a victim as well. The motive was money—Hodge's considerable estate, which Beverly Hodge would inherit; a sizable insurance policy, which named Beverly Hodge as beneficiary; and a preplanned lawsuit against the owners of the building for a "lapse in security." According to Sullivan, all of this information was contained on a tape, which he wanted Maher to retrieve.

"Eschert made a tape of a phone call he had with Beverly Hodge," Sullivan explained. "We believe Beth Eschert is in possession of that tape."

Other than the recorded conversation, there was nothing concrete to link Eschert to the murder, at least nothing Sullivan felt would hold up in a court of law. Without any forensic evidence and in the absence of any clues, Sullivan would be unable to convict Robert Eschert for the brutal slaying of George Howard Hodge.

"Queens doesn't have a strong case either," Sullivan said. "Eschert could walk."

Sullivan painted a horrific portrait of Robert Eschert. Ruthless. Sociopathic. A real monster.

Maher didn't like where this was leading.

"Beth doesn't know anything about the murders," Maher insisted.

"I think she does," Sullivan countered. Sullivan stared a hole in Maher. "You think you could get to her?"

Get to her? Was he crazy?

"You want me to do what?" Maher was indignant. "Fuck some information out of her?"

Sullivan explained that he was under court order not to talk to either Eschert or his wife, Elizabeth, and that using an undercover cop also would violate that order. But a "private citizen" could circumvent that legal detail.

"Besides," Sullivan noted, "anything *I* get would not be admissible in court. A wife cannot be coerced into testifying against her husband. It's privileged information."

Sullivan acknowledged that what he was asking Maher to do constituted a "gray area" of the law.

Maher looked at Doherty, who was being strangely quiet.

"What do you think about all this?" Maher demanded.

In truth, Doherty had mixed emotions. On the one hand, Eschert was not the kind of guy Doherty wanted back on the street. On the other hand, it was a perilous proposition for Maher. And except for a few strands of DNA here and there, Doherty felt Maher could almost be his son.

"It's up to you," Doherty said. But his eyes said *Do the right thing.*

Maher thought about Beth. And little Bobby. Bobby was a sweet kid. Maher couldn't imagine Bobby being raised by a cold-blooded killer.

"Okay," Maher finally said.

Maher leaned back in his chair, his body suddenly limp. He had just agreed to do the single most dangerous thing imaginable: romance a jailed Mafia hit man's wife.

Chapter 5

THE CONVERSATION WITH DOHERTY AND SULLIVAN PLAYED OVER AND over in Maher's head as he drove home. Sure, he owed Doherty a great deal, but not this. *What have I agreed to do? The guy whacked fifteen people and they want me to fuck his wife? Are they crazy? Am I crazy?*

Maher crossed the Third Avenue Bridge into the Bronx and glanced in the rearview mirror at Manhattan, which was now a river away, an isolated island. Although flowing water was merely a physical barrier, one that could be easily crossed, Maher had traversed a psychological perimeter as well. Having had time to think about it, he decided he couldn't do what Doherty and Sullivan had asked.

The phone was ringing when Maher entered his apartment. *Doherty, no doubt. Calling up to apply some pressure, to make sure I don't back out.* Maher rehearsed his speech for a couple of rings: "I'm sorry, Sergeant Doherty, but I can't do this. I'll do something else, but not this." Maher grabbed the receiver.

"Hello?"

"Hey, Kevin, how's it going?" It was Brian Molese.

"Brian?!" Maher was surprised to hear from him.

"I was home on furlough a couple of days ago," Molese continued. "I tried to call you but there was no answer."

"You see the yard? I cleaned it up."

"Yeah. Thanks." There was a long pause. Then: "That *bitch!* That fucking fat bitch!"

The intensity of Molese's rage made Maher shudder.

69

"She's spending all the money. There won't be any left by the time I get out."

Molese was hyperventilating, gasping in noisy rales. Moments passed as Maher listened to a madman breathe. Finally . . .

"Hey, Kevin," Molese said, his voice suddenly calm. "What are you doing still living up there in the Bronx?" The abrupt change in tone was frightening. Molese's mind was moving like a water bug trapped in a rain puddle, darting erratically along the surface of sanity.

"The Bronx is okay," Maher answered.

"Come on, man, you said you'd move out to Jersey. With Alice."

"I said I'd think about it."

Molese's voice changed once again, this time to desperation: "You gotta do this for me. You understand? Please, Kevin. *Please!* I'll take care of you, Kevin. The minute I get out, I'll get you some money."

"I'm working, Brian," Maher said. "I got a job as a doorman. I don't need any money."

"Kevin, listen to me. I've been transferred to Taconic. I'm on my way home, man. This is the last stop before they process me out. It'll just be for a few months, okay? You can keep an eye on the house and that fat fucking wife of mine. You can do that for me, can't you, Kevin?"

Maher didn't respond.

"Move into the fucking house, will you?" Molese screamed.

Then, except for Molese's heavy breathing, there was silence. Finally, Maher sighed. "Okay, Brian."

Maher hung up the receiver and rubbed his eyes. *Doherty. Sullivan. Molese. Everyone wants me to move into that house.* And then the word "fate" popped into Maher's mind. Maybe that's what was at work here. The unseen forces of destiny wanted him at 24 Sanford Road, Fair Lawn, New Jersey. There seemed to be no way to avoid it.

MAHER PARKED IN THE DRIVEWAY OF 24 SANFORD ROAD AND ENTERED the house. Alice, as always, was happy to see him.

"I hope you're staying for a couple of days," Alice trilled. She hugged him tightly. Alice always made Maher feel welcome.

"I talked to Brian," Maher said.

Alice's body went rigid. She was obsessed with Brian Molese. In love, perhaps. Either way, the mention of his name concentrated her mind.

"What did he say?" Alice asked. "Did he say he missed me?"

"Sure, Alice," Maher said with a smile. "He said he can't wait to get out and come home."

Alice beamed. And Maher's dislike for Molese edged toward hatred.

"Alice," Maher began, "Brian thought it might be a good idea if I moved in until he got out."

Beth entered the room.

"Did you hear that, Beth?" Alice bubbled. "Kevin is coming to live with us for a while. Isn't that wonderful?"

Beth smiled and locked eyes with Maher. "Yes. That's wonderful."

And so it was that in August 1975, Maher took up residence at 24 Sanford Road.

From the moment Maher moved into the house, he was strangely paralyzed. By fear. By uncertainty. By the moral implications of it all. As each day went by, Maher grew more fond of Beth Eschert. And Beth Eschert's feelings for Maher seemed to intensify. She had gone from eye contact to body contact, brushing against him often, touching him when they talked. There was an undeniable attraction between them. But more than that, there were the primal urges. Maher was a young man who had spent four years in prison without female companionship. Beth was a young woman with a long-absent husband. Maybe both of them could control their emotions. But Maher wondered how long they could control their sexual appetites.

At first, Maher was able to keep his desires under control, not because of any conscious effort, rather because of the situation. Every time his desire for Beth overtook him, an equally powerful guilt shook him free of the longing. And then there was the fear. What would a hit man do to a man who was screwing his wife? One guess.

The first week passed without event. Maher performed various chores, including baby-sitting for Beth's son, Bobby, when

Beth made her frequent forays to Rikers Island to visit Eschert. On Saturday, Alice announced that she was going to visit Molese at Taconic Correctional Facility in Bedford Hills, New York. She asked Maher and Beth to come along.

Taconic Correctional Facility, the prison to which Molese had been transferred, was a minimum-security facility in upstate New York, approximately an hour from Fair Lawn. Essentially a halfway house where prisoners waited as the final paperwork for their release was completed, Taconic looked more like a camp than a place of incarceration. There were few rules and almost no restrictions. Unlike Rikers Island—where a prisoner was allowed only one visitor at a time—at Taconic an inmate could schedule a family reunion. Thus Alice, Maher, Beth, and little Bobby trekked out to Bedford Hills that sunny Saturday afternoon. And since they were not required to crowd into a cubicle or even share a small visitors' room, Alice had packed a picnic lunch, including two liter bottles of 7UP.

It was an incongruous scene. Alice and Beth standing over a picnic table laying out cold cuts and bread, prying open containers of potato salad. Maher and Bobby running around on the freshly mowed grass. And all this taking place on prison grounds.

Molese approached. He greeted Alice with a hug and a kiss, a show of warmth that surprised Maher.

"You remembered the 7UP," Molese said. Molese poured a cup of 7UP and downed it.

Appearances, of course, can be deceiving. In preparation for a visit to her husband, Alice would pry up one side of the bottle cap and, being careful not to entirely break the seal, replace the 7UP with vodka, Molese's favorite drink.

Molese looked toward another picnic table a few feet away.

"Hey, Ronald," Molese said.

Molese introduced everyone to "my new friend Ronald Scofield," who was picnicking with his parents, his sister Bonnie, and his brother John.

Ronald Scofield was handsome, blond, and blue-eyed, extremely muscular. He seemed civilized enough and well educated, just another white-collar criminal biding his time in a country club setting. However, he had been convicted of armed robbery and assault. Ronald Scofield was more violent than he looked.

The afternoon lazed away, ending in a tearful good-bye between Alice and Molese. Maher watched poor Alice, who was crying real tears. And Molese, who was crying for show. At least that's the way Maher interpreted it. After all, until now Maher had never seen Molese demonstrate any affection toward Alice or even have a kind word to say about her.

Since Maher and Bonnie Scofield had seemed to hit it off— they spent most of the visit huddled together and laughing—she invited everyone to stop by her parents' house, which was just a mile from the prison. Beth was not thrilled.

"You know, Bonnie," she said, "that's very nice of you, but I'm tired and just want to head home."

"I could use some coffee," Maher countered. "Especially after drinking all that 7UP."

Everyone laughed.

Beth glanced toward Bonnie, who was as pretty as her brother was handsome. Then Beth scowled at Maher. Maher walked over to her and whispered: "What's the big deal?"

"Fine," Beth sighed and walked away.

A few minutes later Alice, Maher, Beth, and Bobby were sitting at the Scofield residence. It was a blue-collar home, a cloth existence. The Scofields were friendly people, trusting. Maher smiled. *I bet if I asked them they would say there was some mistake.* Maher could just hear Mrs. Scofield saying: *Ronald is innocent, you know.*

Suddenly Bonnie jumped up from her chair. "Kevin, will you come to the store with me?"

Maher and Bonnie left. Bonnie stopped by the grocery store, then the drugstore, then at a friend's house to drop off a pair of borrowed roller skates. Maher didn't mind. He was enjoying the company. Finally, an hour after they had left, they returned to the Scofield house. Beth was seething. Maher stared at her for a moment and then he got it. *She's jealous. Beth is jealous.*

On a hot and humid August afternoon, Doherty called Maher.

"Kevin," Doherty said, "Bohle called the UC line. You've got to get down here as fast as you can."

The UC—or undercover—line was a secure phone at 1 Hogan Place that undercover cops and confidential informants could give as their "home" number. It was the number Maher had given to Bohle.

The phone was in a soundproof booth about the size of a walk-in closet. Signs covered the walls. DO NOT ANSWER. NO RADIOS. It was perhaps the most guarded area in the building. Earlier that afternoon, Doherty had answered the UC line with a simple "Hello." "Who is this?" a suspicious Bohle had asked.

"I said I was your girlfriend's father," Doherty told Maher.

Maher grilled Doherty: "Did you sound old enough to be someone's father?"

"Are you fucking kidding me?" Doherty reacted. "I've got six kids. Just get in the car and get down here."

Maher made it to 1 Hogan Place in half an hour. Doherty was talking with FBI agent Al Garber. After introducing Maher and Garber, Doherty said: "You know, Kevin, you met a lot of guys in prison. Maybe you can help Al with a case he's working on."

Garber had a book full of surveillance photos taken during bank robberies. He asked Maher to take a look and see if he knew any of the suspects. Maher looked at the first photo and shook his head no. Then the second. Same response. Third and fourth. Nothing. Maher pointed at the fifth photo.

"I know who this guy is," Maher said. "That's Joe Jeffries."

Garber flipped the page. "No, it isn't. We already got that guy. That's Wayne Morris."

Maher flipped the page back. "This picture is of Joe Jeffries."

Maher picked up the book and walked over to Doherty's desk.

"Tell him whose picture this is," Maher said to Doherty.

"That's Joe Jeffries," Doherty said.

Garber looked stricken and left the room to call the U.S. attorney.

"There goes *that* case," Doherty noted.

"Can't they just go and arrest Jeffries?" Maher asked.

"It's not that simple," Doherty said. "The mistaken identity will taint the whole proceeding."

Maher followed Doherty into the cramped UC booth.

"Have you located the tape?" Doherty asked.

"Come on, Sergeant Doherty," Maher whined like a recalcitrant child. "I'm doing the best I can."

The conversation turned to a question that had been bothering Maher.

"Sergeant Doherty, how does ADA Sullivan know about the tape?"

Doherty shrugged.

"Somebody turned state's evidence," Maher speculated. "And told Sullivan about the tape."

Again Doherty shrugged.

"But who?" Maher frowned. "Beverly Hodge?"

"I wouldn't think so," Doherty said. "I'm sure the tape implicates her, too."

"Hemmers! Eschert's accomplice. It *has* to be Hemmers. That's who it was. Hemmers."

Doherty remained noncommittal. "I really don't know who it was, Kevin. Or even if that's how Sullivan found out about the tape."

"Wait a minute," Maher said. "Maybe Sullivan found out about the tape with a wiretap. That's it! A wiretap."

Doherty laughed. "Or maybe Eschert told a cellmate about the tape."

Maher looked at Doherty and realized that even if Doherty knew, he wasn't about to elaborate on the circumstances under which Sullivan had learned of the tape's existence.

"You're supposed to give *us* information," Doherty said, confirming Maher's thought, "not the other way around."

"Okay," Maher responded, "you won't tell me how Sullivan found out about the tape. What about *why?* Why would Eschert make a tape that incriminated himself?"

Doherty sat silently.

Maher squinted his eyes, thinking. "You said the tape implicates Beverly Hodge."

"No," Doherty corrected him, "I said *maybe* the tape implicates Beverly Hodge."

Maher smiled. "Eschert made the tape to keep Beverly Hodge from turning him in."

"I don't know if that's true," Doherty said.

"*I* do," Maher said with a smile.

"Look, Kevin. Forget about who, what, and why. You need to find out *where* the tape is. Locate it. And get it to Sullivan."

Maher thought about Beth and sighed. "To tell you the truth, Sergeant Doherty, I don't know if I can do it."

As Doherty formulated a response, the phone rang. Maher and Doherty looked at each other. It rang again.

"Answer it, Kevin," Doherty instructed.

Maher grabbed the receiver. "Hello?"

It was Henry Bohle. Doherty stood, made a motion for Maher to keep Bohle talking, and slipped out of the booth.

"I told you before, Bohle, it's twenty-five hundred dollars. Five hundred up front."

Maher was insistent.

"And I need a picture of Izzo."

Maher paused as Bohle agreed. Then Doherty slipped back into the booth with ADA Peter Benetiz, who was handling the Bohle case.

"Where in Queens?" Maher said into the receiver.

Benetiz vigorously shook his head no and grabbed a piece of paper. He scribbled something and then held it up for Maher to see: *Get him to come to Manhattan.*

Maher nodded and resumed his conversation with Bohle.

"Look, Bohle. I ain't coming to Queens."

A pause.

"Why not? Because you probably shopped around. That's what you did, isn't it? Shopped around."

Another pause.

"No way, Bohle. I ain't being seen with you in Queens. You want me to do the job, you come to Manhattan."

A very long pause.

"I'll meet you at T. J. Tucker's. Eight o'clock. Take it or leave it."

Maher hung up. "He agreed."

"Good work, Kevin," Doherty said with a smile.

Benetiz detailed what he needed to arrest Bohle for conspiracy: "Make sure you get a picture of his business partner. Make sure you say the money is to buy a gun. Make sure he tells you exactly what he wants you to do." Having issued his instructions, Benetiz left the room.

"We'll wire you up," Doherty said.

Maher nodded, then: "Why was he so bent out of shape about getting Bohle to come into Manhattan?"

Doherty was direct. "Benetiz is an ADA in *Manhattan*. It wouldn't be his case if the conspiracy to commit murder took place in Queens."

Maher leaned back in his chair. Suddenly the idea of justice reformed as something other than the symbolic blindfolded woman balancing a set of scales. Justice was a man with geographic preferences and political ambitions. It wasn't that Maher blamed Benetiz for wanting to take credit for the case. It was that Maher realized he was not engaged in some noble battle against crime; rather, he was a player in a high-stakes game.

Maher left 1 Hogan Place and walked around the city for a couple of hours, musing about the "assignment." In fact, Maher didn't think of himself as an informant. Informants were snitches who traded information for a reduced sentence, cornered animals scratching for a plea bargain, traitors who gave up their buddies to save themselves.

Indeed, Maher's upcoming meeting with Bohle was different in all respects. Maher wasn't bartering information for a reduced sentence. While it was true that Doherty had helped Maher stay out of jail, the Bohle meeting had not been a condition of that help. Maher had agreed to meet Bohle *after the fact* and was doing so solely because of an obligation to Doherty. Nor was Maher seeking any plea bargain. His troubles with the law were, presumably, behind him. And finally, Maher had not been involved in a crime with Bohle, so he wasn't being a traitor.

Maher returned to 1 Hogan Place at about six o'clock.

"So this guy Bohle wants to whack his business partner Louis Izzo," Maher said. "That's backward, isn't it?"

"What do you mean?" Doherty asked.

"Usually the Italian is the whacker, not the whackee," Maher said, laughing.

After a tape recorder and a transmitter had been attached and tested, Maher left for his meeting with Bohle at T. J. Tucker's.

T. J. Tucker's—which was on First Avenue near the 59th Street Bridge—was a popular hangout. Young, upwardly mobile types mixed with former and current professional athletes.

Maher entered at seven-thirty to find a packed bar. Beyond the bar was an equally bustling dining area. But off the dining area was a glassed-in café section, which was empty. Maher decided on a table in the café section.

Maher took a seat at a small wooden table and ordered a beer. Then he whispered into his shirt. "Hey, Sergeant Doherty. You out there somewhere?"

By eight-fifteen it was beginning to look like Bohle wasn't going to show, and Maher was wondering how much longer he should wait. He decided to order another beer and give Bohle until eight-thirty.

"Bring me another Heineken," Maher told the waitress.

Bohle arrived before the beer.

"Sorry," Bohle said as he slipped into a chair across from Maher. "The traffic was—"

"Look," Maher broke in, "I don't have time for your bullshit. You want me to whack your partner, don't keep me sitting in some fucking dive for half an hour."

Bohle looked around nervously. There was no one nearby.

"You bring the money?" Maher asked, then, remembering what Benetiz told him to say: "The money for a gun."

"Five hundred," Bohle said. "Right?"

"And a picture of Izzo? The guy you want me to whack."

Bohle placed a Manila envelope on the table. Maher picked it up, opened it, and looked inside.

"Well, Henry," Maher said, "I guess you just hired yourself a hit man."

They sat in silence for a moment. Then Maher asked: "So why you want your partner dead, Henry?"

Benetiz had asked him to establish a motive.

Bohle was accommodating. "He's been stealing from me for years. I just found out about it."

"So, how we gonna do this, Henry?"

"Make it look like a robbery," Bohle answered. "You can take whatever's in the safe."

Right, Maher thought. *There won't be anything in the safe.*

Bohle looked around him for prying ears, then leaned across the table. "Tomorrow morning. Come to the office. It's a trailer on the lot. Come around eight. I'll leave and walk down the block. Then you go in and take care of Izzo."

"You got it," Maher said.

Fortunately for Doherty and Benetiz, Bohle was new at hiring hit men. Maher's heavy-handedness most certainly would not have worked with someone like "Fat Boy" Parlati, for example. With a wise guy like Parlati, Maher might not have gotten more than a block from T. J. Tucker's. But the novice felon and the rookie informant had managed a decent enough performance to gain raves from at least one of the critics at 1 Hogan Place.

"Great job," Benetiz gushed as he listened to the tape.

Doherty, on the other hand, was not pleased. He chided Maher, not like a cop who was running a CI, but like a father scolding a son.

"First of all," Doherty began, "I can hardly hear Bohle. The glass walls echoed all the sound. And second, you were too eager, too pushy. That kind of mistake can get you killed."

As Doherty ranted on and on about how dangerous CI work could be, Maher tuned out. All he wanted to think about was the rush he got from going undercover, the thrill of having a secret life. It was exciting. Maybe even as exciting as stealing cars. And the best part was, it was legal.

WHEN MAHER RETURNED TO NEW JERSEY, THE REALITY OF WHAT HE WAS doing pierced the fantasy. *Now I'm back on my OTHER assignment: Fuck Beth Eschert and get the tape.* But this assignment wasn't giving Maher any pleasure. He was afraid that if he went through with it, only two things could happen, both of them bad: (1) Eschert would want revenge; (2) Beth would feel betrayed.

"Where were you? Beth asked as Maher entered the kitchen.

"I met a friend for a drink," Maher said as nonchalantly as he could.

Beth studied Maher for a moment. "A friend?"

Maher smiled. Beth seemed jealous. "A *male* friend."

Maher walked to the refrigerator and retrieved a beer. "Where were *you* all day?"

Beth sighed. "I was at the courthouse copying documents. And I went by to see Robert's lawyer. And then I stopped off at Rikers."

"Documents? What documents?"

"Oh, I'm helping Robert with his defense."

Great, Maher thought. *Beth is running around New York gathering information to aid in her husband's defense while I'm about to destroy any defense he could mount.*

After dinner, Maher, Beth, and Alice talked for a while in the living room. As it neared midnight, Alice drifted off to bed.

Maher looked at Beth. She seemed lost, vulnerable, afraid. And beautiful. So beautiful, so sweet. How could she have married a man like Robert Eschert?

"Sometimes I wonder how it all got so screwed up," Beth said, seeming to read Maher's thoughts.

"I know what you mean," Maher said with a laugh. Twenty years old and four years of prison. That wasn't the way Maher had envisioned his life.

Beth brushed a strand of hair from Maher's forehead and smiled. Maher stared at her. What was he supposed to do now? Was he supposed to sweep her into his arms?

The moment passed. Beth stood, said good night, and disappeared upstairs. Maher fell back on the couch and sighed. He realized he really *could* pull it off, he really *could* bang her if he wanted to. Only Maher wasn't thinking of *banging* her, he was thinking of *making love* to her. Somewhere along the way his emotions had crossed the line. And as much as he denied it, he knew what was happening. He was falling in love with Beth Eschert.

MAHER WAS PUNCTUAL FOR HIS RENDEZVOUS WITH DOHERTY AND Sullivan, walking into 1 Hogan Place at 7:00 A.M. Once again he was fitted with a recorder.

"The minute Bohle leaves the trailer we're going to move in," Doherty said. "You run down Queens Boulevard. A couple of cops will chase you, but you'll get away. You got it?"

"I got it," Maher said, anxious to get on with it.

Maher parked a block away from Flushing Car Service and walked to the parking lot. A nervous Bohle exited the trailer and gave Maher a furtive glance before hobbling toward Queens Boulevard. And then all hell broke loose. Sirens. Flashing lights. Cops exploding out of nowhere. Bohle stopped as if he had been struck by a bullet. Maher took off.

"Get him!" Doherty screamed. As had been prearranged, Detective Greg Demetriou chased Maher. Although Demetriou could have easily caught him, Maher "escaped," reaching his car in the nick of time and tearing off down the street.

Back at Flushing Car Service, Bohle was cuffed and dumped in the backseat of a squad car.

Louis Izzo approached Doherty and asked: "What's going on?"

"Your partner hired someone to kill you," Doherty said.

Izzo's face drained. "Not Henry?"

"Yes," Doherty answered. "Henry."

LATER THAT MORNING, MAHER REPORTED TO WORK AT 200 EAST 58TH Street. One of the doormen greeted him with a bit of bad news.

"You've been laid off," the doorman said.

"What?"

"The new owners don't want to pay for part-time doormen anymore."

"But I was a handyman, too," Maher protested.

"What can I tell you?" the doorman said with a shrug.

Maher walked down Park Avenue in a daze. A few days ago he was living in the Bronx and had a good job. Now he was unemployed and living in New Jersey. Maher's mind flashed back to his years of incarceration. At least life on the inside was predictable.

Maher spent much of the day driving aimlessly around the city and trying to put things in perspective. Earlier that day he had nailed Bohle. Tomorrow or the next day he would dig up the tape. Then what? He'd have to find another job. But what job? It wasn't easy for an ex-con to find employment. Maher's desperation presented an obvious solution. *I could always steal a car. Just one more car.* Maher eyed a Mercedes parked on Madison Avenue and started to calculate the profitability of stealing it. And then. *What am I thinking? I don't want to go back to jail.* Maher sped away.

* * *

"HOW WAS WORK?" BETH ASKED AS MAHER ENTERED THE HOUSE.

"I got laid off."

"Oh, Kevin. I'm so sorry."

Alice rushed into the room. Having overheard the conversation, she walked over to Maher and hugged him.

"Now, don't you worry," Alice soothed. "I've got plenty of money."

Maher looked at Alice. Brian Molese's words echoed in his head. *That fat bitch is spending all the money. There won't be any left when I get out.*

Later that evening, after Beth had tucked Bobby into bed and Alice had retired early as usual, Maher and Beth were watching the news when a promo appeared for an upcoming story.

"And the hiring of a hit man," newscaster Ted Kavanaugh read from the cue cards, *"right after this message."*

Maher jolted. Beth got up to change the channel.

"What are you doing?" Maher almost shouted.

"Changing the channel," Beth said. "I don't want to hear about some hit man."

"I want to see it, okay?"

Beth shrugged. "Fine."

Following the commercial break, a video of Bohle being led into the precinct in handcuffs was accompanied by a voice-over detailing the "breaking story."

Maher looked at Beth. He wanted to tell her that *he* was the hit man and that he was working for the cops. But he couldn't tell her anything.

The Bohle story ended, and Maher snapped off the television.

"Beth," Maher began, "I want to talk to you about something."

Beth frowned. She had never seen Maher look so serious.

"Sure, Kevin."

"Beth, why are you protecting Robert?"

"What do you mean?"

"The tape. That's what I mean."

Beth paled. "What tape?"

"Come on, Beth, you know what tape."

Beth stared at Maher for a long moment. Her eyes reflected confusion, uncertainty, mistrust. "How do you know about the tape?"

"I overheard you tell Robert on the phone that the tape was safe."

Maher hadn't overheard anything. But he was gambling that Beth had indeed mentioned the tape in a phone conversation or, if she hadn't, wouldn't remember that she hadn't. Beth stared away, her mind reeling back through the dozens of phone calls from Eschert. Then she looked at Maher.

"He's my husband."

"Yes, he is. And he's also Bobby's father." Maher leaned in on Beth. "Do you want little Bobby raised by a murderer?"

"Robert is *not* a murderer. He's innocent."

"Have you listened to the tape?"

"No."

"Why not?"

"It's none of my business."

Maher pressed: "Maybe you're afraid of what you'll hear."

Beth crossed her arms. "I don't want to talk about it."

"I think you should go to the district attorney and tell them everything you know."

Maher braced for a tirade. Instead, Beth suddenly grew very sad. She stood and walked quickly up the stairs.

Maher thought about Beth's initial reaction, which was that of a woman defending her husband. But now there was something more powerful going on in Beth's mind, something more primal. Beth Eschert also was a mother thinking about the welfare of her child.

The following morning, Beth seemed to have forgotten about the conversation. She was full of energy, chirpy. She fed Bobby breakfast then left to take him to nursery school. Alice also left.

"I'm going shopping," she told Maher as she swept out the door.

Maher could hear Molese's voice echo in his brain: *That fat bitch is spending all the money.*

Now alone, Maher walked slowly and deliberately through the house. *Where would Beth hide the tape?* Maher decided that the first place he would look was a large credenza where Beth was always stuffing things. Recipes. Magazines. Coupons. Maher knelt down and carefully sorted through it. A hair ribbon. A scarf. A catalog. *A tape!* Maher stood and ran to a wall unit, popping the tape into a tape deck. He pressed the "play" button and heard a man's voice. Then a woman's voice. They were planning a murder.

MAHER WALKED UP TO DOHERTY'S DESK AND HANDED HIM A CASSETTE tape. Doherty looked at it.

"The Rolling Stones?"

"It was the first tape I came across. And I wanted to copy it before Beth got back from nursery school."

Doherty shot to his feet. "This is the Eschert tape?!"

"That's the Eschert tape."

Doherty buzzed Sullivan, who charged into the room.

"You got the tape?!" Sullivan asked, gasping.

"That's what you asked me to do, isn't it?"

Sullivan took the tape and returned to his office.

"How you doing for money?" Doherty asked.

"I'm okay."

"How can you be okay? You lost your job."

Maher laughed. "I'm going to steal another car."

"That's not funny."

Doherty opened a desk drawer and took out two $20 bills. He handed them to Maher.

"I can get forty dollars at a time out of petty cash," Doherty explained.

"You don't have to pay me," Maher said. "I'm doing this because of what you did for me."

"Take it," Doherty insisted.

Maher hesitated, then took the money.

After an awkward moment, Maher stood. "I better be getting back to New Jersey."

"Take care of yourself, you hear?"

"I will."

"Keep in touch, Kevin."

"Sure, Sergeant Doherty."

And with that, Maher walked out of the squad room, rode down on the elevator, and exited 1 Hogan Place. He stopped and looked up at the building. He would miss Doherty. And he would miss the excitement of working with the cops. At least he was doing something good, something worthwhile. Now he was back to being just another ex-con looking for work, someone whose future loomed as nothing more than an expanse of time that needed to be filled.

On the drive back to Fair Lawn, Maher resolved to move out of the house. He had accomplished the mission, so why stay? Maher could only think of reasons not to stay. One: he was falling in love with Beth. Two: Beth's husband was a remorseless killer. Three: Beth had a kid. As much as he loved little Bobby, Maher didn't want to get involved with a woman who had a kid. Hell, he was just a kid himself.

Maher walked into the house and found Beth sitting in the living room. From the look on her face, it was obvious she had something to say. Maher stiffened. Had Beth somehow figured out that he had copied the tape?

"I went to Rikers this afternoon to visit Robert," Beth said. "I was telling Robert all about you."

Maher swallowed. "About *me?*"

"Yes. Over the past few visits, I've been telling him how much I like you. How fond of you I am."

Maher frowned. He couldn't really be hearing this.

"So today I told Robert that I was attracted to you. *Physically* attracted."

Maher looked at Beth in horror. "And what did he say when you told him that?"

"He said he wants to see you."

Chapter 6

MAHER CLIMBED BEHIND THE WHEEL OF ALICE'S BRAND-NEW IVORY-colored 1976 Chevrolet Malibu Classic. Beth slid into the passenger seat. The forty-five-minute trip to Rikers Island was mostly silent. Then again, what was there to say? Robert Eschert, killer for hire, wanted to have a conversation with Kevin Maher, who already had seen more trouble than he ever expected.

Maher stared out the window and imagined what the meeting would be like.

ESCHERT: You fucked my wife.
MAHER: No, I didn't. I swear I didn't.
ESCHERT: You thought about doing it, didn't you?
MAHER: Okay. Maybe I thought about it.
ESCHERT: You're a dead man, kid. A dead man.

"Kevin?" Beth said. "Are you all right?"

Maher snapped back to reality. "Yeah. I'm fine." *I'm dead. I'm dead. I'm dead.*

Maher parked the Malibu in a parking lot near Rikers and the two of them boarded a bus that carried them across the bridge to the prison island. They walked into the Rikers reception area, a large one-story building with hundreds of plastic seats bolted to the concrete floor. It looked much like a bus depot, which, in actuality, it was. This was where visitors boarded the prison bus, which wended its way around the island's many structures. There were the cell blocks, of course. Schools for juvenile offenders. Administration buildings. Laundry facilities. Hospitals. Indeed, Rikers Island was a self-contained community.

The guard issued Maher his pass and instructed him to wait outside for the prison bus. Since prisoners were allowed only one visitor at a time, Maher would be making the trip by himself while Beth waited for him at "Reception."

The prison bus arrived, and Maher considered not boarding it. But he did. A few minutes later he was walking into the Rikers Island hospital ward where Eschert was having some tests. Maher was led to the visitors' area, which consisted of five cubicles divided by glass. He took a seat in one of the cubicles, staring at the empty chair across from him. Then Robert Eschert appeared, took a seat, and peered through the glass at Maher. His eyes were cold and emotionless.

"So *you're* Kevin," Eschert said evenly, his icy gaze moving slowly over Maher's body.

Maher started to say something. But he couldn't speak.

Eschert continued, measuring his words. "Beth has told me quite a lot about you. And every time I call the house and talk to Bobby, he's always saying 'Kevin and I did this, Kevin and I did that.' "

Maher slumped a little. *He not only thinks I've stolen his wife, he thinks I've stolen his kid.*

"Bobby's a great kid," Maher finally managed.

"Yeah," Eschert said with a smile. "He's a great kid."

Eschert looked away for a long moment, then snapped his head back toward Maher.

"I'm in jail," Eschert said, stating the obvious. "And you know the worst thing—*the worst thing*—that can happen to a man in jail?"

Maher knew the answer but wasn't about to say it. He waited for Eschert to speak.

"Somebody fucking his wife," Eschert finally said with a sneer.

Maher's heart started to pound. *Eschert is going to have me killed.*

"Yeah," Maher blurted out, "I know what you mean. I was in jail once and found out somebody was fucking my girlfriend."

Maher laughed nervously. Eschert did not seem amused.

"What do you think of Beth?" Eschert asked.

Maher chose his words carefully. "She's very nice."

"You think she's attractive?" Eschert pressed.

Maher held his breath. *What am I supposed to say? Am I supposed to tell him that his wife is unattractive and piss him off? Or am I supposed to say his wife is attractive and have him put a fucking contract out on my life?*

"Beth is a very attractive woman," Maher said.

Eschert smiled. "Beth is a *beautiful* woman. And you know what else she is? She's human, flesh and blood. She has desires." Eschert leaned close to the glass. "She tells me she's attracted to you. Are you attracted to her?"

Maher felt like he was being maneuvered into a confession. It reminded him of an interrogation by cops in which they would ask a series of questions that built on each other like a stack of bricks until they walled you in. Maher sat stone-faced. Eschert stared at him.

Eschert pressed. "Are you attracted to her or not?"

"Sure," Maher said, his voice barely audible. "I'm attracted to her. Who wouldn't be?"

Maher looked directly into Eschert's eyes. This time he didn't see the coldness, he saw fear.

"I love Beth," Eschert said. "I don't want her running around, falling in love with someone. I don't want to lose her."

Suddenly Maher felt sorry for Eschert. But the pity was fleeting. Maher reminded himself that the man on the other side of the glass was a murderer.

"Let me ask you a question," Eschert said. "If you find her attractive, how come you never made a move?"

Maher relaxed a little. At least Eschert knew he hadn't slept with Beth.

"I don't do that kind of thing," Maher insisted. "I don't mess with somebody else's woman."

Eschert smiled. "Beth thinks it's because you're afraid of me."

Maher shrugged. There was no way to respond to that.

"They'll never convict me on the murders," Eschert stated with arrogance. "But I figure I still gotta do four years. That's a long time for a woman like Beth to wait."

Eschert's gaze dropped to the floor. He grimaced. Then slowly raised his eyes. "Kevin. I want you to take care of Beth until I get out."

Maher frowned. *Four years? That's a long time to ask someone to take care of your wife.*

Eschert elaborated. "I want you to take care of her needs. Her *sexual* needs."

Maher gasped slightly. Had he heard correctly?

"You're a young man," Eschert explained. "You don't want to get involved with a woman who has a kid. And Beth would never fall in love with someone like you."

Maher felt vaguely insulted.

"I would be forever in your debt if you would do this for me until I get out," Eschert said.

Maher studied Eschert. *He's asking me to fuck his wife. Sullivan and Doherty wanted me to fuck his wife. Hell, everybody wants me to fuck his wife.*

"Okay," Maher finally said. What else could he say?

"And take care of little Bobby for me, will you?"

"Don't worry, Robert. I'll take real good care of Bobby."

The visit over, Maher stood and walked toward the elevator. Although it was strictly forbidden for inmates and visitors to come in contact, a guard inadvertently led Eschert into the hallway at the same time Maher entered the hallway. Maher and Eschert stood face to face. They shook hands. And then Eschert was taken back to his cell.

MAHER STEPPED OFF THE BUS AND REJOINED BETH IN THE RECEPTION area.

Beth smiled. "Everything okay?"

Maher shrugged. "I guess so."

Maher and Beth took a city bus back across the bridge and climbed into the Malibu. Maher steered the car out of the parking lot and onto 21st Street in Queens. Beth watched him for a moment, then placed her hand on the inside of his leg. He glanced down at Beth's hand and recalled the many trips the two of them had made in Beth's Volkswagen Beetle. Whenever Beth drove him around, it seemed she was always shifting gears. And the entire time her hand would slide along Maher's leg. Maher had chalked it up to the cramped confines of the

Volkswagen, nothing more than unavoidable contact due to close proximity. But now, as he stared at Beth's delicate hand exploring the side of his leg, he realized it had never been an accident.

Maher took Beth's hand and lifted it from his thigh. He looked into her eyes, just for an instant, but long enough for the taxi to dart in front of the Malibu. There was a sudden crunching sound as the hood of the Malibu buckled and the yellow cab slid sideways. As Maher peered through the windshield at the cab—which now resembled a large, banana-colored accordion —several things flashed through his mind, not the least of which was the fact that he had no driver's license and probably a hundred outstanding tickets. Maher's instincts took over. He jammed his foot on the accelerator and took off. The severely damaged cab followed. Suddenly Maher was involved in another car chase. However, this chase was brief. Maher blasted over the 59th Street Bridge and onto the FDR Drive North, quickly losing the cab. He continued north on the drive, crossed the Third Avenue Bridge into the Bronx, and took the Major Deegan Expressway to 230th Street. Then he turned right onto Bailey Avenue, where he parked the Malibu and removed the license plates.

"We can't just leave it here," Beth protested as Maher led her down the street.

"We can't wait for the cops either," Maher countered.

Maher and Beth climbed into a taxi and headed for New Jersey.

"Alice has insurance," Maher noted. "When we get back to Fair Lawn we'll have Alice report the car stolen."

Maher and Beth entered the kitchen, where Alice was reading a magazine. Maher dropped the license plates on the table.

"What's this?" Alice asked.

"License plates," Maher said.

"License plates? For what?"

"They used to be on your car," Maher answered.

Alice was freaked. "My car? Where is my car?"

Maher explained what had happened.

"I just bought it," Alice said with a moan.

"Don't worry," Maher assured her. "By tonight the car will

be stripped. The insurance company will declare it a total loss. And you'll get a new car."

Alice was too stunned to protest. "As long as you're sure."

The patchwork clan that consisted of Maher, Beth, Bobby, and Alice sat down for dinner. The gathering wasn't exactly *Father Knows Best*, but it had all the warmth of a traditional family. At about nine-thirty, Beth tucked Bobby in for the night. And at eleven, Alice went to bed. Then Maher and Beth ended the evening as they always did: They watched the news.

Until now, the nightly event was nothing more than what it appeared—two people sitting in front of a television. Maher would comment about a particular news story. Beth would offer her thoughts. But on this night, both Maher and Beth sat rigid, staring straight ahead. When the news ended, Beth stood.

"Good night, Kevin."

"Good night, Beth."

Beth turned and walked upstairs, leaving Maher sitting alone in the living room. It was quiet. The kind of quiet you could hear because it was *so* quiet. Then Maher heard the creaking of stairs and looked up. Beth was standing on the landing. She was holding a quilt loosely around her. And she was wearing nothing but a pair of panties.

"You coming to bed?" Beth asked.

Maher couldn't speak. Nor could he move. He just sat there staring at Beth.

Beth continued down the stairs and walked up to Maher, taking his hand. "Come, on, Kevin. Let's go to bed."

Maher stood and followed Beth up the stairs. When they reached the bed, she turned and allowed the blanket to drop to the floor. He took her in his arms and abandoned conscious thought, succumbing to the feeling. In a few moments it was over.

Minutes passed. Finally . . .

"Kevin?"

"Yes?"

"When did you first have feelings for me?"

"I guess it was that day in Green Haven when I saw you with that dopey blue bandanna wrapped around your head."

"It wasn't a bandanna, it was a *scarf.*"

"Whatever it was, that's when I first felt something."

Beth smiled. "Well, I *did* notice that you kept dropping your eyes."

"What about you? When did you first have feelings for me?"

"I suppose it was when I first saw you at Green Haven. But I *really* knew I had feelings for you when you took that blond bitch to the store."

"What bitch? Who are you talking about?"

"Scofield's sister," Beth said.

Maher laughed. Beth pouted.

"It wasn't funny, Kevin. I was really pissed."

"Yeah. You were."

Maher and Beth locked eyes and then locked bodies. The long period of abstinence was over, and the pent-up desire would no longer be denied. All night long they alternately made love and talked. At dawn they drifted off to sleep, only to be awakened by the sudden opening of the door and a bouncy little Bobby flinging himself onto the bed.

"Hi, Mommy. Hi, Kevin."

Bobby curled up next to them, oblivious to the implications of discovering Maher in his mother's bed.

The situation made Maher feel uneasy. He looked at Beth. *There's a person in there,* Maher thought. *A real person.* So much of Maher's life had seemed unreal. Then he looked at Bobby, and images played across Maher's mind like a home movie. Little Bobby crawling around on the rug with his Hot Wheels. Little Bobby out in the yard in his hooded jacket. Little Bobby refusing to eat his dinner. Suddenly the uneasiness passed. And it felt like family.

"You ever think about having a little brother or sister for Bobby?" Maher asked spontaneously.

"No!" Beth's answer was both fast and final. "Childbirth hurts."

Maher lay back and stared at the ceiling. *I finally feel like starting a family, and the woman I'm with says no.*

THE NEXT FEW DAYS WERE A BLUR OF EUPHORIA. EVEN ALICE BECAME caught up in the sunburst of emotion that brightened her house. But then—as quickly as a sudden squall can darken the sky—Brian Molese appeared at the door. He was home for a twenty-four-hour furlough.

"Alice!" Molese called out as he entered the house.

When she heard his voice, Alice rushed—sprinted as fast as an obese woman could—and greeted her husband with a bear hug. Molese stood limp, not returning her embrace. Alice stepped away and looked past him. Standing a few feet away was the man she had met on her last visit to the prison in Bedford Hills, Molese's "new friend." Ronald Scofield.

The fact that Scofield had accompanied Molese home on the furlough was not, in itself, unusual. Prison buddies often spent furloughs together. But their behavior was unusual. They whispered constantly, engaged in frequent eye contact, and exhibited odd, girlish behavior toward each other.

At about 9:00 P.M., Molese and Scofield dressed for the evening and left the house. It was embarrassing to Alice. Her husband, whom she hasn't seen for weeks, would rather go out for the evening with a man than spend time with her.

"Good night," Alice said at ten o'clock, which was earlier than she normally went to bed. The pain was etched on her face, the humiliation clouding her eyes.

Maher and Beth went to bed around midnight. Maher was restless, unable to sleep. So he was awake when he heard the front door open at 3:00 A.M. He heard the sound of Molese's voice, and Scofield's voice. He heard them laughing. They were drunk. Then Maher heard the sound of the sofa bed opening. And then he heard Alice's heavy footsteps in the hall. And then Alice's voice.

"Brian, aren't you coming to bed?"

"I'm sleeping down here with Ron," Molese said with a snarl.

"What?"

"I *said*," Molese spewed, "I'm sleeping down here with Ron."

Maher raised himself on one elbow. He heard Alice whimper. And then:

"You get the fuck away from me!" Molese roared. "And stop that fucking sniveling, you fat bitch!"

The next thing Maher heard was the sound of a fist smashing into flesh. A dull thud. And then another one.

Maher bounded from the bed and ran to the stairs. Molese

had Alice by the hair and was slamming blow after blow into her face. Blood was flowing from Alice's nose.

"Brian!" Maher screamed. "What the fuck are you doing?"

Maher grabbed Molese and pulled him away from Alice.

"That fat whore!" Molese roared. He struggled to break free of Maher's grasp. Maher tightened his grip.

Beth knelt and comforted the trembling Alice while Maher led Molese into the kitchen.

"I'm going to kill that fat fucking pig!" Molese said.

Maher frowned. "Why, Brian? What did Alice ever do to you?"

Maher left Molese and Scofield in the kitchen and went upstairs to the master bedroom, where Beth had taken Alice. Alice was shaking, whimpering. Beth rubbed Alice's shoulder. "I'll be right back."

Beth stepped into the hall with Maher and closed the door behind her.

"I'm getting Brian out of the house," Maher said. "Cool him off a little."

"This is so terrible," Beth said, near tears herself.

Maher, Molese, and Scofield went to a nearby diner. Molese, his voice calm, said: "You gotta help me out, Kevin. You, too, Ronnie. We gotta put Alice out of her misery. She's a fat slob. All she does is smoke and eat."

Maher looked at Scofield, hoping for an ally in reasoning with Molese. But Scofield sat quietly, a smirk on his face.

This is sick, Maher thought as he studied the two of them. A pair of pretty boys smitten with each other. And one of them was a potential murderer.

"I *am* going to kill her," Molese insisted. "You better believe me."

"Oh, I believe you, Brian," Maher said.

Molese smiled, seeming to gain some satisfaction from Maher's response.

"Then help me kill her, Kevin."

Maher grimaced. Yet another request from Molese to aid in the murder of his wife.

"I can't do that, Brian."

Molese glared at Maher for a long moment. Then he smiled.

"Let's get something to eat, huh?"

The three of them ate and then left the diner. Molese and Scofield dropped Maher off at Sanford Road.

"We're going into the Village," Molese said as Maher climbed out of the car.

The car screeched away, leaving Maher standing on the sidewalk. It was 6:00 A.M. Quiet. Dead quiet. The sky had an eerie grayish tint as the sun fought its way over the horizon. Maher stood there for several minutes before entering the house.

THE FOLLOWING MORNING, ALICE—HER FACE SWOLLEN AND DISCOLORED —shuffled around the kitchen.

"It *is* my fault, you know," Alice said. "If only I took better care of myself, Brian wouldn't act like that."

Maher sat silent as he listened to Alice make excuses for Molese.

"I'm going on a diet," Alice declared.

Alice left the kitchen. Maher went to the phone and called Doherty, explaining what had transpired the night before.

"He's going to kill her, Sergeant Doherty," Maher whispered into the receiver. "He *really* is. You've got to do something."

But what could Doherty do? A husband threatens to kill his wife. So what? Happens every day.

"Sorry, Kevin," Doherty told Maher. "There's been no crime committed. There's really nothing I can do."

Maher hung up the receiver and was struck with one overriding thought: *I've got to get out of this house before Molese really does kill Alice.* Maher felt a pang of guilt. *Am I being a coward? Can I let Alice die?*

Then again, Alice couldn't shake her pathetic obsession with Molese. She would never believe Molese would harm her, would never get an order of protection. So what could Maher do? What could Doherty do? What could anyone do?

ON NOVEMBER 5, 1975, A MANHATTAN JURY CONVICTED ROBERT Eschert of the Hodge murder. Eschert was given a sentence of twenty-five years to life. His accomplice, John Hemmers, turned state's evidence and received twenty years to life. Beverly Hodge would serve fifteen years to life.

When Maher heard about Eschert's conviction, he wondered what role the taped phone conversation between Eschert and Beverly Hodge had played in the verdict. Since ADA Sullivan had been under court order not to have any contact with Beth Eschert, the prosecution had opted not to enter the tape as evidence. It probably would have been ruled inadmissible. Still, something had caused John Hemmers to have a sudden change of heart and confess. As far as Maher was concerned, the tape was the reason Hemmers caved in. It made Maher feel good to think he had helped put a killer away for life.

Beth's reaction to her husband's conviction was more emotional. She was stunned, then hysterical, then deeply depressed when the realization hit her that her husband—the father of her child—would not leave prison for a long time, if ever.

"The truth, Beth," Maher said as he walked with Beth down Sanford Road, "is that this guy's a fucking killer. You want this guy to come out and raise your kid?"

Beth didn't respond. Maher placed his arms around her.

"You come and live with me, Beth, and we'll see how it works out."

Alice was heartbroken that Maher and Beth wanted to leave. Yet Alice, being Alice, was understanding. She asked only that they stay until she could find someone else to live with her. In short order, Alice found another woman to share the place— Marcia Ferrell, who had known Alice in college. Marcia's husband had recently died and, since she wasn't on speaking terms with her father, she needed a place for her and her three-year-old son, Harold, to live.

The search for an apartment was not easy. What could they afford? Maher had just lost his job. And Beth's income consisted of welfare payments, small loans from Alice, and whatever cash her in-laws could spare each month. Thus both Maher and Beth began job hunting. Neither of them had the greatest résumé. Beth's previous experience ran the gamut from dental assistant to flight attendant at United Airlines. Maher's employment history was, at best, spotty.

Beth was the first one to be successful. Aided by a headhunter at an employment agency, she secured a job working in the circulation department of *New York* magazine. Her salary was $210 a week. Maher's job, in which he would earn $180 a week, came courtesy of his uncle, Paddy Maher.

The history of the Maher family was nothing if not colorful. In 1967 Paddy Maher was a middleweight fighter with three fights, two of them knockouts. Paddy Maher happened to be in a tavern one night when a bar fight erupted and spilled out into the street. Three men began pummeling one man, and so Paddy came to the solo's defense. Paddy threw a punch, knocking down one of the attackers. He threw another punch and knocked down the second attacker. Then he knelt to tend to the bloodied victim, and the third attacker went after Paddy. Paddy rose up and delivered a vicious uppercut. The attacker fell backward. Before the ambulance arrived, he was dead. Paddy panicked and fled to Fort Lauderdale, where he called and asked Kevin Maher's father, Edward, to wire money via Western Union. The cops arrived before the money. Back in New York, a grand jury refused to issue an indictment. But as Maher would often say when relating that story about Uncle Paddy: "He was always fucked up over that." Now Paddy Maher helped his nephew get a job as a laborer in the track department at Penn Central Railroad.

To avoid discovery that he was an ex-convict, Kevin Maher filled out the job application as *Edward* Maher and gave a fake Social Security number that was, in part, his Zip code in the Bronx. While Maher knew they would eventually find out the Social Security number was bogus, he figured he would deal with the problem when it arose. For the moment, the fake number got him a job.

In January 1976 Maher and Beth found a nice apartment at a reasonable rent. It was in the Bronx, at 1634 Mayflower Avenue. One of the reasons Maher and Beth chose the Bronx, and Mayflower Avenue in particular, was the proximity to Robert Eschert's parents, who lived ten blocks away. By living near the Escherts, little Bobby would have a chance to see his grandparents on a regular basis. In addition, Maher and Beth would have a baby-sitter. Everything, it seemed, had worked out. However, there was something that bothered Maher a great deal. He was keeping a secret from Beth—that he aided in her husband's conviction. Maher decided he had to tell her. If that ended the romance, so be it.

When Beth arrived home after work, she could tell that something was wrong. Maher took her into the living room and asked her to sit on the couch. He paced back and forth for a few moments and then sat next to her.

"Beth," Maher began, "I have something to tell you."

Maher stammered about knowing Doherty and what he owed Doherty and then launched into a diatribe about how Doherty always said: *Do the right thing.* Finally, Maher got to the point.

"I helped the DA," Maher said. "I helped the DA get a conviction on Robert."

The words didn't sink in right away. Beth half smiled. "What did you say?"

"I gave the DA some information that helped convict your husband." Maher couldn't bring himself to tell her he had copied the tape.

Beth sat stunned for several seconds. Then she began shaking her head no.

"Robert didn't just kill Hodge," Maher continued. "He's suspected of at least fifteen contract killings."

Beth became hysterical. Maher tried to console her. She pushed him away.

"You used me," Beth said, sobbing.

Maher didn't have a response. He watched Beth cry for what seemed like hours.

"I loved you and you used me," Beth said, sniffling. "Every man I ever loved has hurt me."

Now Maher was the one who was stunned. They had never used the word "love." In fact, they had danced around it like it was a profane thing to say. *I have feelings for you,* Beth might say. And Maher might answer back: *I have feelings for you, too.* But never love.

"I love you," Beth said, no longer using the past tense.

Maher wrapped his arms around Beth. "I love you, too."

DESPITE THE UNUSUAL NATURE OF THE SITUATION, ESCHERT'S PARENTS—little Bobby's grandparents—were fond of Kevin. If the Escherts harbored any resentment that Maher was living with the wife of their incarcerated son, they didn't show it. Perhaps Eschert had explained to them that he had asked Maher to take care of Beth. Whatever the reason, the expanded family coexisted harmoniously and the Escherts treated Maher like an adopted son.

As the weeks fell away, Beth's visits to Eschert dropped from three times a week to twice to once. Then she began missing a week here and there. Clearly, Beth was drawing away, distancing herself from the past, looking to the future.

But the future held some trepidation for Maher. Eschert had been given twenty-five years to life. As harsh as the sentence was, Maher was troubled by the fact that Eschert was sentenced on only *one* conviction. Although unlikely, Eschert might be successful in convincing a court that the sentence was "cruel and unusual." In that case, he conceivably could be out in eight to nine years. Sure, eight years was a long time. But time can pass quickly, and Maher didn't want his life to be thrown into chaos at some future date. The thought of Eschert walking out of prison represented a real threat for Maher. Often, he would stare off and watch the horror unfold in his mind.

Beth in the kitchen cooking dinner. Maher helping Bobby, now a teenager, with his homework. Suddenly a knock on the door. Maher answers it. He gasps. It's Robert Eschert home from prison.

"Thank you for looking out for Beth and Bobby," Eschert says as he enters the apartment.

Bobby stands and runs to his father, embracing him.

"Hello, Dad," Bobby says, sobbing. "Welcome home."

Then Beth rushes from the kitchen and throws her arms around Eschert.

"I've missed you so much, Robert," Beth says. "I love you. I've always loved you."

Eschert then turns to Maher and says: "You can leave now, Kevin."

The scene made Maher sick, and he knew he had to find a way to prevent it. So he resolved to ask Beth to cooperate with Queens ADA Marty Bracken, who was about to take Eschert to trial for the two murders he committed in that borough. Indeed, two additional homicide convictions would ensure that Robert Eschert would *never* get out of prison.

Maher and Beth dropped Bobby at his grandparents' apartment on their way to dinner at a local Irish pub. As Bobby hugged Beth, Maher felt a pang. *I love that kid so much. How could something so good come from someone so evil?*

Once at the pub, Maher didn't waste any time.

"You need to get your life in order, Beth. What are you going to be doing? Visiting jails the rest of your life?"

"He's my husband," Beth protested. "The father of my son."

"That's right," Maher agreed. "And kids are impressionable. What happens if Robert gets out and teaches Bobby the tricks of his trade?"

A look of realization passed over Beth's face.

Maher pressed. "Listen, this guy is a murderer. A fucking killer. He doesn't care about human life. He's a cold-blooded—"

But Beth was no longer listening. She was a mother. And her son's well-being had been brought into question, placed in jeopardy.

"I'll do it," Beth interrupted Maher's monologue.

The next day, Beth met for hours with Marty Bracken. While she didn't have any specifics, she was quite helpful. Robert Eschert was convicted in late January 1976 of the two homicides in Queens. He was given two more life sentences.

Beth never again visited Robert Eschert in prison. Shortly after he was convicted in Queens, she filed for divorce.

WITH ESCHERT PUT AWAY FOREVER, MAHER AND BETH ATTEMPTED TO normalize a relationship that had begun in a most bizarre fashion. They tried to be just another couple making a life for themselves in New York City. Each morning, as they headed off to work, they would say hello to their neighbors. And the neighbors would smile and think: *There goes Kevin and Beth, the nice young couple who live at 1634 Mayflower Avenue.* No one could have guessed that on one brisk February morning, Maher was not going directly to his job. He was stopping off to see his parole officer, Brian Berg.

The meeting with Berg was routine. Indeed, Maher had all the right answers. *Yes, I still have a job. No, I haven't used drugs. Yes, I'm still at the same address.* But then, as the meeting wound to a close, Berg said: "Oh, by the way, Kevin. A homicide detective wants to talk to you. Detective Louis DePasquale."

Maher jolted: "Why does he want to talk to *me?*"

"It's nothing about *you*, Kevin. It's about a case he's working on."

Maher went directly to Doherty's office.

"Sergeant Doherty," Maher said, "some homicide detective wants to talk to me."

Doherty smiled. "Yes, Kevin, I know all about it. Louis DePasquale. He called and asked if he could borrow you."

"Borrow me? For what?"

"The Scofield case."

Maher's mind reeled. "Scofield? *Ronald* Scofield?"

"Yes," Doherty said. "You're a known associate of Ronald Scofield. DePasquale thought you might be able to help nail the bastard."

Maher looked away for a moment, conjuring up the evening in Fair Lawn when Brian Molese and Ronald Scofield arrived on furlough from the prison in Bedford Hills. Maher winced as he replayed the events in his mind. Alice being beaten by Molese. Molese swearing he was going to kill her. But what did Scofield have to do with anything? He was Molese's lover, that's all. Then Maher put it all together. *Oh, my God! I hope that son of a bitch Molese didn't get Scofield to kill Alice.* Maher turned slowly and looked at Doherty.

"Please tell me Scofield didn't kill Alice Molese."

Doherty frowned: "Alice Molese? No, no. He didn't kill Alice Molese."

Maher was relieved. Doherty shuffled some papers on his desk.

"Scofield killed a prostitute in midtown."

Maher slumped in his chair. He was not by nature superstitious. Yet he had always felt an evil presence swirling around the house in Fair Lawn. And now it seemed that the demons of 24 Sanford Road had been unleashed at last.

Chapter 7

MAHER SAT IN AN OFFICE AT 1 HOGAN PLACE AND SIGHED. *I THOUGHT this kind of stuff was behind me.* But clearly it wasn't. Sitting across from Maher were Detective Louis DePasquale and Assistant District Attorney John Malady.

"We think Scofield killed a prostitute," DePasquale began.

(The woman's name has been withheld to protect the privacy of her parents.)

"How do you know he did it?" Maher asked, doubtful that Ronald Scofield actually murdered someone.

"We *think* he did it," Malady said.

DePasquale explained the details of the case.

A white male and a female prostitute, using the alias "Mr. and Mrs. Adams," checked into the Dixie Hotel at 250 West 43rd Street, a pay-by-the-hour hotel just off Times Square. About half an hour later the white male exited the hotel. A maid found the prostitute dead, her body stuffed under the bed. It was a particularly brutal crime. The woman had been struck a total of eight times, detaching her right eye. The killer had used both a telephone and a six-foot floor lamp as weapons. In addition, she had been strangled with the telephone cord.

DePasquale had the place dusted for prints and came up empty. No physical evidence could be linked to the killer. The only lead was the registration card. The name was phony, of course. And so was the address—98 Babbitt Road, Bedford Hills, New York. But although there was no 98 Babbitt Road in Bedford Hills, the *street* actually existed. And the man had inexplica-

102

bly added an *actual* Zip code in Bedford Hills. This led DePasquale to conclude that the suspect had more than a passing knowledge of that town.

"I ran a check of recent parolees and work release participants from the Tuconic prison at Bedford Hills and came up with Scofield," DePasquale remarked. In addition, DePasquale noted that Scofield's family lived in Bedford Hills. "Which means he knows the streets and the Zip codes." Furthermore, DePasquale had learned that the agency handling Scofield's work release program was five blocks away from where the murder took place. DePasquale interviewed Scofield, but Scofield refused to answer any questions. Without some other form of intervention—such as a confidential informant Scofield trusted—Scofield would walk.

"We need you, Kevin," Malady said.

Maher thought about how Scofield just sat there as Molese pummeled poor Alice. Locking up Scofield would not only be an adventure, it would also be a pleasure.

"Sure," Maher said. "I'll do it."

DePasquale and Malady smiled.

"How much?" Maher asked.

"How much?" DePasquale looked at Malady. Malady looked back at DePasquale.

"Well, I ain't doing it for nothing," Maher stated with emphasis. He wanted to be paid. But how much didn't really matter. What mattered was that he would be receiving money to act in a law enforcement capacity.

DePasquale offered $500 for the job. Maher accepted.

MAHER WAS A VETERAN AT WEARING A WIRE. SO HE WAS AS UNRUFFLED as a surgeon when he glided his 1971 Chrysler to a stop in front of Scofield's house in Bedford Hills later that evening. Even the car had been prepped. Standard procedure in situations like these was to remove a fuse, rendering the car radio inoperable. The reason for this slight modification was to prevent sound from obscuring a taped confession. Police had observed over the years that the first thing many suspects did when they climbed into an automobile was turn on the radio and crank up the volume. This behavior was not intended to muddle any recording done in the car, rather it appeared to be a reaction designed to prevent someone *outside* the car from overhearing the conversation. Cops had disabled radios many times, yet suspects never seemed to get it.

Scofield was no exception. The moment he slid into the passenger seat of Maher's car, he reached for the radio and snapped it on. Nothing.

"The radio's broken," Maher said matter-of-factly.

Scofield glanced nervously out the window. The street was empty. After a beat, Maher kick-started the conversation.

"Ronald," Maher said, "what the fuck did you do?"

"What are you talking about?" Scofield's eyes were wide with fear.

"Man, these fucking cops were all over me. They said someone who looked like me killed a fucking whore."

Maher and Scofield *were* similar in appearance. So Scofield bought Maher's line. He mulled over what Maher was saying for a minute or so.

Maher pressed. "The cops kept asking me about Bedford Hills."

Scofield began to look like a cornered rabbit.

Maher grabbed Scofield's shoulders. "Come on, Ronald. What the fuck did you do?"

"I couldn't get it up, Kevin."

Maher studied Scofield for a moment. That's what this is all about. He couldn't get it up?

Scofield, without any further prodding, continued. "She kept playing with me but I couldn't get it up. Then she said she was leaving. I asked for my money back but she wouldn't give it to me. So I hit her with the telephone."

Scofield opened the car door. "I gotta get out of Bedford Hills."

"Where are you going?" Maher wanted to know.

"I don't know. Somewhere in Manhattan." Scofield stepped out onto the sidewalk. "I'll call you."

Maher drove back into the city where he, DePasquale, and Malady listened to Scofield's impromptu confession. When the tape was over, DePasquale seemed happy enough, but Malady had a look of concern.

"Not enough," Malady said with a sigh.

Maher was incredulous. Malady explained that Scofield's confession contained nothing specific about the crime.

"I want to make sure I get a conviction," Malady said. "So I need you to go back and get Scofield to describe the murder in detail."

Maher sighed. Being a cop wasn't so easy after all.

A few days later, Scofield called and asked Maher if he could borrow some money. This time they met at a seedy West 44th Street hotel. Maher, fitted with a tape recorder, handed Scofield $50.

"Ronald, you gotta tell me what happened."

"I *told* you what happened," Scofield retorted. "I hit the slut with the phone."

Maher leaned in. "Listen. I've been in jail long enough to know what they need for an arrest, an indictment, and a conviction. You tell me every detail of what happened from the time you picked her up until you left the hotel room, and I'll be able to tell you, without a fucking doubt, whether or not they're jerking your chain."

Scofield frowned, and Maher thought Scofield was spooked by the straightforward request for a blow-by-blow account of the murder. But then Scofield started into the story.

"Okay, l-l-let's see," Scofield stammered. "She wanted to leave—she was lying on the bed and she started to get up—I got pissed off and whacked her with the phone."

"How many times?"

"I don't know. Three. Four, maybe."

"And that killed her?"

"No! No!" Scofield was exasperated. "When I realized she was hurt bad . . ."

Scofield's voice trailed off.

"How bad?" Maher pressed. "How bad was she hurt?"

"I knocked one of her eyes out."

"Which eye?"

Scofield touched his right eye. "The right one."

Maher grimaced. "But she was still alive?"

"Yeah. She was squirming around the bed. And the bitch wouldn't die. The fucking bitch wouldn't die!"

Maher was sickened by what he was hearing. Scofield continued.

"I couldn't let her live, Kevin."

"Why not, Ronald? Why couldn't you let her live?"

"I was on a work release program. I figured if she talked, they'd violate my parole."

Maher felt like drawing back his fist and driving it into Scofield's face.

Scofield went on with his gory tale. "I choked her with the phone cord, but the bitch just wouldn't fucking die!"

Maher winced at the words.

Scofield continued. "So I threw her on the floor and beat the shit out her head with the fucking floor lamp."

"You left her on the floor?"

"I stuffed the fucking whore under the bed."

"Which way was the body facing?"

"Does that matter?" Scofield asked.

"Maybe," Maher said.

Scofield thought for a moment. "She was face down."

Maher continued to extract specifics from Scofield, including the color of the room and the type of furniture. Feeling he had enough to satisfy ADA Malady, Maher left. He stopped off in the lobby bathroom on the way out.

"I got this motherfucker now," Maher whispered under his breath as he relieved himself. "This stupid motherfucker is going down."

Maher rendezvoused with DePasquale, and he listened to the tape. Scofield was putting himself away for a very long time. Then came the sound of Maher walking into a bathroom, followed by the sound of a zipper. Maher could be heard whispering: *I got this motherfucker now. This stupid motherfucker is going down.* Next came the sound of Maher relieving himself and then a flush.

"I forgot I had the Nagra on," Maher said.

Both Maher and DePasquale laughed.

The next day Malady listened to the tape and immediately issued an arrest warrant. Then Maher testified in front of a grand jury as CI #667903. Scofield, as Maher had predicted, was indeed going down.

*   *   *

COP WITHOUT A BADGE

SINCE MAHER HAD JOINED PENN CENTRAL, THERE HAD BEEN A FINANCIAL restructuring of the railroad with a new name—ConRail. Maher's supervisor informed him that there was an opening in the signal and communication department of ConRail's New Jersey region. The pay would be higher and the work would be a lot easier than the effort required in replacing railroad ties. And so, in mid-October 1976, Maher resigned his job at ConRail New York and signed on with ConRail New Jersey. He would start his new job on October 26. All was well in the Maher/Eschert household. Until the phone call from ADA Malady.

"Kevin," Malady began, "there will be a discovery hearing in a few days and I'm going to have to turn over the minutes of the grand jury hearing."

Although Malady insisted that he was not required to divulge Maher's name, Maher knew that Scofield wasn't *that* stupid. Scofield would know immediately who the unnamed CI was. For the first time since he started playing cop, Maher was frightened. Scofield knew where Maher lived. And even if Scofield were locked up, Scofield had a brother. And he had friends with nasty dispositions.

Still reeling from Malady's call, Maher received another call.

"Hey, Kevin. It's William Hand."

William Hand was an inmate Maher had met during his term at Coxsackie Prison.

"I want to do a bank," Hand said. "I need a wheel man. You interested?"

An invitation to a felony. Maher shook his head. *Is there no way to go forward? Yes, there is a way to go forward. Say no. Hang up the receiver.*

"When?" Maher asked, surprising himself.

"Tomorrow."

They agreed to meet that evening at Maher's house to discuss the job.

Maher tried to reach Doherty but he wasn't in and couldn't be reached. Maher looked at the wall clock. He would be meeting Hand in two hours. He had to talk to *someone* in law enforcement before the meeting. It occurred to Maher that bank robbery was a *federal* crime. And he recalled having met FBI agent Al Garber in Doherty's office.

Maher decided not to waste time on the telephone and drove

directly to the FBI's New York headquarters, an apartment building on East 69th Street. Maher entered the building and walked up to the reception desk.

"Agent Al Garber," Maher said. "Tell him Kevin Maher is here to see him and it's important. Tell him I'm Sergeant Doherty's CI."

A moment later, Garber emerged.

"Hello, Kevin. What can I do for you?"

"I'm going to rob a bank," Maher said.

Garber led Maher down the hall into a small room.

"Tell me about this bank," Garber asked.

"First Federal Savings and Loan. Fourteenth Street and First Avenue. Hand says it's an easy bank." Maher laughed. "He told me a friend of his has robbed it *three times.*"

"When?" Garber wanted to know.

"Tomorrow."

Garber shook his head. "It can't be tomorrow. You'll have to stall him for a few days."

Garber explained that the policy at the Justice Department was to move cautiously. Before they arrested a suspect, the FBI would always "identify" the suspect first, checking to see if another bureau was involved. What if the Bureau of Alcohol, Tobacco, and Firearms was already on Hand's case?

"If you don't take him off now with me," Maher protested, "he'll find someone else and do the job anyway."

Garber remained hesitant.

Maher pressed. "The guy is a heroin addict. And he's running around the city with a gun."

Garber grimaced. Certainly Hand was capable of acting on impulse, knocking off the first bank he saw. At least this way, with Maher, it was a "controlled bank robbery," which was how the FBI referred to such an operation. Garber grabbed the phone and called a group supervisor. It was resolved that they would do the best they could to communicate with other bureaus. The bank robbery was on. For the next half hour, Garber briefed Maher on what he expected. When Garber finished, Maher got to the fee.

"How much do I get for this assignment?"

Garber offered Maher $1,500. Maher smiled. He got $500 from the Manhattan DA's office for the Scofield case. And he would receive three times that much from the feds for his work on the Hand robbery. In the beginning, the adventure had been enough. Now the money was getting good enough to turn the adventure into a career.

But then reality hit him. *Scofield! What about Scofield and the discovery hearing?*

"Agent Garber," Maher said, "I have a problem."

Maher explained the Scofield situation, and Garber suggested that Maher enter the witness protection program.

"We can put you in North Dakota," Garber said.

Maher was not overwhelmed by the idea of living in North Dakota. After a brief discussion of the options, Garber and Maher agreed that, in addition to the $1,500 he was getting as a fee, the FBI would pay an additional $1,000 for "relocation." Maher chose New Jersey. Garber fired back that the FBI did not "relocate" people a few miles across the Hudson River and countered that a destination much farther away would be safer. Maher held his ground: New Jersey. Finally, Garber consented.

HAND ARRIVED AT MAHER'S HOUSE SWEATING AND SHAKING. *NOT A GOOD sign*, Maher thought. Hand was in need of a heroin fix.

"We do the bank tomorrow morning," Hand said, his voice trilling from the involuntary shakes. "Ten o'clock."

Hand asked Maher to meet him at an intersection on Tremont Avenue in the Bronx. Although Maher pressed Hand about an address, it was clear that Hand did not want Maher to know where he lived. Unfortunately, Hand was sitting in Maher's living room. So Hand knew where Maher lived.

Maher sighed. The sooner this job was over and the sooner he got to New Jersey, the better.

The following morning, Maher drove his 1971 cream-colored Chrysler 300 to an intersection on Tremont Avenue and waited for Hand to appear. A moment later, Hand—more than a few convulsions past his last heroin fix—stumbled out of a large frame house near the corner. *So much for his secret address*, Maher thought, laughing to himself. *The dumb fuck makes a big deal about meeting him on a corner, then walks out of a house a few feet away.*

"You're driving *your* car, man," Hand said as he climbed into

Maher's car. His voice was soaked in suspicion. "What the fuck are you doing?"

Maher was quick with a response: "It's got a 440 under the hood, man. You want to get away or not?"

Hand mulled that over for a minute then countered. "They can trace your car."

Maher fired back another volley. "No, they can't. I put on stolen plates."

In fact, the plates were *not* stolen. But it was the best response Maher could come up with on the fly.

Hand reached into his jacket pocket and removed two guns: a .32 and a .357 magnum. The .357 looked new and bristled with power. The .32 clearly was old, even a bit rusty. Hand gave Maher the .32.

"Let's go," Hand said, rocking back and forth in the seat.

Maher navigated the Manhattan traffic and turned onto 14th Street. As had been laid out by Garber, Maher double-parked his car behind a double-parked van. Although the van looked innocuous enough, there were six FBI agents crouched inside, each with an automatic weapon.

Hand nervously scanned the street and then turned to Maher: "Okay. We wait for an old woman to walk into the fucking bank. And then we jump out. You follow her into the bank and grab her and we'll use her as a hostage."

Maher took a deep breath. Taking a hostage had never been part of the plan.

Hand passed Maher a wool ski mask. "Put this on. When we jump out, pull it over your face."

Maher started to say something, something like, "William, it's seventy-five degrees outside. A wool ski mask is a dead give-away." Instead, Maher just popped the wool cap on his head and sat there as Hand scanned the area for an elderly hostage. Five minutes passed. Then ten. Maher's forehead was sweating profusely. *Where the fuck are all the old ladies?* Suddenly Hand's eyes widened. Maher turned to look out the windshield. *Maybe there's an old lady coming down the fucking sidewalk.* But it wasn't an old lady. It was a uniformed police officer, strolling west on 14th Street. The officer ambled past the car, lowering his eyes as he passed. You could hear him thinking: *Ski caps?*

Instead of continuing west, the officer turned and walked

east, once again passing the Chrysler. He stopped a few feet in front of the car and stared through the windshield at Hand.

The steady gaze of the cop made Hand start to tremble slightly. "I ain't going back to prison, Kevin. You hear me? I ain't going back to no fucking cell."

Maher peered through the windshield at the young officer, who didn't look more than twenty years old. He had a shiny new holster and a deep blue uniform that hadn't seen many laundry cycles. A rookie for sure, perhaps a Police Academy graduate with only a few days on the force. Maher tried telepathy. *Please, officer. Walk away. Just walk away.* But the officer kept his eyes fixed on the car.

Hand was now taking breaths in little choked gasps. "I'm telling you, Kevin, I ain't getting taken alive. I'll waste this fucking cop if I have to."

Maher sneaked a look at the FBI van. *Do they realize there's a foot cop out there?* Then Maher glanced back at the officer. Slowly, the officer slid his walkie-talkie off his belt and raised it to his lips. Maher watched in horror as the cop mouthed the words: *New Jersey plates. FMS 953.* Maher's earlier response to Hand's trepidation about the car—*I put on stolen plates*—now had an ominous ring to it as the cop stood waiting for a response on his walkie-talkie.

"You said you had hot plates on this fucking thing," Hand blurted out, then began rocking back and forth again on the seat. Hand slid his fingers over the .357. "I'm going to waste the stupid motherfucker."

Maher decided that no matter what, he couldn't let Hand shoot a cop. Maher grasped the .32. He could feel the grit and the rust. Although he wasn't even sure if the gun would fire, Maher slowly moved the barrel of the .32 toward Hand's side and prepared himself to pull the trigger if it looked like Hand was going to fire at the cop. As the tense seconds ticked by, Maher's mind raced through the repercussions of what he was about to do.

If the cop comes over, what do I do? What if the cop sees my gun? He doesn't know I'm a good guy. I know this fuck beside me is about to kill a cop, so what do I do? Do I just sit here and let it happen? No; I have to shoot Hand. But when the cop sees the gun, is he going to start shooting at me? Or what if I kill Hand and get arrested? Am I going to get charged with murder? How does that work? I was born a Roman Catholic. I was an altar boy. And now I've got to kill a guy? Fuck!

Although Maher wasn't aware of it, an FBI surveillance team had taken up a position in a furniture factory across the street from the bank. The team commander got on radio and instructed the cop to leave the area immediately. But even after the officer received the urgent message, he lingered, his eyes probing the car.

Hand raised the .357 slowly. Maher steadied the .32 and slipped his finger around the trigger. Then he turned his head. He didn't want to see the blood. He would look away and squeeze the trigger. Maher tightened his finger, applying pressure to the trigger. Suddenly . . .

"He's leaving!" Hand said with a growl. "He's leaving!"

Maher—now drenched with sweat—relaxed the tension in his finger and looked through the windshield. The cop was walking away. And an old lady—laden down with shopping bags—was shuffling toward the bank.

"You get out of the car first," Hand yelled. "The minute you get in the bank, you grab the old lady."

Maher and Hand bounded from the car and ran toward the bank.

The FBI would have preferred to arrest Hand in the act. That way, they would be able to charge him with bank robbery. Otherwise, they would only be able to charge him with *attempted* bank robbery, which carried a far more lenient sentence. As illogical as the distinction might seem to a layman, that was the way the law worked.

While it was in the best interests of the FBI not to intervene before Hand had a opportunity to pull off the heist, they couldn't allow a dangerous felony such as an armed robbery to occur. What if an innocent bystander were killed and it was later revealed that the FBI could have prevented the tragedy?

Maher and Hand moved quickly across the sidewalk. As Hand reached out for the revolving door, a flood of tellers and customers burst out of the bank. Then several pedestrians stepped toward him. The hot dog vendor dropped a bun and whipped around. Two Con Edison employees, wearing bright blue hard hats, stopped working and ran toward the bank. A cashier jogged out of a Blimpie fast food restaurant. Suddenly, *every one of them*—the tellers, customers, pedestrians, hot dog vendor, Con Edison employees, even the Blimpie cashier—drew guns. They were all either FBI agents or NYPD cops.

A stunned Hand was tackled and thrown to the sidewalk. He surrendered without incident. So did Maher. They were shoved in a paddy wagon together, booked for *attempted* bank robbery and a weapons charge together, and they were arraigned together at Southern District Court. As Maher and Hand stood before a judge, several federal marshals burst into the courtroom.

"Your Honor," one of the marshals explained, "We have an arrest warrant for Kevin Maher in South Carolina."

After a brief discussion at the bench, Maher was handed over to the federal marshals.

Once outside the courthouse, Maher was uncuffed. The South Carolina warrant, just like the arraignment, was phony—designed to protect Maher's cover.

"Good work," one of the marshals said.

Maher smiled. It *was* good work.

As Maher walked down Centre Street to retrieve his car, he felt a swell of pride. *I'm a good cop,* he thought as he strode along, buoyed by a natural high. But then a sudden depression seized him. He wasn't *really* a cop. In fact, he could never *really* be a cop because someone with a felony conviction was not allowed to be a cop. Maher bolstered himself again by reasoning that he was *kind of* a cop. But that didn't take away the sting of the one thundering realization that shook his senses: *All I ever wanted to be was a cop. Just because I was a wild teenager who stole a car I'll never get to be a real cop.*

It just didn't seem fair.

THE FOLLOWING MORNING—THE MORNING AFTER HE HAD "ROBBED" A bank—Kevin Maher a.k.a. *Edward* Maher reported for his first day of work at ConRail's signal and communication department in New Jersey. As Maher looked around at his coworkers, he smiled. *They don't have any idea I robbed a bank yesterday.* So Maher felt no trepidation when Con Rail's chief inspector, Artie Dunn, approached him. After all, Dunn was a family friend who

looked the other way when Kevin Maher became Edward
Maher to get a job at ConRail.

"Kevin," Dunn said, "what's this all about?"

Dunn handed Maher a *New York Times.*

"Oh, fuck!" Maher said with a gasp as he started to read.

The reason for his consternation was an item in a column
titled "Crime Blotter." The item read as follows:

> A stakeout by agents of the Federal Bureau of Investi-
> gation and members of the New York City Police De-
> partment major-case squad resulted in the arrest of
> two men as they attempted to hold up the First Federal
> Savings and Loan Association at 237 First Avenue,
> near 15th Street. Charged with the attempted robbery
> were William Patrick Hand, a 22-year-old fisherman,
> and Kevin Maher, 22, a truckdriver.

"I was working with the feds," Maher said.

Dunn was not entirely convinced. He studied Maher for a
long time. Maher squirmed.

"Listen, Artie. If I had really robbed a bank yesterday, would I
be reporting to work today?"

Dunn continued to stare at Maher.

"You can check with the feds if you want," Maher said.

"I will," Dunn replied and then walked away.

When Maher got home that evening, he received more than
a dozen frantic phone calls from friends and relatives. They all
wanted to know the same thing: "Kevin! Did you rob a bank?!"

"It's not me," Maher repeated over and over. "It's another
Kevin Maher."

The flurry of phone calls over, Maher sat down with Beth and
informed her they were moving to New Jersey.

"But we just moved to the Bronx," Beth retorted.

"We have to move to New Jersey," Maher said.

"But we can't afford to move," Beth pointed out.

"The FBI is paying for it," Maher explained.

"Fine," Beth responded and then walked into another room.

Beth never asked questions. Even something as major as a
move to another state elicited little more than a mild protest.
Perhaps living with a contract killer had conditioned her not to
be inquisitive.

A few days before Scofield's discovery hearing, Maher was summoned to FBI headquarters by Garber. According to Garber, a cop in the Manhattan DA's office had raised the specter that Maher might have entrapped Hand to gain relocation money from the FBI. The cop had no proof Maher had used any form of entrapment but cited the "coincidental" timing of the Hand bank job and the Scofield discovery hearing, which necessitated that Maher relocate.

Maher was outraged. Doherty offered some solace by telling Maher that the cop in question was suspect of *all* CIs. And Garber further calmed Maher by saying he didn't believe Maher would do such a thing. Still, Garber said, the bureau had to check it out.

Within hours, federal agents had spoken with a friend of William Hand who swore under oath that the idea to rob First Federal had originated with Hand. The source further stated that Hand actively sought out Maher for the job, not the other way around. Maher was vindicated. Yet it left bad feelings. Here he was doing what he thought was the *right thing* and he winds up on the defensive. It just wasn't worth it. He resolved to walk away from it all. And just to make sure he really did walk away, he promised Beth he would never again work undercover.

VIRTUALLY HOURS BEFORE THE SCOFIELD DISCOVERY HEARING, MAHER and Beth moved into a three-bedroom, two-bath apartment in a two-family house in Edgewater, New Jersey. And they decided to get married. But word came back from the attorney they had hired to handle the divorce that Eschert was contesting the action. Unable to get married, Beth did the next best thing. She went to the Division of Motor Vehicles and obtained a driver's license under the name Beth Maher. Next, Beth applied for a new Social Security card under the name Maher. No one asked for any proof of marriage. Both Beth and Maher were surprised how easy it was for a woman to change her identity.

Beth's change of name from Eschert to Maher had no real impact on their day-to-day lives until one of Bobby's classmates called Maher "Mr. Eschert." Maher explained that he was not "Mr. Eschert," he was Mr. Maher. This, of course, prompted

Bobby to ask why *his* name was Eschert but "you and Mommy are Maher."

"My name was Eschert when you were born," Beth replied.

Six-year-old Bobby accepted the answer. And he wouldn't ask that question again for more than a decade.

FOR THE NEXT TWO YEARS, MAHER DID AS BETH AND HE HAD AGREED: He retired his imaginary badge. The frequent queries from various detectives no longer even tempted him. And whenever someone from his prison days surfaced with some felonious scheme, Maher politely declined.

"You better get somebody else," Maher would say. "I'm out of the business."

Life continued to improve for Maher and Beth. They saved some money and moved to a nicer place, in Wood-Ridge. At twenty-five years old, Maher had found contentment. Events prior to his relocation to Edgewater seemed surreal, as if they never had occurred. But then, on the night of March 23, 1979, as Maher and Beth settled in to watch the evening news, there came a bleak reminder about Maher's bizarre past. The demons of 24 Sanford Road returned. And this time the evil was as hellish as it gets.

The news anchor stared out somberly from the television screen: "A mass murder in Fair Lawn, New Jersey. Coming up after this message."

Maher snatched the phone receiver and dialed Doherty. "Sergeant Doherty. Turn on channel seven."

Maher and Beth sat silently through a commercial. On the other end of the phone, Doherty, a receiver pressed to his ear, watched silently as well. Finally the newscast returned.

"A mass murder in New Jersey," the anchor repeated. "For more on this late-breaking story we go to correspondent John Johnson, who is standing by live in Fair Lawn."

The image on the television screen changed to John Johnson standing in front of Molese's house. Indeed, it *was* a late-breaking story—the body bags were just being removed. One normal-size body bag. One gigantic body bag. And one tiny body bag. Maher began to feel ill. Beth placed a hand over her gaping mouth. They knew. Before John Johnson uttered a word, they *knew*.

"A brutal triple homicide tonight in this quiet New Jersey community. The bodies of two women and a boy—their throats slashed—have been discovered inside this house at Twenty-four Sanford Road, in Fair Lawn. The victims have been identified as Marcia Ferrell, her five-year-old son, Harold Ferrell, and the owner of the house . . ."

Johnson glanced at his notes, then looked up, staring directly into the camera.

". . . Alice Molese."

Chapter 8

ALICE MOLESE HAD NOT MERELY BEEN MURDERED, SHE ALSO HAD BEEN sexually mutilated. In addition to a slashed throat, both her breasts had been cut off. And in a particularly grisly display of misogyny, a knife had been inserted deep into her vagina and pulled upward all the way to her neck.

Maher tossed the police report on the desk of Fair Lawn police lieutenant Joseph Messere. Also in the room were Bergen County investigators Francis P. DelPrete and Robert Rehberg, two of the *forty-eight* cops who had been assigned to the case, described by the media as the most heinous homicide in Bergen County history.

Reports of the bloodbath—which had led the newscasts on all local stations in the area and was on the front page of newspapers across three states—included the gory details of how Alice was killed as well as the particulars of how Marcia Ferrell and her son, Harold, were put to death. Harold's head had been almost completely severed from his five-year-old body, with only a piece of skin connecting it to the torso. Marcia Ferrell—who apparently put up quite a struggle—had suffered multiple stab wounds.

The eyes of millions of people were looking apprehensively toward Fair Lawn, New Jersey. What if some homicidal maniac was on the loose? After all, who else would have been so cruel and sadistic?

"Brian Molese," Maher said, then added: "Brian butchered her because he hated her so much."

Maher glanced at the crime scene photos for an instant, which was as long as he could bear to look. Poor fat Alice sat slumped in a corner of the dining room, a look of dull surprise on her frozen features. Maher swallowed hard to keep from throwing up.

"Molese asked me to kill Alice *twice*," Maher told the three cops.

DelPrete and Rehberg exchanged troubled glances.

"Why didn't you report it to the police?" DelPrete asked.

"Why did it take you three years to come forward?" Rehberg followed up before Maher could answer.

"I *did* go to the cops," Maher fired back. "Sergeant Jim Doherty in the Manhattan DA's office."

Messere called Doherty, and Doherty confirmed Maher's statement about reporting Molese's solicitations. Satisfied, Messere hung up the receiver and looked at Maher.

"Molese discovered his wife's body," Messere stated evenly. "Molese and a man named Larry Gallagher."

Messere went on to say that Molese's statement detailed a number of valuable items that were missing from the house.

"He told us it must have been a botched burglary," Messere said.

Molese had been particularly upset about the loss of a large ring that he claimed once belonged to King Farouk. According to Molese, he bought the ring from Frank Sinatra.

Maher laughed derisively. "King Farouk! He's been telling that bullshit story for years."

"You've seen the ring?" Messere asked.

"I *sold* the ring," Maher answered.

Maher related how, in an effort to save the house from being seized for back taxes, he took all of Alice's jewelry into Manhattan and cashed it in at the 47th Street Jewelry Exchange.

"I sold everything except an antique necklace," Maher recalled. "Alice really loved that necklace—it belonged to her mother—so I didn't sell it, I pawned it. At a place called Providence Loan Association in the Bronx. I got thirteen hundred for it."

"You still have the pawn ticket?" DelPrete wanted to know.

"Yeah," Maher replied. "I still have it."

"You have receipts?" DelPrete pressed. "For the items you sold in Manhattan?"

"Yes," Maher answered. "I saved the receipts."

DelPrete and Rehberg took Maher to his apartment to pick up the pawn ticket and the sales receipts, then headed to Fordham Road in the Bronx, where they stopped into Providence Loan Association. The necklace—which had been collecting dust for three years—had been sold less than a week before. Nonetheless, DelPrete and Rehberg were able to confirm that the necklace—listed among the items Molese claimed were taken in the "burglary"—had indeed *not* been stolen.

Next stop for the investigative trio was the 47th Street Jewelry Exchange. The man who purchased Alice's jewelry was still right where he was three years ago. Since the jeweler had been suspicious of Maher at the time, he had photocopied Maher's driver's license and saved all the paperwork pertaining to the transaction.

"What's the problem?" the jeweler asked, now even more suspicious.

"The woman who owned the jewelry is dead," Maher said.

The jeweler gave Maher a look of understanding sweetened with sympathy. "So you need this information for the settlement of her estate?"

"No," Maher shot back. "I need the information for the police. She was murdered."

Maher nodded over his shoulder. "These two gentleman are detectives from Bergen County."

The stunned jeweler quickly rifled through his files and made photocopies of the transactions involving Alice's jewelry.

Mission accomplished, Maher, DelPrete, and Rehberg returned to Fair Lawn police headquarters.

"These may be quite helpful," Rehberg said, referring to the receipts. "It raises the possibility that Molese lied about the jewelry."

Maher was indignant. "Possibility!?"

Rehberg noted that there could be other explanations for why Molese reported the jewelry stolen. For example, what if Molese knew about his wife's jewelry collection but didn't know if she still owned any of it? Discovering that the jewelry was missing after Alice Molese's murder, Brian Molese may have assumed it was stolen.

Maher was only half listening. "He *did* it. He killed Alice. Why don't you just go and arrest him?"

"We don't have enough to charge him," Rehberg countered.

Maher grew agitated. "Don't you understand? The faggot son of a bitch killed Alice. Lock the bastard up!"

"He *is* the prime suspect," DelPrete acknowledged, "but we have no physical evidence to link him to the crime."

DelPrete asked Maher if he would be willing to work undercover to help nail Molese.

"You could wear a wire," DelPrete suggested, "and you could arrange a meeting with—"

"No," Maher broke in, "I can't."

"Why not?" both DelPrete and Rehberg asked in unison.

"I locked up Scofield," Maher answered.

DelPrete and Rehberg sat in astonishment as Maher launched into the story of how Ronald Scofield, Molese's homosexual lover, had murdered a prostitute.

Before he left police headquarters, Maher gave a sworn statement detailing everything he could recall about his association with Molese, from the days at Green Haven to the night Molese battered Alice as Scofield looked on. The following day, Beth also gave a sworn statement.

A week passed. Then a month. Brian Molese still had not been charged with the murder of Alice Molese. Indeed, the case was growing cold, which is why Maher was engulfed in a cloud of frustration when he entered 1 Hogan Place and stormed up to Doherty's desk.

"You have to do something, Sergeant Doherty," Maher exclaimed.

Doherty sighed. "What can I do, Kevin? It's not my case. It's not my jurisdiction. Hell, it's not even my state."

Maher paced for a moment, then stopped and faced Doherty. "If I hadn't moved Beth and Bobby out of the house, that would have been them being carried out in body bags instead of Marcia and Harold. Beth would be in Marcia's grave and Bobby would be in Harold's grave."

That thought had occurred to Doherty. He placed his hand on Maher's shoulder.

"There's nothing we can do right now, Kevin."

Maher knew Doherty was right. And so, at least for the moment, it looked as if Brian Molese had gotten away with murder.

As the shock of hearing about Alice abated, Maher and Beth again withdrew into their private world, doing what any other suburban couple might do. They were parents to Bobby, who was now eight years old, bought a German shepherd named Samantha, took a vacation to Disney World in Florida, and socialized with a circle of friends who included their coworkers and neighbors. By the fall of 1979, they were no longer struggling with life, they were embracing it. And due to Beth's promotion to circulation manager at *New York* magazine and Maher's frequent overtime stints at ConRail, they were earning a combined yearly income of more than $60,000. They could afford more than necessities now, they could afford dreams. And Maher had one overriding dream: a fast car.

Of course, it was a fast car that got Maher into trouble in the first place.

"I'd like to buy a Corvette," Maher had said to Beth in early September.

"If it will make you happy," Beth had answered, "*do* it."

Thus Maher's love affair with speed was renewed when he purchased a 1979 blue Chevrolet Corvette, model L82. The price was $12,500, half of which Maher had to fork over as a down payment because of his credit history.

As fast as the car was right out of the showroom, Maher wasn't satisfied. So he went to Larry Birnholz, a mechanic who was familiar with making high-performance modifications on Corvettes.

"I want to make a few changes on my car," Maher told Birnholz.

At Maher's request, Birnholz installed a high-performance intake manifold and a Holley carburetor, which were designed to increase the speed of the Corvette. When Birnholz was done, Maher had a vehicle that would do a quarter mile in fourteen seconds. And a quarter mile just happened to be the distance of a drag race.

There was a place in Queens where an intersection of parallel roads and bridges crisscrosses in such a way that a perfect quarter-mile course lay between the bridges. The stretch of asphalt —an ideal layout for drag racing—was called Connecting Highway, and every Friday and Saturday night a collection of souped-up cars would roar to the starting line at one bridge and zoom to the finish line at the other bridge. The spectacle would attract thousands of onlookers who gathered on the overpass and looked down on the urban raceway. Wagers as high as $4,000 or $5,000 were made by the drivers.

The weekly racing event had its origins in the 1950s and had become a long-standing tradition. The police did their best to prevent them by asking the fire department to hose down the highway, the wet pavement making it difficult for tires to establish traction. But on summer nights, the water would quickly evaporate, and the show would go on.

When Maher arrived on the scene, a star was born. Weekend after weekend, Maher's Corvette crossed under the bridge in first place, earning the title "Fastest Street Car in Brooklyn and Queens." But just as the fastest gun in the West had to keep looking over his shoulder, so did Maher. Each week, someone showed up at Connecting Highway with a newly modified machine and took aim at Maher's title. Although Maher kept winning, his margin of victory was getting smaller. So he dispensed with the '79 Vette and stopped in at Malcolm Conners Chevrolet in Paramus, New Jersey, where he ordered a 1980 Corvette.

When the new bright red Corvette—a car for which Maher had paid $14,000—arrived, the first thing Maher did was call Chevrolet and order a 1970 LT1 short block engine (1970 was the last year Chevrolet made a high-compression motor with an eleven-to-one compression ratio). Then Maher had a series of special high-performance modifications made, not only to the short block but also to the heads. Triple-angled valve job. Ported and polished angle plug cylinder heads. Doug Nash five-speed transmission. LT1 intake manifold. The cost of the modifications was $5,000. Next, Maher contacted Henry's Axles in Anaheim, California, and phoned in specifications for a custom-designed rear end. To manufacture the design Maher described, Henry's Axles would have to take the drive shaft from a Diamond dump truck and mold two half shafts for the Vette, then modify the ten-bolt Corvette rear end housing to fit a larger twelve-bolt, heavy-duty ring and pinion posi unit, and *then* grind the housing so it would accept a 2.73 rear-end ratio.

"Sure," the man from Harry's Axles said. "We can do it."

A few weeks later a tractor-trailer truck pulled in front of Maher's house. Inside the trailer was the Frankenstein rear end along with a bill from Harry's Axles for $3,700.

Maher took the Vette to Frank's Sunoco in Lyndhurst, New Jersey, where he fitted the car with the Harry's Axles hybrid.

By the time Maher was finished, he had $30,000 invested in a one-of-a-kind vehicle. It was such an extraordinary specimen that word quickly spread about the car. And the legend of Maher's Vette grew as he blasted the beast through a quarter mile at Connecting Highway in an amazing eleven seconds. In short order the car came to the attention of *Vette* magazine and was featured in the December 1980 issue. The nature of the conversion, the legend of its performance at Connecting Highway, the magazine article, all of these things added to its value and mystique.

In 1980 Maher had seemingly escaped his past and had come up a winner, at least the way such things are measured in the blue-collar corners of New York and New Jersey. And, except for the occasional calls from Doherty, there were few reminders of the days before Beth and Bobby.

Doherty had phoned once to tell Maher that Detective Greg Demetriou—whom Maher had met at the Manhattan DA's office—had been shot chasing a bank robber on 42nd Street.

"Greg is so fast," Doherty related, "that he outran the uniformed cops. That's how he got shot."

Doherty went on to say that Demetriou would recover and that he would be awarded the NYPD Medal of Honor.

The second call from Doherty included a humorous bit of news from one of Maher's first cases.

"Remember Henry Bohle?" Doherty asked. "He hired you as a hit man to kill his partner Louis Izzo."

"Yeah," Maher said. "What about him?"

"Well," Doherty began, "I get a call the other day from Izzo. He's panicked. Whispering into the phone. Izzo says: 'Sergeant. Guess who just showed up for work?' And I say: 'Who?' And

Izzo says: 'Henry. He's sitting at his desk like he just got back from a long weekend.' "

Maher and Doherty started laughing.

"What?" Maher said between chuckles. "Bohle gets out of prison and five years later goes *right back to work?*"

"That's right," Doherty continued. "So Izzo asks me: 'Sergeant, what am I supposed to do?' I tell him: 'The guy served his time, paid his debt to society, there's nothing you can do about it. Maybe you should sell your share of the business or buy him out.' "

"That's really funny," Maher observed.

"Not so funny for Izzo," Doherty countered.

And then they both broke out into hysterics. Which is exactly how Maher wanted to remember the past, if at all. With a laugh.

"I'm retiring, Kevin," Doherty said suddenly. "I've had enough."

"You can't do that!" Maher exclaimed. "Who will I call when I need to talk to somebody?"

"You can still call me," Doherty said with a laugh.

But that's not what Maher meant, and Doherty sensed it. Maher was hooked on the undercover action.

"Hey, Kevin," Doherty assured him, "I still know a lot of people on the job."

DURING THE FIRST SIX MONTHS OF 1981, MAHER CARRIED ON WITH HIS relatively sedate life. But then, on the morning of June 9, Maher was shaken by a news report on WINS radio that Brian Molese had been shot. Details of the shooting were sketchy for a couple days, but on June 12 a newspaper article appeared under the headline SURRENDER OF SUSPECT SOUGHT.

> Detectives at the Sixth Precinct are trying to negotiate the surrender of a suspect in the shooting of Brian Molese, the former husband of a Fair Lawn woman murdered in her home in 1979.
>
> Molese, 39, and his roommate, Christopher Crosthwaite, 20, were both shot Monday night with a .22-

caliber handgun, allegedly by a couple they invited for
a drink at their East 10th Street apartment.

Molese and Crosthwaite, who had both been shot in the
mouth, had been treated and released from St. Vincent's Hospital in Greenwich Village. The article stated that police knew the
identity of the suspect—which was being withheld pending further investigation—and that the suspect's lawyer was former
U.S. attorney general Ramsey Clark.

Maher put the paper down. *Ramsey Clark? Who the hell could
have shot Molese?* And then it occurred to Maher exactly who it
must have been. Molese had mentioned meeting him at Manhattan House of Detention, a place known by inmates as "The
Tombs." And the man Maher had in mind, a notorious contract
killer, always used a .22.

Maher checked in with his police sources, and although he
was not given the suspect's name, he *was* told that the suspect's
initials were J. S., which confirmed what Maher already knew.
A few days later, the suspect was identified: Joseph "Mad Dog"
Sullivan, perhaps the most feared hit man working the murder-
for-hire territory.

The legend of Joseph "Mad Dog" Sullivan began in 1971
when, on Good Friday, he became the only man ever to escape
from the maximum-security confines of Attica Prison. He was
captured six weeks later and, after completing nineteen years of
the original twenty- to thirty-year sentence for manslaughter,
was paroled in 1975 at the age of thirty-six.

By summer 1981, Mad Dog had become the suspect in several homicides. And now he was being sought in connection
with the shooting of Brian Molese. (Molese and his roommate,
Crosthwaite, were extremely lucky, having survived only because of a faulty silencer, which fragmented the small-caliber
.22 slugs and slowed their velocity as they exited.)

But *why* did Mad Dog shoot Molese? Did it have anything to
do with Alice Molese's murder? More to the point, did Molese
hire Mad Dog to kill Alice?

Police were speculating that the shooting occurred because of
a narcotics deal gone bad. But Maher thought otherwise. Whatever it was that caused Sullivan to shoot Molese, Maher was

certain it had something to do with the grisly murders at 24 Sanford Road.

When Sullivan was apprehended in early 1982, he remained silent about his role in any of the homicides with which police had charged him. (His wife, Gale, who had been in Molese's apartment when the shooting occurred, was also arrested.) In fact, the only statement Mad Dog gave to anyone about anything was to Bergen County detective Frank DelPrete when DelPrete visited him in an upstate prison.

"I'll tell you two things," Mad Dog said. "I'm no snitch. And I don't kill kids."

Since Maher knew people on both sides of the fence, he went fishing for a clarification of Mad Dog's statement. An explanation filtered back from the street, and it was corroborated by two police sources.

According to those sources, in autumn 1978 Mad Dog had indeed been hired by Molese to "kill everyone in the house." But when he cased 24 Sanford Road, he found out that one of the occupants was a five-year-old boy. This infuriated Mad Dog, who had a son about the same age.

"I don't kill kids," Mad Dog said with a snarl at Molese.

He offered to "whack the two women but let the kid live." Molese countered that "the kid has to die, too." Even Mad Dog was shocked at Molese's heartlessness.

Although Mad Dog was not going to carry out the contract, he demanded that he be paid for "the time I put in so far." Molese told him that he didn't have any money right then but promised to pay immediately after Alice, Marcia, and Harold were dispensed with.

A week after this conversation about killing Alice, Fair Lawn Police received an anonymous phone call.

"There's going to be a murder this Thanksgiving," the voice said. "At Twenty-four Sanford Road. Everyone in the house is going to be killed. And it will be made to look like a robbery. The killer will be Brian Molese."

Maher's street source insisted Mad Dog made the call, which would explain one element of his statement to DelPrete: "I'm no snitch." Mad Dog was saying to DelPrete: *I called you guys and told you about the murders, but I'm no snitch. I did it because of the kid.* Now the statement, each half taken in context, made perfect sense. "I'm no snitch. And I don't kill kids."

Fair Lawn Police treated the anonymous call seriously. They went to 24 Sanford Road and spoke with Alice. But Alice assured the cops that it had to be some kind of mistake.

"Brian would never harm me," Alice said. "He *loves* me."

Maher found this part of the account comforting. It confirmed his belief that Alice could not be convinced Molese wanted to kill her. She had been warned. And she chose to ignore the warning.

Maher's sources picked up the story two years after the murders. Fugitive Mad Dog came out of hiding, went to Molese's apartment, held a gun in Molese's mouth, and said: "Where's my money?" Obviously Molese gave Mad Dog the wrong answer. Mad Dog shot Molese three times in the mouth and then went after Crosthwaite.

Mad Dog was not someone to fuck with. Maher's street source related how Mad Dog shot and killed a man in a bar one night for stepping on his shoe. How Mad Dog, at the age of twenty-four, instigated the Rahway Prison riots in 1963. How Mad Dog, shortly after being released from prison, accepted and carried out the Jimmy Hoffa contract.

"Mad Dog whacked Jimmy Hoffa?" Maher asked his source incredulously. "Is that *true?*"

But it didn't really matter whether Mad Dog was the contractor who made Jimmy Hoffa disappear. Where legends are concerned, in the case of both heroes and villains, the lines of demarcation between the factual and the apocryphal are always blurred. The point was, Mad Dog *could have* killed Jimmy Hoffa.

Ironically, Mad Dog's father—who died when Mad Dog was twelve years old—had been an NYPD detective. A friend who knew Mad Dog as a child told a newspaper reporter that after his father died, his mother would make him kneel down in front of a photograph of his father and pray that he would grow up to be half the man his father had been.

He showed her.

BY 1982, MAHER'S WINNINGS FROM THE DRAG RACES AT CONNECTING Highway had allowed him to buy two additional cars—a

$21,000 1982 Cadillac El Dorado for Beth, and a $14,000 1982 Camaro, which was a replica of the Indianapolis 500 pace car. Although he never intended to race the Camaro, the blue and silver beauty was still too slow for Maher's sensibilities; so he replaced the 305-cubic-inch engine with a 400-cubic-inch engine.

As much as the Corvette was a symbol of Maher's skill with automobiles, the Camaro was a symbol of his lost dreams. *If only I had had a chance*, Maher would think every time he looked at the Indy 500 trim on the Camaro, *I could have won in Indianapolis*. While most people have reason to contemplate what could have been, few would be likely to purchase a constant reminder of some long past missed opportunity. Yet that was exactly what Maher had done by parking an Indy 500 replica in his garage.

IN APRIL 1982, DETECTIVE FRANK DELPRETE PHONED WITH A BIT OF good news. The Bergen County district attorney was ready to go to the grand jury in the Molese case. Notwithstanding the evidence the Bergen County prosecutor's office and the Fair Lawn Police Department had painstakingly gathered over the previous three years, DelPrete had a request.

"I'd like you to testify before the grand jury," DelPrete said. "And don't worry, the testimony will be sealed."

"I'd love to put that bastard away," Maher answered.

On a beautiful April morning, Maher arrived at Bergen County Courthouse in Hackensack, New Jersey, and took the witness stand. He told the grand jury about the day Molese sat in Green Haven Prison and said with a sneer, "I married the fat bitch for her money," and then said: "I want her killed. You'll be out before I am. And I want you to kill her for me."

Maher held the panel entranced as he described how Molese came home on furlough with homosexual lover Ronald Scofield, brutally beat Alice, and then, at a diner in Fair Lawn, New Jersey, solicited him a second time to murder Alice. "Brian said, 'We gotta put Alice out of her misery. She's a fat slob. All she does is smoke and eat. Help me kill her, Kevin.' "

There was a hush in the room when Maher stepped down from the witness stand.

After a month of examining evidence and hearing testimony

from twenty witnesses, the grand jury returned a four-count sealed indictment in which Molese was named as one of three coconspirators in the slayings of Alice Molese, Marcia Ferrell, and Harold Ferrell. One of the other coconspirators was unidentified, and the third was identified only as J. S. J. S., of course, stood for Joseph "Mad Dog" Sullivan.

At 3:00 P.M. on May 6, 1982, Brian Molese was arrested at his 10th Street apartment in Greenwich Village. But it would be a while before he would stand before a jury in New Jersey. Molese, it seemed, was facing criminal charges in New York. So instead of being extradited across the Hudson River, Molese was deposited in Manhattan Correctional Facility to await trial for embezzlement.

Following Molese's arrest, there was a surge of media attention focused on him and the murders. As pieces of Molese's story were revealed day by day on the front pages of newspapers in three states, the events leading up to the killings exhibited plot twists worthy of a Hitchcock thriller.

In March 1979, Molese found himself deeply in debt and was facing foreclosure on the house at 24 Sanford Road. Coincidentally, in February, a month before the murders, everyone at 24 Sanford Road—Alice Molese, Marcia Ferrell, and Harold Ferrell—took out a $90,000 insurance policy. Then, six days before the murders, Marcia's mother died, leaving her a house and $21,000 in cash. With her estate now valued at more than $150,000, Marcia named Brian and Alice Molese as trustees.

The stage was set. If Marcia died, her estate went to Harold. If Marcia *and* Harold died, Alice would take control of the Ferrell estate. But if Marcia *and* Harold *and* Alice died, Molese would come into a small fortune in insurance money. Adding to the windfall was a triple indemnity clause in all three policies. Essentially the clause specified that should Alice, Marcia, or Harold die in an accident involving public transportation, or *should they be murdered*, the insurance company would pay *three times* the $90,000 face amount on *each* policy. Now that Alice, Marcia, and Harold actually had been murdered, the death benefits totaled $810,000.

A short time after the triple homicide, Molese sought to collect on Alice's insurance and also wrote a letter to the insurance company evoking his power as trustee and executor of Marcia's estate. However, since he was the prime suspect in the homicides, the Bergen County prosecutor's office instructed the insurance company to withhold payment of death benefits pending further investigation.

Molese, no better off financially than he was before the murders, was now desperate. So when Marcia's father asked Molese to step aside in order that Marcia's estate could be settled in an expedient manner, Molese demanded money. Incredibly, in order to gain control of his deceased daughter's affairs, Marcia's father paid Molese—whom he knew was almost certainly his daughter's murderer—$7,500 to relinquish any and all claims to the estate.

Maher, of course, was following the Molese story closely. The more he read, the more nauseated he became. Brian Molese was more of an animal than Maher had ever imagined.

It had been six years since Maher had worked with cops on a case. Yet every day he thought about the action, the thrill, the danger. Indeed, the two professions he most coveted as a kid—a race car driver and a cop—were among the most dangerous. He had transformed himself once into a modern-day bounty hunter and was now a hero at Connecting Highway, but these were approximations of the real thing. So he had spent the six years between 1976 and 1982 in an endless postmortem. *Why did I steal the Roadrunner? Why did I run from the cops? Why did the DA come after me like that? Why didn't I give up the Cross Bay bank robbers?* Depression set in.

Exacerbating Maher's depression was the fact that his mother was going through a rough time. Once again divorced and alone, she had moved in with Maher and Beth for a short time and then moved to Maher's sister's house. But Susan—now married and with a son to raise—didn't seem as welcoming to her mother as Maher thought she should be. Maher and Susan argued often. Soon they weren't speaking at all.

About the only thing that seemed to lift Maher's spirits during this period was a visit to Doherty.

Doherty had tried retirement for a couple months in 1980 and had hated it. So he took a job on Long Island working for the Defense Department that involved investigating applicants who were seeking a security clearance.

The lowest-level clearance enabled someone to view documents labeled Official Use Only. The second level of clearance provided access to files designated Secret. The next level, Top Secret material. The highest level, which meant that there were no restrictions on an individual so designated, was called Q Clearance. The president has Q Clearance, of course. And only a handful of others.

Doherty also investigated breaches of security. While his job sounded exciting, Doherty was not happy. As a police detective, he had always followed a case through from the beginning to its conclusion. As a federal investigator, however, he often handled only a portion of an investigation. For Doherty, accustomed to being in charge of an investigation, it was a frustrating experience. So he looked forward to Maher's visits, when he could reminisce about the good old days.

On one particularly hot summer afternoon in 1982, Maher left his job at ConRail early and drove his Indy replica to Long Island to see Doherty.

"I never worked like this before," Doherty said. "I find out something but I don't go any further. I just get the piece of the investigation pertaining to Long Island. I'm not allowed to go to Washington, where the case *really* is."

After venting his frustration, Doherty asked Maher:

"So, Kevin. You been staying out of trouble?"

Maher shrugged. "Staying out of trouble and staying bored."

"Well," Doherty said with a smile, "better bored than dead."

Maher looked away.

"What is it?" Doherty wanted to know.

Maher took a breath and said: "I met a couple car thieves in Queens who specialize in Corvettes. They're selling Vettes to a chop shop in Jersey."

Doherty raised his eyebrows. He could see where this was leading. But what *should* he do? Should he make every effort to dissuade Maher from stepping back into the fray? Or should he act the cop and question Maher further?

"What do you know about these auto thefts?" Doherty finally asked, the cop in him winning the inner struggle.

"All I know is that some guys are grabbing Corvettes in Queens and dumping them in a body shop in Kearny."

"If they're stealing cars in New York and selling them in New Jersey," Doherty pointed out, "that's interstate transportation of stolen property. A *federal* crime."

Doherty wrestled with himself again. Then: "Maybe you should talk to an FBI agent over in Jersey."

Maher smiled. Fighting it, Doherty smiled, too, then stood and walked across the room, disappearing into an office. He returned a moment later and handed Maher a piece of paper that contained a name and a phone number.

"The auto theft guys tell me you should talk to agent Bob DeBellis. FBI office in Newark."

PRIOR TO MEETING WITH MAHER, DEBELLIS HAD PLACED SEVERAL CALLS to verify that Maher was who he said he was. So when Maher walked into the FBI's headquarters on Raymond Boulevard in Newark, New Jersey, he got right to the point.

"There's a body shop in Kearny that's receiving stolen vehicles," Maher said.

DeBellis jotted down the name of the body shop.

"If this checks out," DeBellis told Maher, "I'll pay you a thousand dollars."

"It'll check out," Maher said with emphasis.

And then Maher smiled. After a six-year hiatus, he was back on the job.

Chapter 9

A WEEK AFTER MAHER HAD GIVEN DEBELLIS INFORMATION ON THE stolen car operation, Maher picked up a newspaper and saw an article about a raid at the Kearny body shop. A jubilant Maher grabbed the phone and called DeBellis.

"I told you, Agent DeBellis," Maher said, laughing, into the receiver, "I told you the place was chopping cars."

"That's right," DeBellis answered, his voice flat.

After a moment of silence, Maher said: "You raided the place, didn't you?"

DeBellis didn't respond.

Maher suddenly had a sick feeling, like he was about to be screwed. He restated what he knew with a little more force. "I saw a thing in the paper this morning. You raided the place."

We didn't raid the place," DeBellis answered.

"What?" Maher was confused.

"I'll call you right back," DeBellis said.

Maher paced next to the phone for a few minutes until DeBellis called back.

"I found out what happened," DeBellis reported. "The *State Police* raided the place."

Now Maher *knew* he was going to get screwed. "Yeah. *Right.*"

DeBellis' intercom buzzed—another incoming call—and he told Maher he'd get back to him shortly. But the morning turned to afternoon, and afternoon dissolved into night. No Bob DeBellis. Maher was resigned to the fact that attempting to re-

134

vive his undercover career had been a mistake. *If you can't trust the fucking FBI, who can you trust?*

In the midst of inner tirade, the doorbell rang. Maher went to the door. It was Bob DeBellis.

DeBellis entered, walked to a table, and counted out ten $100 bills.

"A thousand dollars," DeBellis remarked. "Like we agreed."

Maher picked up the money and looked at it for a moment. "But you said the FBI didn't get the bust."

"That's correct," DeBellis answered. "But what I told you was: If the body shop checks out, I'll pay you a thousand dollars. The body shop checked out. It just so happens that the State Police got there first."

Maher looked at DeBellis. *This is a stand-up guy.*

And so began Maher's relationship with Agent Bob DeBellis.

A few days after the chop shop in Kearny had been shut down, DeBellis stopped off at a local bar to meet a longtime friend, Robert Colaneri. Colaneri had a weight lifter's build, broad shoulders and bulky arms, and his entire body—from his ankles to his neck—was covered with tattoos. Indeed, one could have assumed DeBellis had tracked down a dangerous suspect. But Colaneri, despite his appearance, was not a felon. He was a cop. Specialty: undercover.

Among other things, DeBellis and Colaneri talked about the increasing auto theft problem in the New York/New Jersey area. At least the chop shop in Kearny had been shut down, but there were bigger operations than that.

"Like Marconi," Colaneri noted. (The name of the chop shop owner has been changed because he was never indicted.)

Anthony Marconi ran a legitimate business called, appropriately, Marconi Body Shop. Located in Belleville, New Jersey, Marconi Body Shop was recognized by car owners in three states for its professional body work. It was also recognized by every law enforcement agency within a hundred miles as a high-volume stolen-car factory. The problem was, Marconi was so good at receiving, modifying, and then selling stolen vehicles that even the constant surveillance by several police forces failed to turn up any concrete evidence. Colaneri himself had recently impounded a Corvette that he knew was a Marconi "tag job" but was forced to return the car when he was unable to prove it. Marconi wasn't an amateur by any means. He had an "operation," with a corporate structure as well put together as General Motors.

"I have an informant who might be able to get inside Marconi's organization," DeBellis said, referring to Maher.

"That's the only way you're going to get him," Colaneri remarked.

Undercover cops had tried to snag Marconi before, but he was too crafty. No matter who went in, Marconi either knew they were a cop or sensed they were a cop. Indeed, Marconi Body Shop seemed impenetrable.

"He's an interesting kid," DeBellis said. "Real good with cars."

"What's he trading off?" Colaneri asked.

"Nothing," DeBellis answered. "He's a paid informant."

Colaneri nodded. "But he's got a record, right?"

"Not much of one," DeBellis said with a shrug. "A couple of convictions resulting from a stolen car charge back in 1971. No previous record. Nothing since."

"You said he was a kid," Colaneri pointed out.

"Basically he is. He's twenty-seven."

Colaneri calculated the years for a moment then reacted: "Then he was, what, sixteen, seventeen when he stole the car?"

DeBellis nodded. "Got four years."

Colaneri shook his head. "Four years? No priors? A minor? What the hell happened?"

DeBellis shook his head. "Who knows?"

Colaneri—who was also twenty-seven years old—recalled what he was doing when he was sixteen. He wasn't stealing cars, but he knew kids who were. Had the impulse struck him, he might have stolen a car back then as well. After all, it wasn't a big deal. Usually the charges were dropped. Worse case might have been juvenile detention. But *four* years? In a *prison*? Colaneri took a deep breath. *There but for the grace of God . . .*

The similarities between Colaneri and Maher were striking despite the obvious differences—Colaneri was Italian/Irish and Maher was all Irish; one had grown up in New Jersey and the other in the Bronx. But beyond the genealogy and the geography, there was little to separate them. Both were born in 1954

—Maher on April 18, Colaneri four months later, on August 16. Both spent their youth in working-class communities where there were few choices and little opportunity. Both resisted donning a spirit-choking blue collar and were driven to seek adventure, a yearning that manifested itself in a fascination with fast cars. And both planned to prolong the adventure by becoming a cop. Now Colaneri was a cop and Maher was an ex-con. However, had it not been for one cold November night in 1971, a night on which Maher stole a car and Colaneri thought about stealing a car but did not, then Maher could have emerged the cop and Colaneri could have been cast as the ex-con.

Colaneri's grandparents had emigrated from Italy at the turn of the century, and his father, John, was born on Baxter Street in the heart of Little Italy. His father moved to Jersey City, where he met and married the red-haired, blue-eyed Grace Gilligan. Shortly after the marriage, John and Grace bought a small house in Wood-Ridge, New Jersey, and in the late 1940s they moved to Hasbrouck Heights, where they started an American family of Italian *and* Irish descent. First born was daughter Marilyn. Then *three* more daughters—Barbara, Joan, and Margie. But John was undaunted. He wanted a son and was determined to have one. In fact, he had three: John, Jr., Robert, and Michael.

By this time, John Colaneri and his brother Joe had a thriving cutlery business in East Rutherford called Colaneri Brothers and had just expanded the business to include lawnmowers and snowblowers. (The business still exists today and remains family-owned.) Then, on January 18, 1964, a crisp Saturday morning, John suffered a heart attack at the store. Despite the efforts of another of John's brothers, Dr. Anthony Colaneri, John did not recover.

Following his father's death, nine-year-old Bobby changed. He became difficult for his mother to handle, often getting into trouble. As the years passed, he grew more restless. During his sophomore year he bought a motorcycle (a 64 BSA Thunderbolt), and during his senior year he bought a 1968 Corvette—dark blue with powder blue interior, a white convertible softtop and removable blue hardtop, and a 350-cubic-inch engine with 350 horsepower. He raced the Corvette every Friday and Saturday night on Route 80 in Lodi, New Jersey, where a quarter-mile stretch of the highway that led from Lodi to Hasbrouck Heights had been marked with paint. Cars from a hundred-mile radius would be trailered in like they were at a legitimate race-track. And Colaneri's Corvette would beat them.

Even serving as captain of the undefeated 1972 state champion Hasbrouck Heights High School football team didn't seem to lessen his wild streak. When Colaneri wasn't drag racing, he was running with motorcycle gangs. Neither of these things would have been allowed if his father were still alive. And his decision not to go to college would not have set well with John Colaneri either.

Despite his star athlete status in high school, Colaneri knew that he wasn't pro football material. He enlisted in the Army immediately upon graduation in 1973, and after reporting for duty he was among six other enlisted men to be singled out as candidates for West Point. But Colaneri couldn't see himself at a military academy either and declined the offer. Instead, he went through boot camp and then was assigned to a base in Vencenzia, Italy, where he became an MP. At nineteen, Colaneri had accomplished at least one of his goals. He was a cop of sorts. A military cop.

In 1974, Grace Colaneri was hospitalized with a liver infection, and Colaneri obtained an emergency leave to visit his mother. Temporarily stationed at Fort Monmouth, New Jersey, Colaneri befriended the personal secretary of the base commander, often taking him home for dinner, sometimes fixing him up with a date. Their friendship resulted in a discussion about how Colaneri might extend his leave. Permanently.

Following a flurry of paperwork, the commander's secretary was able to get Colaneri a hardship discharge to care for his ailing mother. Colaneri was out of the Army after just a year and back in his hometown, once again buzzing around on his motorcycle or behind the wheel of his Corvette. In his travels, he met Frank Sassani, president of the Bronx Motorcycle Club. With Sassani's help, Colaneri got into the laborers' union and began working with the construction crew that was building the Meadowlands Sports Complex.

Colaneri still courted trouble. Hard-drinking. Volatile. Angry. And the tattoo gallery that was his body made him look the part. Colaneri got his first tattoo—a motorcycle—at sixteen. A few months later he added two more. Before long, *both* his arms, from the wrist to the elbow and from the biceps to the shoulders, were covered with ink. The designs were so numerous and closely spaced that he acquired what is known as "sleeves." When he ran out of room on his arms, chest, and back, he began to fill in the skin on his legs.

Over the next two years Colaneri surfed just above the law. He was solicited to steal cars, observed various petty crimes, and heard about all manner of criminal activity. Miraculously, he never got involved in any of it. Miraculously because it wasn't always his sense of right and wrong that stopped him. Sometimes it was the circumstances that kept him from tripping up. A sibling's birthday party or a chance encounter with an alluring girl or any number of serendipitous events had often prevented him from meeting with his growing collection of corrupting friends. Then he would hear about the arrests. And he would know that if he had been there he would have been arrested, too. Any hope of ever becoming a cop would have evaporated. Colaneri felt lucky. *Maybe my father's looking out for me*, he would think when he missed becoming a felon by minutes. Somehow Colaneri managed never to be at the wrong place at the wrong time.

On his twenty-first birthday, in 1975, Colaneri, who was now vice president of the Bronx Motorcycle Club, was celebrating with members at a local hangout in Paterson, New Jersey, when he spotted a blonde at the bar. He leaned over toward Peter and Robert "Mickey" Schultz, two gang members.

"Who's the girl with the white pants on?" Colaneri wanted to know.

Mickey frowned. "That's my sister. Believe *me*, you don't want to get involved with *her*."

As it happened, Peter and Mickey kept a tight rein on their "little sister" Patti.

"Yeah," Peter added. "Tommy the Prospect wanted to go out with her, too, but we wouldn't let him."

Colaneri laughed. Tommy the *Prospect*. A "prospect"—in gang vernacular—was someone who wanted to join the club. Prospective inductees became probationary members and were given a motorcycle jacket that had only one patch—"MC"—

which stood, of course, for Motorcycle Club. Prospects were not allowed to wear patches that read "Bronx" or to display the center patch logo of the club: crossed pistons. Those adornments would be added to the jacket when the club deemed a prospect worthy of full membership. However, after more than a year, poor Tommy still had not been granted the full colors of the Bronx Motorcycle Club, and it seemed he would forever remain a "prospect." Hence the moniker *Tommy the Prospect.*

"I'm *not* Tommy the Prospect," Colaneri pointed out.

There was a tense moment. Preventing Colaneri from talking with sister Patti was about to lead to a confrontation. Finally Mickey smiled.

"Hey, Bobby. It's *your* fucking life."

Colaneri walked over to Patti Schultz and said: "I'm going to wind up marrying you."

Patti raised an eyebrow. "What is that, some kind of line?"

In the meantime, Tommy the Prospect was watching Colaneri and Patti closely. Tommy was not thrilled. So Mickey walked over to his sister and took her aside.

"These two guys come to blows over you, Patti," Mickey said, nodding toward Colaneri and Tommy the Prospect, "and *you're* going to have a problem."

But there was no fight. Tommy backed off.

For the next three weeks Colaneri and Patti were inseparable. She often went with him to the clubhouse on Lemoine Avenue in Fort Lee, home of the New Jersey chapter of the Bronx Motorcycle Club. On the night of September 11, 1975, a call came into the clubhouse at 6:00 P.M. Mickey Schultz had been in an accident in New York and had been taken to Lenox Hill Hospital in critical condition. Colaneri decided not to tell Patti that her brother had been injured, saying only that there was an emergency and he had to leave immediately. Colaneri jumped on his cycle and raced across the George Washington Bridge into Manhattan. Patti went to the home of Terry Snodgrass, the girlfriend of another club member.

By the time Colaneri arrived at the hospital, Robert "Mickey" Schultz was dead.

Colaneri was told that witnesses reported seeing a car take a sharp left turn and plow into Mickey's motorcycle. More than a half an hour after the accident, an ambulance finally arrived.

Paramedics carefully braced Mickey's neck, placed him on a stretcher, and loaded him into the ambulance. But then the ambulance wouldn't start. So there was a fifteen-minute wait for a second rescue vehicle.

Patti called her mother's house and was told by her Aunt Pat to get home as fast as she could. Although Patti was still unaware that her brother had been killed, she knew something terrible had occurred. She was verging on panic when she climbed into Terry's beat-up 1967 Oldsmobile and headed for the Bronx. Unfortunately, the Cross Bronx Expressway had been closed due to construction, and the snarl of traffic Colaneri had skirted on his cycle was almost unnavigatable in an automobile. After a tortuous trip from Jersey to the Bronx, Patti rushed into her mother's house. Several family members were gathered there. They were crying. Patti, shaking and emotionally spent, sought the consoling arms of her sister Donna.

"Mickey's gone," Donna said softly.

As tragedy can sometimes do, Mickey's death drew Colaneri and Patti closer. Two weeks later Colaneri proposed and Patti accepted. They were married on Valentine's Day 1976. And they moved to Carlstadt, New Jersey, where their first child, Bobby, was born on September 4 that same year.

Now that they had a son, Patti began to express her displeasure over her husband's lifestyle. Drag racing. Motorcycle gangs. And the full complement of hangers-on who skim along the periphery of those activities. Drug dealers. Pimps. Prostitutes. Car thieves. Worse, Patti could sense that Colaneri had begun to lose his direction, veering perilously close to the wrong side of the law on too many occasions.

Colaneri quit drag racing and resigned from the Bronx Motorcycle Club. He became a weekend warrior, riding his motorcycle solo along the back roads of New Jersey. Actually, there wasn't a clubhouse to go to anymore. The night Colaneri and Patti were married, somebody blew up the place.

For the balance of 1976 and 1977, Colaneri drove a construction truck. He was laid off in December 1977 and collected unemployment until the spring of 1978, when he was supposed to go back to work. However, the only job available was driving an "emulsion" truck—the vehicle that transported hot tar—between Newark and Bogota. Due to the toxicity of the tar, a special, protective suit was required. It was an undesirable, dangerous job. Colaneri declined. But then he got a bit of a shock from Patti.

"I'm pregnant," Patti said one afternoon.

By summer, the unemployment checks stopped. Faced with providing for two children and coupled with the unreliability of construction work, Colaneri began to wonder if maybe he shouldn't follow up on some of the less legitimate opportunities that presented themselves. All he had to do was steal one Corvette and he could walk away with a grand. That would solve both Colaneri's problems—his need for income and his reawakened hunger for excitement. Once he was a high school football star. Once he had the fastest Corvette on Route 80 in Lodi, New Jersey. Now he was married with one kid, another on the way. Out of work. He felt a failure.

In Maher's case, fate had been unkind. In Colaneri's case, fate saved him. Someone mentioned to Colaneri that there was a test about to be given by the Carlstadt Police Department. This was good news. So he took the test and waited to see if he had made the cut.

As the days passed, Colaneri's thoughts were troubled. He knew himself well enough to know that if he didn't get on the Carlstadt police force, he would probably go the other way. He would probably do something stupid to get cash. And he would likely try to convince himself it was for his kids.

Colaneri was notified that he had scored extremely high on the test. He was sworn in as a Carlstadt police officer on July 17, 1978. Then, on December 2, Gina Marie was born. Whereas once they seemed to threaten his sense of adventure, now Patti and his children offered stability.

For the first year on the job, Colaneri patrolled the streets of Carlstadt in a uniform. But he craved more action than just cruising around in a squad car, and he volunteered for undercover work. Considering his burly appearance and, of course, the full body of tattoos, Colaneri was a natural. In fact, no one ever guessed he was a cop until it was too late, although there was one time in October 1979 when Colaneri's cover was blown.

Colaneri had been working a drug case with Detective Sergeant John Occhiuzzo for months and was about to make a major buy at the suspect's house. Colaneri—dressed in a T-shirt emblazoned with a swastika—was sitting in the suspect's kitchen when the suspect's wife returned home. As it happened, the suspect's wife was good friends with Colaneri's sister-in-law. Recognizing Colaneri's face from family photos, she pulled her husband aside and told him that Colaneri was a cop.

Still, Colaneri was considered to be the best undercover operative Carlstadt had ever seen, which is why he was sitting in a bar talking with FBI agent Bob DeBellis. Colaneri was the guy to talk to when the cases got tough.

Colaneri snapped back to the present and looked at DeBellis.

"Tough break," Colaneri said, referring to Maher's harsh sentence for car theft.

Yet, while Colaneri could grimace about what he knew to be similarities between him and Maher, he had no way of knowing the many other commonalities he shared with DeBellis's CI. The house where Colaneri's parents once lived in Wood-Ridge was only two blocks from where Maher currently was living. And Patti's mother's home in the Throgs Neck section of the Bronx was just a few blocks from where Maher and Beth had previously lived. Besides their coincidental geographic proximity, Maher and Colaneri shared a passion for Corvettes and had often shopped in the same auto parts stores.

"I'd like to meet this kid," Colaneri told DeBellis.

"I'm sure you will," DeBellis answered.

DURING THE SECOND MEETING BETWEEN MAHER AND DEBELLIS, DEBELLIS explained who Anthony Marconi was—how difficult it had been so far to get anything on Marconi—and outlined what would be expected of Maher in an undercover operation aimed at Marconi Body Shop.

"We'll work out the price later," DeBellis advised Maher.

Maher nodded. He trusted DeBellis now. He knew DeBellis would come through.

After receiving his "assignment" from DeBellis, Maher didn't waste time. He went straight to Marconi.

"I got a couple of guys good with Corvettes," Maher told Marconi.

Marconi studied Maher for a long time before answering,

then told Maher he would get back to him in a couple of days. Marconi wanted time to have Maher checked out. But Maher wasn't concerned. He was known in Corvette circles by the locals and had a conviction for grand theft auto. Wherever Marconi turned, Maher would look like someone who could deliver Corvettes.

A few days later, Marconi contacted Maher and told him: "I'll pay eight hundred to a thousand a car."

Marconi explained the difference in price. Most Vettes would command the eight hundred dollars. A Vette with glass roof panels—not *fiber*glass—would warrant the higher amount.

"I can take five a week," Marconi told Maher. "If you're good and don't bring no heat, you can make five thousand a week."

Maher left Marconi's garage and went to see Larry Birnholz, the mechanic who worked on Maher's Corvettes, and told him about the conversation with Marconi.

"I need some guys to help me steal a few Vettes," Maher said.

Birnholz, who wasn't averse to stealing Vettes for parts, told Maher he often teamed with three men who specialized in stealing Corvettes: Randy Anderwkavich, Richard Blasso, and Franco Torre.

"I want to meet them," Maher told Birnholz.

"Let's go," Birnholz said.

The first thing Maher said when he met Anderwkavich, Blasso, and Torre was: "I know Anthony Marconi."

The band of thieves were impressed.

"Yeah," one of them said. "We've heard of him."

Maher was now in control. He took the four car thieves to Marconi Body Shop in Belleville and introduced them to Marconi. Again Marconi asked for a couple of days. And again the thieves—all of whom had prison records—checked out. Marconi was in business with a bunch of felons, and he knew felons could not be cops. The sting was set.

On September 23, Maher met with DeBellis and briefed him on the situation. Instead of being thrilled, DeBellis was concerned. The band of thieves Maher had enlisted were not a group of punks snatching cars off the street with a slaphammer. At least one of them—Richard Blasso—was a reputed Mafia soldier who had a penchant for armed robbery.

"I'm telling you two things right now," DeBellis said with

emphasis. "I cannot condone a sting in which a stolen car is used in the theft of another car."

"I'll use *my* car," Maher responded.

DeBellis continued. "And you are *not* authorized to participate in an armed carjacking."

"Don't worry," Maher countered. "They never said anything about an armed carjacking. All we talked about is delivering a Vette to Marconi."

"As long as there are no guns involved," DeBellis asserted.

DeBellis looked at Maher. He seemed too self-assured, too cocky.

"Look, Kevin," DeBellis said, "what I'm trying to tell you is, you do a stickup and you'll go to jail. I won't be able to help you, you understand?"

Maher was sobered by the thought. "I understand."

At nine o'clock that night, Maher met the car thieves at a predetermined location in Queens. Maher was driving his Camaro with its Indy 500 markings. They were driving a Pontiac Trans Am, which was stolen.

"Let's go," Blasso said, motioning for Maher to get into the Trans Am.

"I'm not getting in no fucking hot car," Maher said. "Come in *my* car and we'll go cruising for a Vette."

The four men climbed into Maher's Indy pace car replica. Anderwkavich was in a particularly good mood.

"What are you so happy about?" Maher asked.

"I just came from the hospital," Anderwkavich said, his voice effervescent. "I just had a baby girl."

"*You* didn't have nothing," Maher pointed out. "Your *wife* had a baby girl."

Everyone laughed. And then the five men set out to steal a Corvette.

For the next two hours Maher cruised around Queens looking for Corvettes, particularly Corvettes with glass roof panels. Street after street. Neighborhood after neighborhood. No luck. Maher's passengers were restless.

"What about this jeweler?" Blasso asked.

"He's got hundreds of thousands of dollars in gems," Anderwkavich said. "The only time to get him is when he walks from the car to his house."

The men began directing Maher.

"Turn here," Anderwkavich said. Then a few minutes later: "Try that street."

The next thing Maher knew he was in the section of Flushing at the intersection of 151st Street and Bayside Avenue. Anderwkavich instructed Maher to stop the car across the street from a brownstone.

"That's the house," Anderwkavich told Blasso.

Maher checked out the driveway. It was empty.

"No Corvette," Maher noted. "Let's go."

"Fuck Corvettes," Blasso barked. "That's the jeweler's house. We wait here till he comes home."

Maher glanced nervously around the car. *These guys are talking about a fucking stickup!* DeBellis's words echoed in Maher's mind: *You do a stickup and you'll go to jail. I won't be able to help you, you understand?* Maher understood. But now he was in a car with four men seemingly about to engage in armed robbery. Worse yet, it was Maher's *own* car, with identifiable markings, no less.

"We're going to knock off the fucking jeweler," Blasso said with a growl.

"Get the fuck out of here," Maher told Blasso.

"Don't worry," Blasso said. "It's gonna be easy."

"I ain't knocking off no fucking jeweler," Maher insisted.

"He's gonna be carrying fifty, a hundred grand in gems," Blasso explained.

Maher pressed: "Who the fuck turned you on to this jeweler?"

"This guy. Beamen," Anderwkavich answered.

Maher had heard of Beamen. He was a small-time drug dealer.

"And how do you know that this guy's going to be carrying fifty to a hundred thousand in jewels?" Maher asked, snickering. "Beamen tell you that?"

"Yeah," Anderwkavich said. "Beamen took the jeweler off once before. He was a pushover."

"A pushover, huh?" Maher was growing concerned. The momentum for a holdup was building all around him. "If it's that easy and he's carrying that large and walking into a dark alley like that"—Maher pointed to the darkened driveway—"why ain't Beamen doing it? Huh? Why did he give it to you?"

"He's in jail," Anderwkavich said.

"We're supposed to take care of Beamen later," Blasso chimed in.

Maher looked at the tree-lined driveway. *A guy carries a hundred grand in jewels home every night at midnight? And these jerks know about it?* Something wasn't right. And whatever was about to go down, Maher wanted no part of it.

"I ain't knocking off no fucking jeweler," Maher said again.

Maher reached for the gear shifter. At the same time, Anderwkavich slid a .32-caliber snub-nosed Smith & Wesson from his jacket, and Blasso pulled out a single-barreled sawed-off shotgun.

Maher withdrew his hand from the shifter and fell back against the seat. Now *what the fuck do I do?*

Chapter 10

MAHER GRABBED THE STICK SHIFT AND JAMMED THE CAR INTO FIRST GEAR, then slammed his foot on the accelerator. The Camaro catapulted from the curb. Summoning all the bravado he could muster, Maher looked over his shoulder into the backseat and stared directly into Blasso's eyes.

"Marconi's gonna pay us five grand a week and *you* want to stick up some fucking jeweler? Fuck you, man! *Fuck* you."

Blasso was not amused. "Hey, you don't want to do it? Then fuck *you!*"

Maher drove like a maniac until he reached the spot where the stolen Pontiac Trans Am was parked. Blasso, Anderwkavich, Birnholz, and Torre climbed out of Maher's Camaro and piled into the Trans Am. A moment later, the Trans Am pulled away, disappearing into the night.

Maher's heart was pounding as loudly as the pistons in the Camaro. He drove home and fell into bed. Beth looked at him and sensed something was wrong.

"Kevin? What is it?"

"I took another assignment with the FBI," Maher said.

Beth winced slightly. A betrayal. A broken promise.

"I thought we agreed you wouldn't do that anymore," Beth said with a sigh.

"Beth . . ." Maher didn't know what to say.

"Fine," Beth said with emphasis.

Maher tried to explain. "It was going to be a big payday."

"Fine," Beth said again. This time her voice was barely a whisper.

Maher continued. "But then these guys set me up. They wanted to do a jewel heist. Before I knew it, I was in front of this jeweler's house. I backed out, and here I am."

Maher shrugged. Beth gave Maher a little half smile.

"Fine," Beth said once again, then rolled over, turning away both physically and emotionally.

Maher stared at the ceiling. *Fine. That's what she always says when she's upset. Fine.* Maher hated that word. It twisted him up inside. Maybe he didn't want to admit it to himself, or perhaps he didn't fully realize it, but there was a good reason why the word "fine" ravaged his emotions so completely. Somewhere, deep within his subconscious, he could hear Beth slipping away with each utterance of the word. He was losing her.

Maybe he already had.

THE FOLLOWING MORNING, MAHER WAS ABOUT TO SLAP HIS HAND DOWN on the clock radio's snooze alarm when the all-news station WINS broadcast the following report:

"In Flushing, Queens, four armed men wearing ski masks ambushed an off-duty policeman in his driveway last night in a botched holdup attempt. The officer shot and killed one man. Three other suspects fled the scene."

Maher shot straight up. *Flushing? Four suspects?*

Maher turned up the volume. Details of the attempted robbery were sketchy, according to the report, since the police had just begun their investigation.

Maher looked toward the door to the bathroom, where Beth was taking a shower. He realized, after hearing the newscast, that the case he thought was over might just be beginning. *Do I tell Beth?* Maher decided he wouldn't say anything to Beth. He couldn't bear to hear her say "fine" again.

Twenty minutes after the first bulletin, an update identified the off-duty police officer as Frank Ciasullo from the 13th Precinct. Another twenty minutes later, as the headlines rolled around again, Maher heard the name of the suspect who was killed: Randolph Anderwkavich.

Maher jolted. *The dumb bastards went to the wrong house and tried to jump a cop!*

The newscast also identified Richard Blasso, who had been wounded during the attempted robbery. Blasso had been arrested at a nearby hospital where he went to seek treatment. In addition, the newscast gave Officer Ciasullo's account of the incident. According to police sources, Ciasullo's report stated that when he returned home from his four-to-midnight shift, two armed men approached him from the direction of the rear yard. At the same moment, Ciasullo said he was grabbed from behind by two additional males and that a shopping bag he was carrying in his left hand had been ripped free. Although one of the armed men hit him in the face with a gun, Ciasullo said he was able to draw his off-duty revolver and fire three shots. One shot struck and killed one man, and another shot wounded a second man. The report added that "no guns were recovered at the scene."

Maher knew how that might work against Ciasullo. Blasso would swear he was unarmed. And it would be Blasso's word against Ciasullo's.

The report concluded on an ominous note, at least as far as Maher was concerned.

"Police believe the suspects escaped in a car driven by a fifth man."

Maher frowned. *A* fifth *man?* What *fifth man?*

And then the realization slowly washed over him. *DeBellis is going to think I was the fifth man.*

Maher rushed to the phone and called DeBellis, explaining every detail of what happened the previous night.

"I left them in Queens," Maher insisted. "I got the fuck out of there, I *swear* I did."

"I believe you, Kevin," DeBellis assured him, then explained that because the case was now a homicide it was out of the FBI's jurisdiction. "I'll call this detective at NYPD I know and—"

"No," Maher interrupted. "I'll call someone *I* know."

Maher called Doherty at the Defense Department. After hearing Maher's story, Doherty might have suggested that Maher call a detective from the 109th Precinct, which was the precinct covering the area in Queens where the shooting had occurred. However, Doherty felt that, under the circumstances, he should recommend someone he knew very well, someone who had met Maher before, someone who understood that Maher was not your usual one-step-ahead-of-the-law informant.

"Give Tom Harkins a call," Doherty suggested.

Tom Harkins was one of the few remaining detectives from Doherty's stint at the Manhattan DA's office.

Born in Brooklyn in 1938, Harkins found his way out of the neighborhood by joining the Marines when he was twenty years old. He wound up stationed in Oahu, where he attended classes at the University of Hawaii. Harkins was discharged from the Marines in 1966. After his discharge, he received a master's degree in clinical and counseling psychology from the New York Institute of Technology.

In April 1966 Harkins married Ann Collier. And in September he became a uniformed officer out of Manhattan's 25th Precinct, whose headquarters was on 126th Street between Second and Third avenues; while in the precinct he did a tour of duty on foot patrol. He graduated to the radio and motor patrol, cruising the drug-ravaged uptown streets in a squad car.

In 1969 Harkins was assigned to the Manhattan South Narcotics Squad, and was stationed out of the 1st Precinct, which was referred to as Old Slip because of its location. The 1st Precinct was near the entrances to the Brooklyn-Battery Tunnel and the Brooklyn Bridge, looking out over New York Harbor.

In those days, the path to detective was simple: Put in the time and ultimately be rewarded with a gold shield. Harkins spent two years in plainclothes and was closing in on a shield when the findings of the Knapp Commission sent the NYPD into a state of near chaos.

The Knapp Commission—named after prosecutor Whitman Knapp—convened in early 1970 after cops Frank Serpico and David Dirk made allegations about widespread corruption within the New York City Police Department. (Both became famous when a series of books and movies was done about the commission, particularly the 1973 film titled *Serpico*, which starred Al Pacino.)

Due to what was termed "the Blue Wall of Silence," two years of investigation and public hearings failed to net much more than a handful of low-level officers. But the long, drawn-out process—during which rumors that hundreds of cops were about to be charged with various crimes—rattled the department. To prevent the wholesale devastation of any particular precinct, top police brass began reassigning many of the roughly eight hundred officers in the Narcotics Squad. Narcotics cops were allowed to select a precinct, and Harkins chose the 7th Precinct, headquartered on Delancey Street at the foot of the Williamsburg Bridge.

Following two years in the Anticrime Unit, Harkins returned home one evening to find a message from a police lieutenant. The telephone number was 232-7300—the courthouse. Harkins knew that the department was putting together a "Court Division," and he wanted no part of it. Everyone knew that officers assigned to the Court Division would be nothing more than clerks monitoring the flow of paperwork. Consequently, Harkins ignored the call. But the lieutenant called back again the next day.

"You better call that guy," Harkins's wife, Ann, said when he returned home. "He was really upset."

Harkins returned the call.

Instead of being given an assignment in the Court Division, Harkins was invited to interview with the prestigious Manhattan District Attorney Squad under the direction of DA Frank Hogan. With only seven years on the job, Harkins merely was biding his time and hoping for a promotion to detective. But to become a detective in the DA's office was beyond anything he had hoped for.

A year after the interview, Harkins was notified of his promotion to detective and appeared at headquarters to receive his gold shield. Police Commissioner Michael Codd addressed the new detectives by telling them that, in the wake of the Knapp Commission, "they put us through the ringer." Codd explained that each of those who were gathered to receive a shield had undergone such intense scrutiny that all their previous arrests had been carefully examined. Codd concluded: "Anyone here getting a shield, deserves it."

Following Codd's remarks, name after name was called and the orders were read, assigning the freshman detectives to various precincts. Harkins was assigned to the DA Squad.

A year after Harkins joined the DA's office, Dick Condon—who had been a Knapp Commission investigator—took over

Kevin Maher, six years old, at his First
Holy Communion.   (Kevin Maher)

Bobby Colaneri, eighteen years old,
as an Army MP.   (Bobby Colaneri)

Maher in the Marines at fourteen
years old. 1969.   (Kevin Maher)

Maher's inmate card from Green Haven Correctional Facility, 1975. (Kevin Maher)

Jim Doherty at the Manhattan District Attorney's office in 1975. (Jim Doherty)

Jim Doherty (front, center) and his team of Detectives at the Manhattan District Attorney's office. From left to right: Joe Clabby; Bob Mercado; Greg Demetriou; Pat Carroro; Josh Wainright; Tom Harkins; Jim Maguire; John Justy. Christmas, 1975.

(Jim Doherty)

Manhattan District Attorney Robert Morgenthau displays the Oriental rug Maher helped Doherty recover.

(Jim Doherty)

According to Maher's sources, Brian Molese tried to hire Joseph "Mad Dog" Sullivan to kill his wife Alice Molese.

'Mad Dog' guilty in slaying

Alleged hit man Joseph John (Mad Dog) Sullivan (center), 43, of Richmond Hill, Queens, leaves court in Rochester after being convicted of second-degree murder in the slaying of Teamsters official John Fiorino. Sullivan, a suspect in about a dozen murders across the state, is the only man ever to escape from Attica prison.

Prison mug shot: Ronald Scofield.

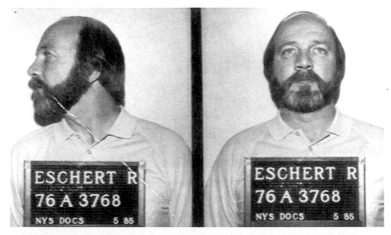

Prison mug shot: Robert Eschert.

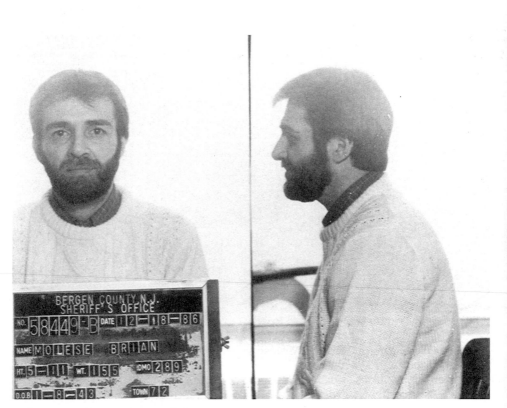

Police mug shot: Brian Molese.

Alice Molese's home at 24 Sanford Road where Maher lived briefly after being released from prison. Alice Molese, Marcia Ferrell, and Harold Ferrell were slain here by Alice's husband Brian Molese. Two other murderers had a connection to this house. (Andy Tomasko)

Maher and former wife Beth (sitting to his left on the couch) at a party in 1983.

(Kevin Maher)

The house at 30 Fourth Street in Wood-Ridge, New Jersey that Maher and Beth purchased in 1984. (Andy Tomasko)

Maher and former wife Beth (sitting to his left on the couch) at a party in 1983.

(Kevin Maher)

The house at 30 Fourth Street in Wood-Ridge, New Jersey that Maher and Beth purchased in 1984. (Andy Tomasko)

The quarter mile stretch of road at Connecting Highway in Queens, where Maher would race his Corvette. (Andy Tomasko)

Colaneri on his
motorcycle, 1976.
(Bobby Colaneri)

Maher and his 1980
Corvette which was
featured in the
December, 1980 issue
of *Vette Magazine*.

Maher's business card from M.A.P. Auto Sales

Maher's 1987 928 S4 Porsche.   (Kevin Maher)

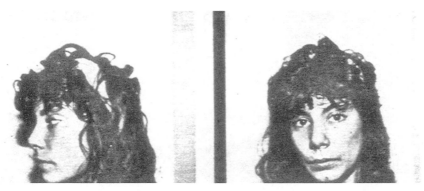

Beverly Merrill's mug shot taken following her arrest in 1986.

Gallagher's, one of the clubs where Beverly Merrill worked as an exotic dancer.

(Andy Tomasko)

Robert Eschert, Jr. in a customized Corvette at M.A.P. Auto Sales, 1991.
(Kevin Maher)

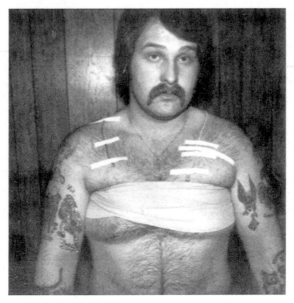

Colaneri being fitted with a wire. (Bobby Colaneri)

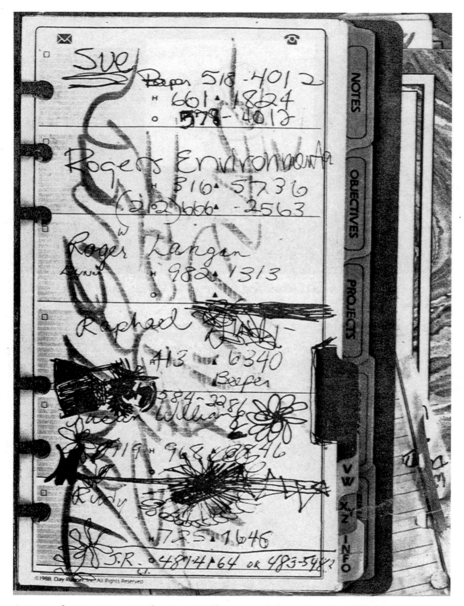

A page from Mary Catherine Williams' address book with Joel Rifkin's phone numbers, (next to his initials J.R. at bottom of page).

A photograph of Mary Catherine Williams that appeared in the August 9, 1993 issue of *New York Magazine*.

From left to right: Author Charles Kipps, Kevin Maher, Bobby Colaneri, Patti Colaneri, and Jim Doherty at Elaine's Restaurant in New York, 1995.

Maher and his girlfriend, Courtney Chandel, 1995.

the squad. The following year, Condon's partner, Sergeant Jack Vobis, joined Condon as a squad supervisor. Since Vobis and Doherty had worked together on the French Connection heroin theft, Vobis brought Doherty in. And, of course, a few months later, Doherty introduced his new informant to Harkins—Kevin Maher.

Over the next five years, Harkins saw quite a bit of Maher. But when Doherty retired in 1980, Maher had stopped coming in. So, on a cool September morning in 1982, there was no reason for Harkins to expect a phone call from Maher.

Harkins had just settled in at his desk and was working on his first cup of coffee when his intercom buzzed.

"There's a Kevin Maher on line two. He asked for you."

Harkins stared at the blinking telephone light for a moment. *I wonder what he wants?* Harkins pressed line two. Instead of hearing "hello" or some other greeting, Harkins was hit with a sudden barrage.

"Okay. So you got two of the guys, right? One guy in the hospital and the other guy dead at the scene. Well, let me tell you, I know the whole story and—"

"Kevin?"

"Yeah?"

"Kevin, what the hell are you talking about?"

"Ciasullo."

"Who?"

"The off-duty cop from last night. He shot and killed Anderwkavich and wounded Blasso."

"Anderwkavich? Blasso?"

Maher sighed. "Don't you listen to the news?"

Harkins took a deep breath. "Kevin, I *just* got in. I haven't seen a newspaper, and no, I haven't listened to the news. So why don't you start from the beginning."

Maher explained the situation to Harkins. Since Maher was jumping all over the place without regard for chronology, it took Harkins half an hour to get the details.

"I could be in big trouble here," Maher said. "And I didn't do anything."

"Calm down," Harkins said. "I'll call you back."

Harkins hung up the receiver and rubbed his forehead. This wasn't his case. The shooting had occurred within the 109th

Precinct. It was *their* case. And the attempted robbery was a matter for the Queens Central Robbery Squad. But now Harkins was involved whether he liked it or not.

From a procedural standpoint, Harkins was required to pass along the information he had just received from Maher. But it wasn't just the procedural hook that was into Harkins, it was also an emotional one. Kevin Maher wasn't just a faceless informant, he was a person. A kid who used to hang out at 1 Hogan Place. Harkins felt he had to do something to help him. Or at least make sure Maher had an opportunity to be heard.

Harkins spoke with Captain Eddie Baccaglini, who then spoke with Chief of Detectives Joseph Borelli. Borelli told Baccaglini to send Harkins to the 109th Precinct to provide assistance on the case.

After stopping by the 109th Precinct and meeting with Detective Robert Kiselewsky, Harkins spoke with a detective from the Queens Central Robbery Squad, Patrick Mockler. Since Maher was Harkins's informant, it was decided that Harkins, Mockler, and Kiselewsky would work together in a kind of joint task force borne out of necessity.

Harkins and Mockler headed across the George Washington Bridge to Maher's home in Wood-Ridge. For more than two hours, Maher and the two detectives went over the incident minute by minute, word by word. Clearly the suspects were unaware that Ciasullo was not merely a jeweler, rather he was a *cop* who *moonlighted* as a jeweler.

"So they said someone named Beamen told them to rob Ciasullo?" Harkins pressed.

"Yes!" Maher answered, growing exasperated. He wondered: *Why are they so obsessed with Beamen?*

The conversation turned to each of the individual suspects and what Maher knew about them. Maher explained that he had only come in contact with the four men because of the FBI stolen car sting.

"Anderwkavich is dead," Maher noted, "and you've got Blasso cold."

Harkins smiled. "Not really. He denies knowing anything about Ciasullo or Beamen."

"Of course he's going to deny it." Maher grew animated. "But he got shot with a bullet from Ciasullo's gun, right?"

Harkins nodded.

"Okay," Maher went on, "so maybe the bullet's still in him."

"It is," Harkins confirmed, explaining that someone fitting suspect Birnholz's description had dropped Blasso off at a Queens hospital. When doctors discovered Blasso had been shot, they immediately called police.

Maher held his arms open. "Okay. You got Blasso. And he's got a bullet in him. You take the bullet and run a ballistics test, which places him at the scene." Maher shook his head. "I've got to tell you guys *everything?*" Maher laughed.

Then Harkins said: "Blasso refused to allow doctors to remove the bullet."

Maher stopped laughing.

"My guess," Harkins suggested, "is that Blasso doesn't want the bullet used as evidence."

For a moment, no one spoke. A man who would conceal evidence in his bleeding gut was scary.

Ultimately the question of a possible "fifth man" arose. Harkins made it clear that if there was indeed a "fifth man," he didn't believe it was Maher. Rather, Harkins told Maher he wanted his help.

"We may need you to wear a wire," Harkins said.

Since it was Friday evening and nothing much could be accomplished over the weekend, the next meeting was scheduled for Monday morning.

The moment Harkins and Mockler left, Beth emerged from the kitchen. She and Maher stared at each other for a long time.

"Are you going to help them with the case?" Beth finally asked.

"Look, Beth, this cop is in trouble and—"

"Fine." Beth spun on her heels and walked back into the kitchen.

THE FOLLOWING MORNING, MAHER FLIPPED THROUGH THE PAGES OF THE *Daily News* and came across a story with this headline:

MASKED MAN IS SLAIN AT POLICEMAN'S HOME

The story recounted the attempted robbery by Blasso and company and then continued:

Details of the shooting were disclosed yesterday in Queens Supreme Court, where two brothers—Richard Beamen, 22, and Marc, 18, of Murray St., Queens— were on trial. They are charged as two of the four armed robbers—all wearing ski or Halloween masks— who invaded the Ciasullo home last August, terrorizing Ciasullo's wife, her sister and her children and made off with $60,000 in jewelry.

Maher frowned. *That's right! Blasso said Beamen had robbed Ciasullo before.*

The article went on to say that when the Beamens' defense lawyers asked for a mistrial, Justice Robert Groh consented.

Maher's mind began to reel. *Is there some kind of connection between the mistrial and the robbery? What if Beamen told Blasso to whack Ciasullo and make it look like a robbery?*

Maher felt nauseous as the realization hit him. *Blasso wasn't asking me to go on a robbery. He was inviting me to a contract killing.*

THE WEEKEND PASSED SLOWLY. FINALLY, AFTER A SLEEPLESS SUNDAY night, Maher jumped into his Camaro and raced into Manhattan. When he entered 1 Hogan Place, he found a somber-looking Tom Harkins.

"We have a problem," Harkins said.

"You're damned right we do," Maher said. "This Beamen mistrial might be connected to—"

Harkins cut him off. "Kevin! Queens chief of detectives Michael Willis thinks *you* were involved with the robbery."

Maher wasn't shocked. He had a sick feeling all along that this could happen.

But why shouldn't a chief of detectives question an informant's veracity? After all, any seasoned cop had dealt with hundreds of informants and, in most cases, the informant wound up being a sociopathic liar. Perhaps Willis was weary of the tenuous cop/informant alliance. Besides, Willis had never met Maher and did not know his history with Doherty and the Manhattan district attorney's office.

As Maher fumed, Harkins added, "The bosses want you to take a polygraph test."

"I've got nothing to hide," Maher retorted.

"You can have a lawyer present if you like," Harkins added.

Maher was stung by the question. "I don't need no fucking lawyer."

Harkins escorted Maher to the police lab, where a polygraph test was administered. The results were conclusive: Maher was *not* involved in the robbery.

Following the polygraph, Harkins and Maher discussed the possible relationship between the Beamen trial and the attempted robbery. They both agreed that Blasso, Anderwkavich, Birnholz, and Torre had *not* made an error in going to Ciasullo's house in Flushing. Officer Ciasullo *was* in the jewelry business. However, as they explored the facts, the case seemed to fold back on itself. Ciasullo was set to testify against the Beamen brothers the next day. Several threatening calls had been placed to Ciasullo's phone warning him not to testify against the Beamen brothers. There certainly seemed to be a connection. Where Maher and Harkins disagreed was whether a tie did or did not exist between the two incidents.

"Beamen told Blasso and Anderwkavich to kill Ciasullo and make it look like a robbery," Maher speculated.

Harkins, less willing to make leaps of logic without a thorough investigation, disagreed.

"All we know is that Beamen gave one or more of the suspects information about Ciasullo," Harkins countered. "We do *not* know that Beamen encouraged the robbery in order to affect his trial. Nor do we know that Beamen asked any of the suspects to kill Ciasullo."

If the *second* robbery had been designed to prevent Ciasullo from testifying in court about the *first* robbery, the plan had not only accomplished the goal of preventing Ciasullo's testimony, it also resulted in a mistrial. The point could have been argued forever. There was only one way to find out for sure.

"Kevin," Harkins said, "we'd like to wire you up and send you to talk to Birnholz and Torre."

Maher would be compensated. Harkins had already spoken with the Policeman's Benevolent Association, which had agreed to $2,500 for the assignment. Two hundred dollars would be advanced in cash as expenses, and the remaining $2,300 would be paid by check on the date of the grand jury hearing pertaining to the case against Blasso, Anderwkavich, Birnholz, and Torre.

"We need to know every detail about how they escaped," Harkins emphasized, "and it's critical we know where they discarded their weapons."

"Without the guns," Maher noted, "Ciasullo's in trouble, isn't he?"

"Not necessarily," Harkins countered.

"Come on," Maher protested. "He was getting threats at his house. He was robbed once before. Blasso, Anderwkavich, Birnholz, and Torre could all swear they had no guns. And some lawyer could say that Ciasullo was paranoid and trigger-happy, then put Ciasullo on the stand and hammer him. *You say they had a gun? Okay, where's the fucking gun, officer?*"

Harkins didn't agree or disagree with Maher's appraisal. He simply restated the objective. "Ciasullo reported seeing a sawed-off single-barrel shotgun and a nickel-plated .32-caliber snub-nosed Smith & Wesson handgun. We would like to recover those weapons."

Maher nodded and stood to leave.

"One more thing," Harkins said. "Emphasize in your conversations with Birnholz and Torre that you told them not to do it."

THAT EVENING, MAHER, WIRED UP BOTH ELECTRONICALLY AND EMOTIONALLY, drove across the George Washington and Bronx-Whitestone bridges and into Queens. He found Birnholz pacing in his living room.

"I told you not to do it," Maher bellowed, "but you fucking idiots did it anyway."

"They got Blasso in the hospital under arrest," Birnholz whined. "We're fucked."

Maher was unsympathetic. "Didn't I tell you not to fucking knock off this guy?"

"Yeah," Birnholz said with a sigh. "You told us."

Although the conversation had lasted only a few seconds,

Maher was well on his way to accomplishing one thing: clearing himself.

"All right, you dumb fuck," Maher said, sighing, "tell me what happened."

Birnholz rattled off the events of the previous Thursday night, often jumping back and forth in the chronology. But Maher didn't stop him. It was all being recorded.

"Blasso was bleeding bad," Birnholz said at one point. "We were running, and the more he ran the more he was bleeding."

Maher shook his head. *Of course he was bleeding worse the more he ran. That's what happens when you run. Your heart pumps faster.*

"I took Blasso to his father's house," Birnholz continued. "The father looked at Blasso and said, 'Get the fuck out of here' and slammed the door. Can you believe that? His fucking son is bleeding to death and he slams the fucking door?"

Birnholz then told Maher that he pounded on the door again. This time he asked Blasso's father to call an ambulance. According to Birnholz, Blasso's father responded by saying "I ain't calling no fucking ambulance."

"So I said, look, your fucking son is bleeding to death and I asked him if I could borrow his truck to go to the hospital. See, there was this plumbing truck in the driveway—Blasso Plumbing and Heating. The old man gave me the keys to the truck and I took Blasso to the hospital."

Maher almost laughed. *Birnholz takes Blasso—who is obviously a fugitive—to the hospital in a truck emblazoned with the name* Blasso?

"I'm in trouble, man," Birnholz said with a moan. "I took Blasso to the fucking hospital."

"Don't worry," Maher said. "They don't know it was you. It could've been anybody off the street who brought him in."

As Birnholz relaxed a little, Maher came back with a question.

"Why'd you do it, Larry?" Maher asked, shaking his head. "First I tell you guys not to do it, then I drive away from the fucking house."

Birnholz was rubbing his forehead.

"Am I right?" Maher pressed. "I tell you not to rob no fucking jeweler and I drive you jerks away from the house."

"You're right, Kevin. You're right."

Maher was going to make absolutely certain that there was no doubt as to his lack of involvement.

"Okay, Larry. So why'd you go back?"

"I didn't want to, Kevin. But Blasso kept saying, 'We gotta rob this guy tonight, it's *gotta* be tonight.' "

"Why *that* night, Larry? Why not another night?"

"I don't know," Birnholz replied, sighing.

But Maher did. In Maher's mind, it all had to do with the Beamen trial. Indeed, Maher was more convinced than ever that Beamen ordered a hit on Ciasullo.

"Did you ever talk to Beamen yourself?" Maher asked.

"No," Birnholz replied.

Maher studied Birnholz for a long moment. He was telling the truth. He had never spoken with Beamen.

"So you go back to the house," Maher prodded. "Then what happened?"

Birnholz explained how he and Torre waited in the front while Blasso and Anderwkavich hid in the backyard.

"The guy comes home carrying a shopping bag and Blasso and Anderwkavich run out of the backyard."

"Armed?"

"Yeah. Blasso had a shotgun and Anderwkavich had a thirty-two."

So far, so good. Maher had cleared himself of any involvement *and* had established that there were weapons.

Birnholz continued: "Anderwkavich gets him around the neck with his arm and twists his right arm up behind his back. Blasso says, 'Give me the bag or I'm going to fucking kill you.' Then me and Torre run up."

Maher envisioned the scene as Birnholz was describing it. Blasso holding Ciasullo at gunpoint. Anderwkavich, his arm around Ciasullo's neck in what thugs call a "dope fiend yoke."

"Sounds like you had him," Maher observed. "What the fuck happened?"

Birnholz shook his head, disbelieving his own recollection.

"The fucking guy reaches in his jacket and comes out with a fucking gun! He shoots over his shoulder and hits Randy. Kills Randy, man. Fucking shoots Randy dead. Then he fires at Blasso."

Maher felt a twinge of awe for Ciasullo. *The guy is facing two*

*guns and locked in a dope fiend yoke and he has the balls to go for his
gun.*

(Actually, there had been more than courage at play, there
had been a fatal error by Anderwkavich. Although Anderwkavich had done exactly what he surely had done in previous
armed robberies—approached from the back, locked his left arm
around the mark's throat, then twisted the mark's right hand
behind his back—there was a simple reason why this otherwise
effective "dope fiend yoke" didn't hinder Ciasullo. Ciasullo was
left-handed, *not* right-handed, and his left hand was free.)

Birnholz then described how he and Blasso headed off in one
direction and Torre went in the other direction. Ciasullo followed Birnholz and Blasso.

"But we managed to lose him," Birnholz said.

Maher took aim at the burning question. "What happened to
the guns, man? Where are the fucking guns?"

"I don't know."

Maher leaned in on Birnholz. "Come on, Larry. *Where are the
fucking guns?*"

"I don't know, Kevin. I *swear.*"

"Then who *does* know?"

Birnholz didn't respond.

"Look," Maher said. "You want me to help you or not?"

Birnholz looked away. "Maybe Torre knows."

IT TOOK TWO DAYS TO TRACK DOWN TORRE AND SET UP A MEETING. IN THE
interim, Maher turned over the Birnholz tape to Harkins. Harkins was pleased on two counts. Maher, as Harkins had always
believed, was not involved in the robbery; and the presence of
guns had been established.

"Now we need to find the weapons," Harkins said.

"Don't worry," Maher said, "I'll find them."

Maher, once again wearing a wire, drove to Torre's apartment
in Queens. Torre, as Birnholz had been, was extremely nervous.
After all, it had been a week since the robbery, and neither
Birnholz nor Torre had been arrested.

"I think I better get out of town," Torre told Maher.

"If they haven't nailed you yet," Maher said matter-of-factly,
"they probably never will."

Maher began his conversation in the same manner as he began the conversation with Birnholz.

"I told you fucking guys not to do it," Maher chastised Torre. "And you fucking jerk-offs do it anyway."

As Birnholz had done, Torre agreed that Maher had warned them against the robbery.

"*So I drop you guys off at the car,*" Maher said slowly and with emphasis. "Then what the fuck happened?"

Torre's story essentially was the same as Birnholz's story, including the fact that Blasso insisted the robbery be done *that* night. And, like Birnholz, Torre claimed never to have spoken with Beamen. The two accounts were identical up to the point at which the shots were fired.

"The guy chases Blasso and Birnholz," Torre recounted, "so I circle back to the driveway. Anderwkavich is lying there hurt bad. He says, 'I'm dying, I'm dying. Help me.' So I roll him under the car and tell him I'll get help."

"He had a gun, right?" Maher asked. "And Blasso had a gun. What happened with the guns?"

"I picked up the shotgun—it was there on the driveway—and I took the pistol from Anderwkavich."

"And what did you do with them?" Maher wanted to know.

Torre hesitated. Maher thought he had lost him.

"I hid the shotgun in a driveway," Torre finally said.

"Which driveway?"

Again Torre hesitated. This time Maher pressed.

"It's only a matter of time, man. They're going to find the gun. Tell me where it is and I'll take care of it."

Torre explained exactly which driveway contained the shotgun. "I threw it under some bushes on the right side."

"What about the other gun? Anderwkavich's gun?"

Torre laughed.

"What's so funny?"

"I'm running through the neighborhood and this fucking squad car comes out of nowhere and hits me with a light. I hear 'Freeze!' So I drop the gun between two parked cars and walk out into the street. This fucking woman cop comes up to me and starts looking at the arm of my shirt. It's splattered with red. And for a minute I think *Oh, fuck! Blood!* But then I realize it's *red paint.*"

Both Maher and Torre started laughing. The fact was, Torre was a painter by occupation, and most of his clothes were dotted in some kind of paint.

Torre continued, "So this broad sees that it's paint and I tell her I'm a painter and she says 'Sorry but there was a robbery in the area and it looked like blood.' And then she lets me go."

After all these years, Maher had become familiar with police procedure. If an officer encounters someone suspicious in the area in which a shooting occurred, procedure dictates a "stop and frisk," if for no other reason than the officer's own safety. Additionally, procedure dictates that a person stopped be positively identified.

"Did she ID you?" Maher asked.

"Yeah," Torre said with a laugh. "Then the broad lets me go."

Maher smiled. Torre could now be placed in the neighborhood at the time of the shooting.

"Okay," Maher said, "she lets you go. Then what?"

"I go back and pick up the gun."

"Where's the gun now?"

"I hid it somewhere else."

"Where?"

"I can't remember."

Maher leaned close to Torre. "Look, you fuckhead, tell me where you hid the pistol and let me get rid of it."

"I told you, I don't remember."

No matter how hard Maher hammered, Torre couldn't seem to recall where he hid the Smith & Wesson .32. Maher gave up and headed into Manhattan to rendezvous with Harkins.

"IMPOSSIBLE," HARKINS SAID WHEN HE HEARD TORRE'S TAPED ACCOUNT of where he hid the shotgun. "There were two hundred cops and Emergency Services Unit guys out there searching a ten-block radius."

"Well, I guess they missed it, then," Maher said with a shrug.

Maher and two detectives from the 109th Precinct left for Queens immediately. They pulled up to the driveway Torre had specified and walked to the shrubbery under which Torre had said he hid the shotgun. One of the detectives pulled back a branch. A single-barrel sawed-off shotgun was lying on the ground.

Despite repeated phone calls and visits to both Torre and Birnholz, Maher never recovered the .32. But Harkins had three things he didn't have before Maher called him. The suspects implicating themselves on tape; the shotgun; and the logbook report of the officer who stopped Torre for having red paint on his shirt, thus placing Torre in the vicinity at the time of the shooting. Birnholz and Torre were arrested and charged with armed robbery.

On a crisp morning in October 1982, Maher dressed for an appointment at Kew Gardens, where the Queens grand jury was set to convene in the matter of Blasso, Birnholz, and Torre. The hearing was scheduled for 9:30 A.M.

At 8:00 A.M., Harkins called Maher and announced: "I have the check for you, and I'm on the way to the grand jury. See you at nine-thirty."

Maher was proud of himself. He had acted as a cop, saved a cop, and felt very much back in the game. Even better, he was on his way to pick up a check for $2,300. But it wasn't the money, it was the self-esteem the money evoked. *I am a cop,* Maher told himself. *I'm being* paid *as a cop.*

Ten minutes later, the phone rang again. It was Harkins.

"Queens chief of detectives Willis still believes you had something to do with the robbery," Harkins stated flatly. "He has refused to sign off on the payment."

Maher went from shock to anger.

"And he still expects me to testify at the grand jury?"

Without Maher's testimony, there was no way to tell how the jury would react to the tape of Birnholz and Torre talking about the crime. While reason might dictate that such definitive recorded evidence certainly would ensure an indictment, Harkins had seen how the absence of a flesh-and-blood witness could create doubt in the mind of a jury. Harkins desperately needed Maher to take the witness stand in Kew Gardens. Yet there was only one response Harkins knew Maher would respect.

"Whatever you decide to do I'll stand by you," Harkins said quietly.

"Fuck him! I ain't testifying."

Harkins understood Maher's reaction and didn't blame him. But, as a cop, Harkins had to make every effort to change Maher's mind.

"Look, Kevin, I know how you feel. But we need your testimony."

"What? This guy wants to make a complete fool of me. Hey, I risked my life several times, took three vicious criminals off the street, recovered a gun, saved a cop."

Harkins had known Maher long enough to know there was no way he was going to turn him around.

Maher did not testify.

Even without Maher taking the witness stand, Blasso was indicted "by reason of belief," a legal term that was perhaps one of the more logical statutes contained in the code of law. Simply stated, if there was every reason to believe that a suspect was guilty, then the suspect can be indicted based on that "reason of belief." In Blasso's case, the bullet in his stomach seemed to indicate *someone* shot him and didn't have any other plausible explanation as to why he was carrying around a slug in his body. (Blasso ultimately was convicted of armed robbery in the first degree and sentenced to three to six years in prison.)

However, in the absence of Maher's testimony, the prosecutor elected not to introduce the tape. The grand jury refused to indict Birnholz and Torre. The case against them was dismissed.

Maher was happy about the grand jury decision. *I proved a fucking point to Willis,* Maher chuckled when he heard that Birnholz and Torre would walk. *And besides, Birnholz is a helluva mechanic. If he's in jail, who the fuck would I get to fix my car?*

Chapter 11

ALTHOUGH MAHER TRIED TO SHAKE IT OFF, HE WAS DEEPLY HURT BY HIS experience in the Ciasullo case. The truth was, he had not been treated like a *real* cop, and it forced him to face the fact that he *wasn't* a real cop. Disillusioned by what he considered shoddy treatment at the hands of a suspicious NYPD chief of detectives, Maher had second thoughts about his undercover exploits. *Maybe I should just forget it*, Maher told himself. Besides, there was something else that was troubling him even more than his future as a quasi-cop. His marriage.

Maher could no longer deny that something had changed between him and Beth. It could be written off as the inevitable fading of passion that often occurs when two people have been together for a long time. But Maher's gut told him it was something more than that. At first Maher thought it was his undercover work. Beth had never really been comfortable with what he was doing. Then Maher wondered if it might be Beth's career, which was on a rapid rise. In 1978 she had left *New York* magazine for a job as circulation manager of *Esquire*. In 1980 she had helped launch a new magazine called *Prime Time*. When that folded after a year, Beth had joined *The Economist* as circulation director. Maybe, Maher speculated, Beth's increasing responsibilities in her ever higher positions were sapping her energy. But he knew that wasn't it either. While the distancing between them seemed to have begun at about the time Beth went to *The Economist*, there was another factor. A coworker named Richard O'Rourke.

After her first day at *The Economist,* Beth had returned home late. She was drunk.

"Where were you?" Maher had asked.

"Oh," Beth had said with a giggle, "an accountant at the office took me out for a drink."

"Who?" Maher had demanded.

"Richard O'Rourke."

Maher had felt a twinge. Not of anger. Not of jealousy. But of sudden loss. His intuition told him Beth was enamored with someone else. As the weeks passed, Maher became convinced she was having an affair. It wasn't that Beth mentioned the name Richard often, which she did, it was the *way* she said the name Richard, the inflection she used, dragging it out: *Ri-ri-ch-ch-ard.* It drove Maher crazy, made him feel physically ill. Yet, when he finally confronted her, she denied it. But Maher knew.

Seeking a way to shut off his mind, to stop the images of Beth with another man, Maher turned his attention to drag racing. On most weekends he could be found at the "strip" on Connecting Highway. He once again set about modifying his Corvette, making the undisputed fastest car even faster. And he went back to his old mechanic, Larry Birnholz. *Why not?* Maher told himself. *Larry doesn't know I was an FBI informant.*

As Maher and Birnholz worked on Maher's Vette, Maher decided to tell Birnholz a variation of the Ciasullo story. *I want this fucker indebted to me,* Maher reasoned.

"I'm an FBI informant," Maher said one day.

Birnholz dropped the wrench he was holding.

"Look, Larry," Maher said with a laugh, "I was never going to lock you up. Grand theft auto? You'd get ninety days, maybe less."

Birnholz, a look of terror and confusion in his eyes, was speechless.

Maher continued: "But when you took off that fucking cop, they wanted me to testify against you. I had no choice. They were going to subpoena me."

Birnholz stared at Maher, his mouth gaping.

"But I refused to testify, Larry. I told them I wasn't going to turn on my friend. Otherwise you'd be locked up right now. And you know that as well as I do."

"So *that's* what happened," Birnholz squeaked. Then: "Thanks, Kevin."

"Forget about it, Larry," Maher said.

They returned to the job at hand.

Maher and Birnholz removed the LT1 engine they had dropped into the Vette two years earlier and replaced it with a 427-cubic-inch L88 Big Block motor, which packed more than 550 horsepower. Total cost: $8,000.

Besides the automotive changes, Maher added creature comforts not often found in a race car. He tweaked the engine to idle at a thousand revolutions per minute instead of the standard twelve hundred rpms, which enabled him to run the air conditioning without the car overheating. And he installed a $4,000 sound system consisting of a twelve-hundred-watt Blaupunkt radio and a speaker array that included ten-inch woofers. The resulting sound was so big that when Maher sat in the Corvette and cranked up the volume, the hair on the back of his head would part.

After having sunk $12,000 into the Vette, Maher not only had the fastest vehicle in the area, he also had the most expensively appointed. Now he had to pay for all these modifications. So every weekend he would head up to Connecting Highway and wait for one of two types of drivers: someone who didn't know him or his Vette, or someone who had gone off to modify his own car and had returned to the strip believing his could finally beat Maher. Maher didn't care who showed up. He would bet $4,000, blast through a quarter of a mile, and pick up the money.

On one Friday night in the fall of 1982, a hotshot in a Camaro appeared. The driver was so certain his Camaro could take Maher's Corvette that he spotted Maher a full car length.

When the Corvette and the Camaro were positioned at the starting line, the driver of the Camaro arrogantly motioned for Maher to move ahead a car length. With $4,000 at stake, Maher didn't mind. He edged in front of the Camaro. A moment later, the signal was given and both cars revved up.

The torque of the Big Block motor in Maher's Corvette (torque is the force an engine produces as turns) generated so much momentum that the car's fiberglass body contorted to the right while the left wheel rose off the ground. For an instant, as the Vette wound up to sixty-five hundred rpms, it seemed frozen in time. Then, in an explosion of raw power, the car shot forward. Seconds later, it was over. Maher had won by ten car lengths, an incredible margin of victory in a quarter-mile dash.

Maher screeched to a stop, climbed out of the car, and popped the hood. Dozens of people crowded around Maher's Vette, pushing and shoving to get a better view. Among the mesmerized onlookers was a twenty-two-year-old Colombian named John Uribe.

Maher had met Uribe a year earlier when Uribe arrived at Connecting Highway in a stock 1978 Silver Anniversary Corvette. At only 160 horsepower, Uribe's car rarely won. Uribe regarded Maher's Corvette—which by now had been featured in three national car magazines and a book about Corvettes—as the ultimate machine.

"Hey, Kevin!" Uribe shouted as he squirmed through the masses. "You put another engine in your Vette!"

Uribe finally made his way to the side of Maher's car. He glanced at the Big Block, then looked up at Maher.

"What'd you do with the other motor?"

"I still got it," Maher responded.

"Can I buy it from you?" Uribe asked, his eyes pleading.

Maher smiled. John Uribe was a nice kid. It wasn't *his* fault he was born into a family-run drug cartel.

Over the past year, Maher had often asked Uribe what he did for a living. At first Uribe would say, "Nothing." Ultimately, after he felt he could trust Maher, Uribe had acknowledged that he was laundering money for the family.

"I take leaf bags full of cash out of the house," Uribe had explained, "and I get the small bills changed into large denominations and money orders."

"Doesn't anyone at the bank get suspicious?" Maher had wondered aloud.

"No," Uribe had said with a laugh, "*I* don't do it myself. I've got a bunch of guys who go to banks all over the city."

Then Uribe had offered Maher a job. "I'll pay you five hundred dollars for every bag of money you change."

Maher had declined.

Now young John Uribe, standing there by Maher's new, improved Corvette and looking very much younger than his twenty-two years, was angling for an opportunity to have the second-fastest car at Connecting Highway.

"I want your old motor," Uribe pressed. "I want the LT1."

"Sure, John. You can have it."

Maher told Uribe he wanted $6,000 for the motor. Maher would not only install it, he also would throw in a myriad of extras, including a 400-turbo three-speed transmission, headers, and a heavy-duty radiator.

Maher contracted the job to Frank's Sunoco Station in Lyndhurst, New Jersey. Every day Uribe would call Maher and check on the progress.

"Now this is going to make me the fastest guy at Connecting Highway?" Uribe would ask over and over.

"*Second* fastest," Maher always would correct him. "*I'm* the fastest."

One day, as Uribe rattled on about what was being installed in his Vette, Maher mentioned that it might be good to have an engine oil cooler.

"Yeah," Uribe agreed. "I need that."

"And what about a transmission oil cooler?"

"I need that, too, don't I, Kevin?"

"It wouldn't hurt."

Multiple spark discharge, special shielded spark plug wires, water injection, special motor mounts, you name it, Maher sold it to Uribe. At a profit, of course. The original $6,000 quote quickly ballooned to $10,000. But Maher didn't feel guilty. Everything he was putting in Uribe's Vette did in fact improve the performance. *And besides*, Maher thought, *he's a drug dealer with bags of cash. I'm going to bang him.*

When the modifications were complete, Uribe showed up at Connecting Highway and blew every other car away. Except Maher's, of course. Even so, second fastest was a lot better than being the slowest.

Besides his new status at Connecting Highway, Uribe underwent another transformation. He no longer had the demeanor of a shy kid. He was flashing a lot of money. And he was showing up with a different leggy bimbo every weekend. At first Maher attributed this to Uribe's sudden popularity as a winner at the races. Maher knew that winning not only built confidence, it also generated cash. Then, Maher realized that Uribe wasn't just carrying thousands he was carrying *tens of thousands*. And he had begun carrying something else.

Cocaine.

One night—a humid summer night in 1983—Maher noticed a pretty brunette standing by the side of Connecting Highway. Uribe watched Maher watching the girl.

"That's Julianne," Uribe said. "I fucked her."

Maher jolted back from some fantasy and looked at Uribe. Sure, he was a good-looking kid, but Maher didn't think of himself as any less appealing. Still, Uribe was the one getting all the action.

Uribe pointed across the highway at a blonde.

"Fucked her, too," Uribe stated without any real emotion.

Maher found himself wondering: *How does he do it?*

"You know how I get all these bitches?" Uribe said, reading Maher's mind.

Maher raised an eyebrow. "How, John?"

Uribe slowly reached into his pocket and pulled out a plastic sandwich bag filled with white powder.

"I give these dopey bitches some of this and they'll do anything I want them to," Uribe said with a smile.

Uribe offered Maher the bag of cocaine. "A present for you, my friend."

Maher hesitated. He had never done coke.

"Go ahead," Uribe urged. "Take it. Try it. You'll see."

Maher tentatively took the coke from Uribe and stuffed it in his pocket.

"There are two ounces in there," Uribe noted. "That should last you for a while."

Uribe handed Maher a tiny spoon. "Here. You'll need this."

Maher took the spoon and then slowly ambled over to Julianne. She looked even better than she did from a distance. High-heeled boots. Black leather miniskirt. And a tiny white feather dangling from one earlobe. Julianne glanced up as Maher approached her.

"Wanna hang out?" Maher said.

Julianne shrugged. "You got any hits?"

Maher showed her the two ounces of coke Uribe had given him. Julianne's eyes widened and she reached for the bag. As she held out her right hand, Maher noticed something. The fingernail on her pinkie was about a half inch longer than her other nails. And she had a tiny diamond embedded in it.

"This cost me five hundred dollars," Julianne pointed out, holding up her diamond-studded fingernail.

The utility of the fingernail became apparent when the two of them climbed into Maher's Corvette. Julianne dug into the bag and used her fingernail to scoop out a small mound of coke, which she quickly snorted. Maher, using the coke spoon, followed suit. He waited for something to happen. Nothing did. *Coke ain't so amazing*, Maher concluded. *What the fuck is everybody talking about?* But a few minutes later, Maher took a second hit. And then a third. Now *I see what everybody's talking about.* He was overcome with euphoria. *Everything is wonderful. The world is fantastic.* This *is what living is all about.* Suddenly his mind was firing like the multiple spark discharge under the hood of the Vette. And his thoughts mimicked his driving technique. Fast. Dangerous. Out of control.

For the next hour, Maher and Julianne cruised Queens, snorting coke and listening to the radio with the volume cranked. Maher was giddy and felt totally uninhibited. Julianne seemed in the mood for anything. So when Maher found himself in front of the Kew Motor Inn on Queens Boulevard, he whipped the car into the parking lot.

Once in the room, Julianne pulled off her miniskirt and blouse, then fell across the bed. Maher shivered slightly as he let his eyes caress her long, slender legs, which were now open and inviting. *Those legs go from here to New Jersey*, Maher mused. A momentary flicker of confusion hit him. Until that night, he had never snorted coke. And he had never cheated on Beth. Never even thought about it. Now he was high and about to screw a girl with a feather earring and one long fingernail. It seemed bizarre, surreal. Maher dug another spoonful of coke out of the plastic bag and snorted it up his right nostril. The curtain of confusion parted. And there was Julianne, waiting on the bed.

Maher undressed and slid on top of her. The world disappeared in a blaze of lust, and Maher's emotions churned inside him like his mind was a blender. In the midst of it all it struck him that the last time he felt this kind of unbridled thrill was when he took the cops on a chase to the Catskills. What never seemed to occur to him were the consequences. Not then. And certainly not now.

MAHER ENTERED THE HOUSE QUIETLY AND, AS HE USUALLY DID AFTER A night at Connecting Highway, tiptoed into the bedroom. He looked at Beth, who was sleeping, and she seemed angelic. *How could I do this to her?* Maher tortured himself. *How could I fuck some dopey bitch?* Then he undressed and slipped into bed. Beth stirred and wrapped her arms around his waist.

"Did you win?" Beth whispered.

"Yeah," Maher said. "I won."

"That's good," Beth said with a yawn, then cuddled against him.

Maher felt waves of guilt. He ached for his mind to stop, longed for sleep. But Maher was about to learn a lesson about cocaine. The drug-induced euphoria dissolves long before the pharmacological effect of the stimulant wears off. And so he lay awake, wondering if he would ever be the same. Toward dawn, rationalization set in. *What am I feeling guilty about? Beth's fucking some guy at the office. Fuck Beth. Fuck her.*

The following morning, as Beth made a pot of coffee, Maher brooded.

"What's wrong, Kevin?" Beth asked.

"I tried cocaine last night," Maher blurted out.

"You did?" Beth seemed only half surprised.

"It's weird stuff," Maher said with a sigh. "I couldn't sleep."

"Of course you couldn't sleep," Beth noted. "Cocaine is a stimulant. Stimulants keep you awake."

And that was the extent of the conversation. This was 1983. Cocaine was no big deal. Even doctors were shrugging off its potential for abuse and addiction.

Throughout the day, Maher found it difficult to concentrate. The effect of his first taste of coke. The remorse over his encounter with Julianne, which even the possibility of Beth having an affair would not quell.

Later that night, Uribe stopped by his house.

"A present for you, my friend." Uribe smiled as he offered Maher a hit of coke.

Maher shook his head no.

"Kevin," Uribe said, "when a Colombian offers you a *present*, you must not refuse. It is an insult."

Maher accepted the plastic bag of coke and the tiny silver coke spoon from Uribe, then took a hit in both nostrils. He felt better immediately. Maher was learning lesson number two about cocaine: The more you used, the more you wanted.

Maher returned the bag of coke to Uribe, but Uribe handed it back to him. "This is for *you*, my friend. My present."

That simple exchange would set the tone for their entire relationship. Maher would teach Uribe all he knew about Corvettes. And, in return, Uribe would offer "presents."

"The reason I stopped by to see you," Uribe explained, "is that I want you to put an LS-seven four-fifty-four in my Corvette."

Maher's eyebrows raised. An LS7 was even more powerful than the Big Block engine in Maher's Vette.

"John," Maher pointed out, "that's a twelve-thousand-dollar conversion."

"I've got the money," Uribe countered.

"You'll need to change a lot of trash bags to pay for it," Maher said with a laugh.

Uribe did not laugh. The solemn expression on Uribe's face confirmed what Maher had always suspected—that Uribe had long since graduated from laundering cash to dealing.

Maher ordered the LS7 engine and had a mechanic at Frank's Sunoco drop it in Uribe's Corvette. Then Maher transferred the Vette to his garage, where he performed additional modifications. Uribe would stop by every day to see how the conversion was coming. One afternoon, Uribe arrived to find Bobby working next to Maher. Bobby was now twelve years old and he loved learning from Maher, watching his "father," the automotive alchemist.

"How's everything going?" Uribe asked.

"Getting there," Maher replied.

Bobby was busy cutting and splicing heavy-duty steel spark plug wires. In the process, the stiff cables had cut his fingers. His hands were bloody.

"Your fingers are bleeding," Uribe reacted.

"It's the wires," Bobby said with a shrug.

The following day, Uribe showed up with a $1,500 Kawasaki dirt bike, a helmet, and knee pads.

"A present for you, Bobby," Uribe said.

Maher was so touched by Uribe's display of concern for Bobby that he gave only a passing thought to the source of the Uribe's funds. *John's all right*, Maher convinced himself as he watched Bobby test out the new motorcycle.

For the next week, while Maher worked on Uribe's Corvette, Uribe over and over asked the same question: "When you finish, I'll have the fastest car at Connecting Highway, right?"

"Right," Maher responded each time. "But like I told you, with this configuration, you won't be able to go Porsche hunting on Long Island."

"I don't care about that," Uribe insisted. "I just want to have the best Vette on Connecting Highway."

Porsche hunting on Long Island was a pastime of an elite group of Corvette owners who had designed their cars for both speed *and* distance. Stock Corvettes would always win a quarter-mile dash against a stock Porsche, while a stock Porsche would consistently beat a stock Corvette over distance. On the open highway, Porsche drivers would sneer at Corvette drivers, then kick their car into high gear and spend the next few minutes watching the Vette fade away in the rearview mirror. Those Corvette owners who had built hybrid vehicles like Maher had, loved to cruise the Long Island Expressway, pull up next to a Porsche, then watch the shocked expression of the Porsche's driver as the Vette roared away. But Uribe didn't have dreams of Porsche hunting. He only wanted to be king of the universe he knew: Connecting Highway.

When the modifications on Uribe's Corvette were done, Uribe tested his new machine at the Connecting Highway strip. As Maher had promised, nothing could touch the "Silver Bullet." It seemed Uribe had gotten what he asked for: supremacy in the quarter mile at Connecting Highway. Of course, he had yet to race Maher.

One Friday night, the inevitable contest was set up: Maher versus Uribe. Uribe—with the greater horsepower—had the edge. But driving experience triumphed over horsepower, and the student was unable to beat the master. Maher won by half a car length. Uribe was miffed. He had paid all this money for an LS7—the most powerful engine you could put in a Vette—and still finished in second place. Uribe stared at Maher. The look in Uribe's eyes said: *Maybe you didn't do everything you were supposed to do.*

"Hey, John," Maher offered. "Let's go again."

This time Uribe won.

"Congratulations," Maher said when it was over.

"A present for you," Uribe said with a smile, holding out a bag of cocaine.

Over the next several weekends, Uribe racked up victory after victory. But the glory was costly. One night, he blew a transmission. Another night Uribe burned out a torque converter. Still another race cost Uribe a rear end. Uribe was just beginning to understand how expensive a hobby drag racing could be. And Maher had begun to realize that Uribe's drug dealing was not fueling the hobby, *the hobby was fueling the drug dealing.* Uribe was dealing more and more drugs to keep pace with the repair bills and the constant upgrades that would allow his Corvette to maintain an edge. While Maher didn't believe he had been the cause of Uribe's change of occupation by introducing Uribe to the bottomless pit of vehicular modification, he *did* feel that he had hastened the transition.

Once, in an attempt to justify his dealing, Uribe told Maher, "Did you know that if one drug dealer in the United States gets busted, two hundred and fifty Colombian farmers don't eat?"

The bit of clever propaganda provided a *raison d'être* for a legion of Colombians who were perhaps only months removed from staring poverty in the face.

IN MID-1983 THE HOUSE AT 83 JEFFERSON STREET IN WOOD-RIDGE THAT Maher had been renting was sold, and the new landlord declined to renew the lease. So Maher and Beth found a place in Waldwick, a town about ten miles away. But almost immediately upon moving in, there were problems. Bobby missed his friends in Wood-Ridge. Beth missed her neighbors. Maher missed his local gas stations and auto part stores. Even Samantha the German shepherd seemed depressed. So Maher and

Beth decided to look for a house to buy in Wood-Ridge. They were doing well financially, and it seemed time they owned a home. But they had to save enough for a down payment. Maher stopped pouring money into his Corvette. And, with the prospect of a real home in the future, he started spending less time at Connecting Highway and more time with Beth, Bobby, and Samantha. The only thing still threatening his future was his cocaine habit.

One evening in December 1983, Maher returned home from work. Before getting out of his car, he took a hit of white powder. He was bolstered by the rush and strode into the house. Suddenly he felt excruciating chest pains and staggered to the sofa, falling onto it. Beth rushed to him.

"Kevin! Kevin! What is it?"

As Beth ran to the phone to call an ambulance, Maher stopped her.

"Beth. I'm all right. I'm feeling better."

Maher recovered enough to get to the dining room table.

"Tomorrow," Beth insisted, "you're going to see a doctor."

Maher took the next morning off and stopped by to see a doctor in Waldwick. A few days later the tests came back.

"As far as I can tell," the doctor said, "there's nothing wrong with you. It could have been an anxiety attack. If I were you, I'd take some time off."

"Would you write a note to my job?" Maher asked.

"Of course," the doctor agreed.

That afternoon, Maher walked into the office of New Jersey Transit (formerly known as ConRail) and informed them he needed to take an extended sick leave, doctor's orders.

A month later, Maher's allotted sick pay expired and he was put on disability, which was not full pay. So when Uribe stopped by one evening and renewed an offer Maher had previously declined, this time it seemed more appealing.

"Why don't you change a little money for me?" Uribe asked. "Like I told you before, I'll give you five hundred dollars for each bag of small bills you change into large denominations."

When Maher didn't answer immediately, Uribe pressed: "It's easy. You drive around to different banks and change two, three hundred at each bank. That way no one gets suspicious."

Maher still didn't respond. He glanced out the window at

Bobby, who was tossing a stick to Samantha. *The money* would *help,* Maher thought.

"Sure," Maher finally said. "Why not?"

AMONG THE PEOPLE MAHER MET AT VARIOUS CORVETTE GATHERINGS AT Astoria Park, where car owners would congregate and show off their cars, was a cop named Vincent Caldera. Caldera drove a 1983 Monte Carlo Super Sport, and since Maher was *the man* when it came to automotive modifications, Caldera would often ask questions about improving performance. As they got to know each other better, Maher told Caldera about his work as a confidential informant. Caldera then confided in Maher about something he normally didn't discuss.

"I'm on modified assignment," Caldera told Maher one day.

The term "modified assignment" was a euphemism. Those on "modified assignment" were being disciplined in some way. In Caldera's case, he was assigned to traffic detail.

"What the fuck did you do?" Maher asked.

Caldera explained that a year before, he was off-duty and driving along in Queens when a taxi cut in front of him and almost hit his car. Caldera pulled his car up beside the cab and flashed his shield, but the cabdriver pressed the accelerator and raced away. Caldera pursued the cab until it got stuck in traffic.

"So," Caldera said, "I jumped out of the car and, with a shield in one hand, drew my gun. I approached the cab and pointed the gun at the fucking driver."

Maher was loving every minute of the story.

"Good for you, man. Fuck him. *Fuck* him."

Caldera continued: "A passenger in the back of the cab screamed at me: 'Hey! You can't pull your gun on him!' So I pointed the gun in the backseat and said: 'Shut the fuck up.' "

Maher laughed. "That's great, Vinny."

Caldera was stone-faced. "The guy in the back was a former U.S. congressman."

"Fuck!" Maher reacted.

"The bastard filed a complaint and I got modified assignment. Now I hear they're thinking of firing me."

Maher shook his head. "Look, Vinny, I know people at the district attorney's office. Let me talk to them."

The following day, Maher spoke with Harkins. Unfortunately, there was nothing Harkins could do. When Maher told Caldera, he shrugged.

"Thanks for trying," Caldera said. "But I think I have it solved."

"How?"

"I know this lawyer," Caldera said, "who represents somebody big in the department. He says he can guarantee me my job back." (Caldera's lawyer represented a high-ranking law enforcement official who cannot be named.)

"That's great," Maher observed.

"Problem is," Caldera added, "he wants twenty thousand. In cash."

Maher knew what that meant. Bribery.

"Promise me you won't say anything about this, Kevin," Caldera said. "I just want my job back, that's all."

"Okay," Maher assented.

Since Caldera didn't have the money himself, he called his father. Then Maher, Caldera, and Caldera's father drove to a bank and withdrew twenty thousand in cash. Next stop was the lawyer's office, where Caldera delivered the bundle of currency.

A short time later, Caldera was reinstated.

Maher had promised Caldera he wouldn't do anything or say anything about the payoff. He would keep that promise. Even so, Maher deposited the information in his memory. A former U.S. congressman. A high-ranking law enforcement official. And twenty grand. Not a bad deposit.

IN JANUARY 1984 MAHER WAS FEELING WELL ENOUGH TO RETURN TO work. However, when he reported for duty, he was told by the assistant supervisor, Moe Sykes, that he had been taken "out of service."

Maher was furious. He had done everything he was supposed to do, filed every bit of paperwork.

"William French's orders," Sykes said.

French was Sykes's superior.

"But here are the test reports from my doctor," Maher said. "And the forms I filled out."

Sykes was unsympathetic. Maher would have to go to a hearing if he wanted to be reinstated.

"Show the paperwork to the hearing officer," Sykes said.

Maher started to say something. Sykes cut him off.

"William French's orders," Sykes said.

On January 24, Maher appeared at a New Jersey Transit hearing.

"I hear you've been taking off a lot of work," the hearing officer said.

"Yeah," Maher responded. "I've been sick."

Maher handed the hearing officer a stack of various letters, test results, and forms. Sykes entered the room as the hearing officer was reading Maher's documentation.

"There's no case here," the hearing officer said. "Why didn't you give these notes to your supervisor?"

"When I tried to give them to him," Maher said, pointing at Sykes, "he said give them to *you*."

The hearing officer looked at Sykes. "Is that true?"

"Yes," Sykes replied. "Bill French already took him out of service."

After chiding Sykes, the hearing officer reinstated Maher, ruling that Maher would be paid for the days he was prevented from working.

"I want you to go to a company doctor," the hearing officer said, "to make sure you're able to return to work."

On February 9, Maher was examined by a New Jersey Transit doctor, and it was discovered that Maher couldn't see out of his right eye.

"I was shot with a BB gun when I was a kid," Maher explained.

Maher reported to work on February 16, and Sykes handed Maher a pair of goggles. Sykes explained that there was a regulation that required anyone with impaired vision to wear protective eyegear. The pertinent regulation, Rule 15, read as follows: "An employee blind or practically blind in one eye must wear protective goggles at all times while on Company property."

"Let me guess," Maher said with a sigh. "William French's orders."

Sykes nodded.

Over the years Maher had adapted to his impaired sight by making use of his peripheral vision. The side shields that were part of the goggles prevented him from doing that.

"I can't wear these things," Maher told Sykes. "I'll get hit by a train and get killed."

"You *have* to wear them," Sykes insisted. "William French's orders."

Maher was getting sick of hearing those words: "William French's orders." It was beginning to feel like harassment.

Maher left work and went to his eye doctor, David A. Kaplan, who agreed that it was more dangerous for Maher to wear the goggles than not to wear them.

Presented with a letter from Maher's doctor, Sykes said: "Go to *our* doctor, and if he concurs, we'll exempt you from the rule."

On February 27, Dr. Bernard Sarn, a New Jersey Transit physician, concurred.

Maher was allowed to resume work *without* goggles. Word around the lot was that the supervisor was definitely not pleased. Neither was Maher. And from that moment on, Maher decided he would watch William French very, very closely.

Chapter 12

Over the next three months, Maher met a number of drug dealers. In virtually every home he entered there were telltale signs of illegal activity. A scale. Residue on a coffee table. Ledgers. Stacks of cash or piles of plastic-wrapped coke. Kilo after kilo after kilo. Maher had no idea that there was that much cocaine in New York City.

Maher distanced himself from the actual distribution and sale of cocaine. If cocaine were being transported—even by Uribe—Maher made sure he wasn't in the car. And since Uribe never charged Maher for coke, Maher was never engaged in a drug buy. It was, of course, a fine line, yet he *was* in a safer position than Uribe. Should the walls of the Uribe cartel crumble around him, the most Maher could be charged with was cocaine possession and whatever the district attorney could come up with regarding the changing of money. It wasn't *really* laundering, Maher kept telling himself. Laundering involved the conversion of illegal money into legal assets. All Maher was doing was transforming illegal money into illegal money with a larger denomination. Maher felt reasonably safe from any prosecution that would lead to jail time. And there was no way he was going back to jail. That's why, when Uribe once asked Maher if he'd like to get into dealing drugs, Maher made it clear that he wanted no part of sales or distribution.

"I'll change money for you, John," Maher had said, his voice firm, "but there's *no way* I'm dealing. *No fucking way.*"

"That's cool," Uribe had responded.

The subject was never broached again.

Despite the convoluted reasoning and his propped-up bravado, Maher sometimes found himself getting scared. *What if I do get caught? And what if I get a tough bastard of a judge and get sentenced to jail time?* The scenario made Maher shiver. *Maybe it's time to quit. Maybe I should tell Uribe that I'm out.* But Maher never seemed able to mouth the words "John, I ain't doing this anymore." And so he kept picking up trash bags full of cash—often as much as twenty thousand in a bag—and exchanging George Washington's likeness for portraits of other presidents.

Most of the drug dealers didn't mind when Maher accompanied Uribe. Maher met José. Carlos. Louis. Usmelia, Uribe's drug-dealing girlfriend. They were all satisfied that if Maher were with Uribe, he must be okay. A few dealers seemed suspicious, but when Uribe vouched for Maher, they backed off. And then there was Hector Comancha. (Not his real name.)

Hector reacted violently the first time Uribe and Maher arrived at his Queens Boulevard apartment. He grabbed Uribe by the arm and took him to a corner of the room, where they screamed at each other in Spanish. Maher didn't understand Spanish, but he got the drift of the conversation. Once in a while, Hector motioned toward Maher and shrieked *"¡Federale!"* Each time, Uribe shook his head no. The confrontation ended when an exasperated Uribe exclaimed in English:

"You don't like it, I'll take my shit elsewhere."

Hector threw up his hands in resignation. But, as first impressions go, neither Maher nor Hector had created a good one.

Before getting down to business, Hector pointed out his new large-screen television. It was one of the first large-screen televisions on the market, and Hector was proud of it. He also made much of his new gray marble table.

"Cost me six thousand," Hector boasted as he lovingly ran his hands over the smooth marble surface.

Uribe and Hector set about negotiating a drug deal. While they talked, Maher noticed a large safe in the corner of the living room. At one point, Uribe, *not* Hector, went to the safe and spun out the combination, opening it to reveal several kilos of cocaine and stacks of cash. Maher found it odd that Uribe was the one who seemed in control of a safe in someone else's apartment. So when they left Hector's place, Maher asked Uribe about the safe.

"That's my safe house," Uribe said.

Maher had heard the phrase "safe house" before—in spy movies. It was a place to hide. To Uribe, however, the term "safe house" represented a more literal description. As Uribe explained it, high-level dealers never kept cash and cocaine in their own apartments. Instead, they would find someone like Hector who would agree to the placement of a safe in *their* apartment. The resident of the apartment did not know the combination of the safe; he merely provided the space. For his trouble—and risk—the "safe keeper" was either paid in cash or, if he were a dealer himself like Hector, was given steep discounts on purchases.

A week later, Uribe and Maher stopped by Hector's apartment again. Maher, trying to be friendly, greeted Hector.

"Hey! Hector! How ya doin'?"

Maher, who was carrying his car keys, tossed them on the marble table as he entered the apartment. Hector exploded into a rage.

"You motherfucker! You scratched my table!"

Hector got in Maher's face. Uribe stepped in and pushed Maher and Hector apart.

"Hey," Uribe said with a laugh. "You guys cool it, okay?"

Maher and Hector stared at each other. Maher held his ground. Hector backed off. But Maher's emotions churned. *I'm going to bang the fucker. I'm going to lock up this little bastard.*

Maher grabbed his keys and headed for the door.

"I'll wait for you outside," Maher told Uribe.

Maher exited the apartment, slamming the door as he left. Once outside, he paced on the sidewalk and fumed. He walked over to where Hector's car was parked, took a pen out of his pocket, and wrote down the license number on a book of matches.

Maher fumed all the way home. *Fuck this. Fuck changing money. Fuck hanging out with dope dealers.* Suddenly it hit him. And he knew exactly what he had to do.

Maher rushed into his house, pulled a phone book from the closet, and looked up the number of the Drug Enforcement Agency. He dialed the number. After explaining to a receptionist that he needed to talk to an agent, Maher's call was put through to the duty agent at the time, Tom Slavanki.

"Agent Slavanki. How can I help you?"

"My name is Kevin Maher. I'm a confidential informant."

"Are you registered with us?"

"No. But I've worked with the NYPD and the FBI. And I have some information you might be interested in."

Maher offered Detective Tom Harkins as a reference.

"Why don't you come in tomorrow," Slavanki suggested. "Twelve o'clock."

"I'll be there," Maher said and hung up the receiver.

Maher fell back on the couch and thought about all the drug dealers he knew. *I can put a dent in the New York City cocaine business.* And the truth was, he could. *And I can put that little fuck Hector in jail.* He could do that, too.

The next day, at twelve noon, Maher entered a high-rise building at 555 West 57th Street and proceeded to the twenty-eighth floor, where the offices of Drug Enforcement Agency Group 43 were located. He was directed to a large open room lined with desks. Agent Tom Slavanki was sitting at one of the desks. Slavanki was more than six feet tall, blond, and blue-eyed. Maher thought he looked German.

"Hi," Slavanki said as he stood to greet Maher. "I'm pleased to meet you."

(Slavanki had called Harkins earlier that day, and Harkins had characterized Maher as the "ultimate informant to the point of being reckless." Then Harkins added a few words of caution: "If you don't have a lot of experience working with informants, you're in for an awakening. You might think you're the dog wagging the tail, but with Kevin, the tail wags the dog." Harkins offered a bit of advice: "There's only one way to work with Kevin. Let him think he's running the show." Finally, Harkins told Slavanki that Maher always acted on instinct. "He won't work with anyone he doesn't trust.")

Maher took a seat across the desk.

"You guys pay?" Maher asked abruptly.

"Yes. We pay."

Maher leaned in on Slavanki. "I just got screwed by the NYPD."

"Detective Harkins told me what happened."

"I'm doing this for pay, just like you are. I don't have some charge I'm trying to work off, no court cases pending, no sentence to reduce. So I don't want to be jerked around. I want to be paid."

Slavanki smiled. "You won't get screwed here. I guarantee it. You do right by me and I'll watch your back like you were my own brother."

Maher pressed. *"When* do I get paid? On arrest or on conviction?"

"Forget all of that," Slavanki said. "This is going to be like a business."

Maher challenged him. "Even if there's no court case, I get paid."

Slavanki had the right answer. "You bring us cocaine, you bring us arrests and seizures of money, you'll get paid."

"How much?" Maher fired back.

Slavanki paused a moment before answering.

"A thousand dollars per kilo of cocaine up to ten per case. Three thousand dollars per arrest up to five per case. And twenty-five percent of all cash seized up to one hundred and twenty-five thousand per case."

Maher thought about all the dealers he had met over the past year, all the kilos of cocaine he had seen, all the cash that was stacked in endless rows.

"I could be rich in six months," Maher exclaimed.

"Slow down," Slavanki said with a laugh. "If you do it right, you could make a career out of this."

Maher mulled over what Slavanki said for a moment, then frowned.

"Agent Slavanki, I have a steady job with New Jersey Transit. I own my own home. I have a child. I do not want to be uprooted and relocated."

"Don't worry," Slavanki said. "You won't have to be a witness."

"If I'm not going to be a witness, how are you going make the arrests stick?"

"For now," Slavanki insisted, "all I want you to do is observe and get the information to me."

"Then what?" Maher pressed.

"At some point," Slavanki answered, "I'll swear out a warrant."

"Isn't my name going to be on the warrant?"

"No. Just your CI number."

Maher still wasn't convinced.

"But if you go in the next day, the guy will know I was the one who told you."

Slavanki had an answer for that as well.

"A warrant is good for fourteen days. We'll wait the full fourteen days if we have to. The legal work will read 'on or about such and such a date SCI number such-and-such observed cocaine residue, large amounts of money, and, based on his observations, a search warrant was obtained.' They'll never know it was you."

"And another thing," Maher said. "If I do this, there's one dealer I don't want arrested: John Uribe."

Slavanki leaned back in his chair. "We will not take off John Uribe."

Maher felt in control. Slavanki seized it back.

"I've got a couple conditions, too. You can't be selling drugs or engaging in any illegal activity."

Maher seemed uncomfortable.

"Occasionally I have to take a snort," Maher confessed. "When a Colombian offers you a present, it's an insult to refuse."

Slavanki looked away for a moment, his lack of response neither condemning nor condoning the "occasional snort," as Maher characterized it.

"Any other illegal activity you have in the past or are now currently engaged in?" Slavanki asked.

Maher told Slavanki he had been "changing money."

Again, Slavanki responded with silence.

"So where do I sign?" Maher asked.

Slavanki took Maher into the next room, where Maher's fingerprints and photographs were taken. Then Maher filled out some paperwork and became registered DEA informant number 000128.

"Now what?" Maher asked.

"The next step," Slavanki said, "is to ID all the suspects. We can't make an arrest until each suspect is identified, whether it be through police or immigration records."

Slavanki stressed that the DEA had a policy of checking with all federal bureaus and appropriate local police departments to ascertain whether the suspect was the subject of another investigation.

"Just like the FBI," Maher said, showing off his knowledge of procedure among federal agencies. And then: "I can give you one guy right now: Hector."

"Hector who?"

"Comancha. Hector Comancha."

"You got an address?"

Maher gave Slavanki Hector's address on Queens Boulevard. And then he pulled out the matchbook with Hector's license plate number on it.

"Here's the license plate number on his car."

Slavanki was impressed.

The ID came back immediately—not because Hector had a record, but because he had taken a police test two years earlier.

Maher shook his head. "The little bastard wanted to be a cop."

Maher told Slavanki about the safe. "Last night I saw a large amount of cash and several kilos of cocaine in the safe."

"Okay," Slavanki said. "I'll get a warrant."

Slavanki started for the door.

"Agent Slavanki?"

Slavanki turned and faced Maher.

Maher finished his question. "Don't you have the power to seize property?"

"Yes," Slavanki said. "If it was acquired with drug money."

Maher smiled. "Hector has a new television and a marble table. Can you do me a favor and seize those things along with the safe?"

"Sure, Kevin," Slavanki said. "We do that anyway."

THE FOLLOWING DAY, MAHER MET WITH SLAVANKI AGAIN. SLAVANKI introduced Maher to Agent Jerome "Jerry" Becker, with whom Slavanki had been teamed. Becker was five feet, nine inches tall, with brown eyes and red hair. The tall, blond Slavanki and the carrottop Becker were referred to around DEA Group 43 as "Tom and Jerry."

"We want to start a list of dealers," Becker said. "Addresses. License plate numbers."

"I don't know the addresses offhand," Maher said, shrugging. "But I can take you there."

Maher and Becker rode the elevator down to the garage where Becker's car, a Chevy Camaro Z-28, was parked.

"Nice car," Maher observed.

"Fastest car in Group 43," Becker boasted.

Maher looked toward a Porsche 928. Becker noticed Maher ogling the car.

"The Porsche was seized in a drug bust," Becker explained. "The group supervisor uses it now."

Maher smiled. *Big paydays. Fancy cars. I'm definitely in the right place.*

Maher and Becker climbed into the Camaro and went hunting for drug locations.

"That's Carlos's house," Maher said as they slowed on a Queens street. He pointed to a brownstone.

In another section of Queens, Maher motioned toward a small four-story building. "That's Louis's apartment," Maher said. "And that's his car. The BMW with Florida plates."

Dealers would often register cars in Florida under a phony name to thwart, or at least delay, being identified.

Becker jotted down Louis's address and the license plate number of the BMW. Maher imagined that he was Becker's partner, Agent Kevin Maher. *Me and my partner are going to bang these motherfuckers.*

Maher and Becker returned to the DEA offices in late afternoon with a list of a dozen addresses and license plate numbers.

"Nice work," Slavanki noted as he perused the list.

Maher shook Slavanki's hand and Becker's hand.

"Good working with you guys," Maher said, then walked out of the DEA offices with the jaunt of a federal agent.

A FEWS DAYS LATER, SLAVANKI, BECKER, AND SEVERAL DEA AGENTS waited outside Hector's apartment. Hector emerged at about 8:00 P.M., climbed into his car, and drove away. The DEA agents then swooped into the apartment and seized the safe, the television, and the marble table. As they were leaving, they taped a search warrant on the door. The warrant itemized what had been confiscated.

The seizure proved to be a good one. Inside the safe were $64,000 and eight kilos of cocaine. Based on the pay scale that Slavanki had previously outlined, Maher's payday would be $24,000—$1,000 each for the eight kilos of cocaine, and $16,000, which represented 25 percent of the $64,000 seized.

When Hector returned home an hour later and saw the search warrant on the door, he panicked and drove to Uribe's house, where he found Maher and Uribe sharing a hit of coke.

Maher had called Uribe earlier and said he was stopping by. Indeed, Maher knew Hector would run straight to Uribe after the DEA seizure, and he didn't want to miss the fun.

"Look at this," Hector screamed, waving the search warrant in the air. "They raided my fucking apartment."

Maher fought back a smile. *And they took your fucking marble table, didn't they?*

"They took my fucking marble table," Hector said with a moan.

Maher stared at Hector. *And they took your fucking television too, didn't they, you little fuckhead?*

"And they took my television," Hector said, gasping.

"The safe!" Uribe screamed. "What about the safe?"

"They took it, man. They took the fucking safe."

Hector—holding his head with both hands—paced in a little circle.

"I talked to a lawyer," Hector said. "He wants a ten-thousand-dollar retainer."

Uribe stared off for a long moment. Then: "I'll have the money for you tomorrow. Where you gonna be?"

"I had my girlfriend rent a room at a hotel on the East Side," Hector said.

"Beep me tomorrow," Uribe told Hector, "and we'll arrange a place to meet."

Hector, a little calmer than when he arrived, scurried out the door.

Uribe looked at Maher: "What do you think?"

Maher could barely contain himself. *This'll teach that little prick to get in my face.*

"You gotta do *something*," Maher said. "Otherwise he'll rat you out the minute the cops pick him up."

"So I should give him the money?"

"No. Don't give him the money. What if his attorney gets him to rat you out? You wouldn't know until it was too late."

Uribe was angry. What was left? A contract on Hector's life? Maher offered the perfect solution.

"You've got a lawyer, don't you, John?"

"Yeah. One of the best."

"Okay. When Hector beeps you tomorrow, show up with your lawyer's business card. That way, if Hector is going to flip, you'll know right away."

Uribe relaxed.

"Good idea, Kevin."

The next morning, Maher and Uribe met Hector at the corner of First Avenue and 57th Street in Manhattan. Uribe handed Hector a business card.

"This is your lawyer," Uribe said.

"Wait a minute," Hector reacted. "I told you. I already have a lawyer."

"*This* is your lawyer," Uribe repeated.

Uribe's eyes were narrowed and suspicious. Hector's eyes were widened and full of fear.

"Okay," Hector relented, "I'll go see this lawyer."

A day passed, and the lawyer called to tell Uribe that Hector had not contacted the office. Uribe was concerned. Maher fueled the fire.

"I told you about that little bastard," Maher said. "He's probably sitting somewhere ratting you out right now."

But Hector was not informing on Uribe, he was hiding in a hotel room trying to summon up a little courage. On the third day following the DEA seizure, Hector finally went to see Uribe's lawyer. And after meeting with Hector, the lawyer called Uribe.

"I spoke to the lawyer," Uribe told Maher. "Hector came in."

"Just watch him closely," Maher warned.

Four days passed before Hector surfaced again at the lawyer's office. In a tense meeting, it was decided that Hector should surrender. So the lawyer dialed Slavanki, whose name was at the bottom of the DEA search warrant.

The lawyer identified himself and then told Slavanki: "I'd like to make arrangements for my client to surrender."

Slavanki waited a beat before answering. "What makes you think we are planning to arrest your client?"

The lawyer was stunned. "Are you saying you have no plans to arrest Hector Comancha?"

"None whatsoever," Slavanki said and hung up the receiver.

Indeed, Slavanki was happy to have the cash and have the drugs off the street. Arresting Hector was meaningless at this stage of the investigation into the Uribe family. But now Hector had a serious problem, a problem that was far more consequential than if he were facing a jail term. Maher put it most succinctly.

"If they don't want to arrest him," Maher told Uribe, "maybe there was nothing in the safe. Or else he'd be at Twenty-six Federal Plaza right now being arraigned."

"He didn't have the combination."

Maher shrugged. "What? A hundred gees' worth of coke and cash won't buy you a safecracker?"

Uribe began to take long, measured breaths. Maher piled it on.

"The only other reason they wouldn't arrest him would be if Hector was cooperating."

"I'm going to talk to Tia," Uribe said.

Maher savored his revenge. *That little fuck is in big trouble now. Tia's going to have him killed.*

As fearless as Maher was, he was terrified of Uribe's Aunt Maria. She had the coldest eyes Maher had ever seen. No drug dealer, no street punk, no hired killer had such compassionless, vacant eyes. *She'd kill you as soon as look at you,* Maher had thought when he met her.

Maher suddenly felt sorry for Hector. All Maher had wanted to do was teach Hector a lesson. He certainly didn't intend to get him killed.

Hector, demonstrating a little sense, dropped out of sight. Maher and Uribe tracked down Hector's girlfriend. She related how a trembling Hector stopped by the hotel room to say good-bye then went directly to the airport, where he boarded a plane for Puerto Rico.

Maher's first collaboration with the DEA had been an unqualified success.

"I still don't like what you're doing," Beth said when Maher spread dozens of hundred-dollar bills across the dining room table. "I worry about you."

"Slavanki and Becker are going to look out for me," Maher insisted. "So there's nothing to worry about. And if I do this for a year—just a year—we'll be set for life."

Beth didn't argue. She knew it wouldn't do any good.

Maher fanned the stack of hundred-dollar bills.

"Now we can buy a *really* nice house," Maher noted. "And now that I'm making all this money, I can buy a Porsche."

Beth half smiled. So much for being set for life.

Maher and Beth contacted a realtor who showed them a house in Wood-Ridge at 30 4th Street. A wood frame house built in the 1920s, the exterior was blue vinyl siding trimmed in white vinyl. The interior was filled with dark wood—molding, windowsills, door frames. There were two bedrooms downstairs and one large bedroom upstairs.

"This could be Bobby's room," Beth said as they toured the second floor.

There was a detached garage about fifty feet from the residence, a perfect home for Maher's Corvette. And there was land around the house—a half acre. Samantha the German shepherd would like that.

"This is the house we want," Maher announced.

The next day, Maher and Beth went to the Boiling Springs Bank and applied for a loan as Mr. and Mrs. *Edward* Maher. Maher chose to use the name and Social Security number the FBI had arranged for him following the Hand bank robbery because neither would show a felony conviction. When the loan was approved a few days later, Maher and Beth went to see attorney James Lappin, who was handling the closing.

"What was the date of your marriage?" Lappin asked.

Maher and Beth looked at each other.

"We're not actually married," Beth said. "We're common law."

Lappin reacted. "The loan was approved based on the fact

that you were married. Since you're *not* married, it could effect your eligibility."

"I can't see where that matters so much," Maher said.

"You lied on your application," Lappin said with a sigh. "There's a good chance you won't get the loan."

Maher and Beth were crestfallen.

"Of course, you *could* get married," Lappin said, laughing.

Maher and Beth looked at each other. Why not get married? But then they both realized why not.

"My husband is contesting the divorce," Beth said.

Beth gave Lappin the full story of her hired-killer husband. Lappin's eyebrows raised more than a few times.

"Since he's in prison," Lappin offered, "why don't you try abandonment?"

It was almost too obvious a solution.

IN MID-MAY, MAHER STOPPED OFF AT DEA GROUP 43 AND TOLD Slavanki that he had been making rounds with Uribe and had compiled a list of unpublished phone numbers used by dealers. (Whenever Maher stopped by a dealer's house, he would ask to use the phone. Before making an actual call, he would dial 958, which was a code used by telephone repairmen to determine if they were on the correct line. The code returned a recording that announced the telephone number.)

Based on what Maher had observed in various apartments, a conservative estimate yielded a potential payoff well into six figures. Maher felt like a cop again. *And* he was going to get rich. What could be better? What could go wrong?

But something did go wrong, and it had nothing to do with the DEA. Maher returned home one evening to a ringing phone. He grabbed the receiver. It was Frank DelPrete.

"Kevin," DelPrete said, "I need to talk to you."

DelPrete arrived at Maher's house an hour later and brought Maher up to date on what had turned out to be a five-year struggle to bring Molese to trial for the triple murders in Fair Lawn. DelPrete explained that Molese had been convicted of fraud in New York two years earlier, served his time, and now had been extradited to New Jersey to stand trial for the triple murders in Fair Lawn.

"The trial is scheduled to start on June fourth," DelPrete said. "If you're willing to testify, I think it would help the case against Brian Molese a great deal."

Maher didn't hesitate. "Sure. I'll testify against the fucking baby-killer."

Then—like a hammer to the side of his head—Maher was struck with a realization: The grand jury testimony was sealed. The testimony in the trial would be public record.

"I'd like to get you together with the prosecutor," DelPrete said.

"Sure," Maher answered, his voice flat. "Let me know when."

DelPrete handed Maher the transcripts from the grand jury hearing.

"I want you to study these transcripts before you meet with the prosecutor."

Maher nodded and took the transcripts from DelPrete as he left.

"What was that all about?" Beth asked as she entered the room.

Maher explained the situation to Beth, adding: "When I testify against Molese, it's bound to come out that I've worked as an informant. Uribe hears that, I'm dead."

The smart thing would be to decline to take the stand and continue working with the DEA. But Maher couldn't countenance the possibility that Molese might get away with murder. Even when Maher factored in all the money he would lose if he stopped working with the DEA, it didn't tilt the scale. In Maher's mind, the deaths of Alice Molese, Marcia Ferrell, and Harold Ferrell had to be avenged. He *would* testify. As far as Uribe was concerned, Maher decided he would handle the problem the way he always handled a problem: head-on. And then Maher walked out of the house and went in search of John Uribe.

MAHER DROVE AROUND QUEENS TELLING HIMSELF OVER AND OVER THAT Uribe was a friend and that somehow he would make Uribe understand. After stopping by Uribe's house and cruising by his favorite hangouts, Maher finally spotted Uribe's Silver Corvette under the Triborough Bridge in Astoria Park. Maher rolled his Vette to a stop and climbed out. Uribe was standing a few feet away.

"Hey, Kevin," Uribe said, happy to see him.

Uribe made his usual offer.

"A present for you," Uribe said, holding out a plastic bag of coke.

Maher held up his hands in a gesture of refusal. Uribe seemed vaguely hurt. Maher didn't care.

"I gotta tell you something," Maher said.

Uribe sensed Maher's anxiety and became anxious himself.

"What?" Uribe asked, his voice rising. "What do you have to tell me?"

"You and I have been friends for a long time," Maher said. "And you know there is nothing I would do to hurt you or your family."

Uribe's face morphed in fear. Something was *very* wrong.

Maher paused for a moment, then went on.

"There's something about me you don't know. I haven't told you this up to now because if you or any members of your family had been arrested, you'd think I was involved."

Uribe laughed. "You trying to tell me you're a *cop?!*"

"I do undercover work for the FBI," Maher stated somberly. "And I work for the cops as an informant."

Uribe staggered back a step. He stopped laughing.

Maher reached into his pocket and produced court transcripts from the grand jury hearing in the Molese case. He flipped to a page and held it so Uribe could see.

"The man on trial is Brian Molese," Maher explained. "He killed a baby. He needs to be convicted."

Maher related the sad tale of Alice, Marcia, and Harold, but Uribe wasn't listening. His eyes were fixed on the bottom section of the transcript.

DA: Have you ever been an informant before?
Maher: Yes.

"Oh man, no!" Uribe finally said, his hand pressed to his forehead. "I can't believe this! No, man! I can't believe this!"

Maher grabbed Uribe by the shoulders. "Look. John. If I

wanted you and your family locked up, you'd be in jail by now. Don't you see that?"

Uribe stepped back. He looked at Maher for a moment, then looked away. Maher tried to reestablish eye contact, but Uribe refused to look at him.

"I'm being straight up with you, John," Maher said. "Man to man. Whatever you do, don't go back and tell your aunt, because she'll kill me."

Uribe, his eyes diverted, started toward his Corvette. Maher followed him.

"John!"

"I gotta go, Kevin."

"John! Listen to me, will you? I'm not going to do anything to hurt you."

Uribe jumped into his Silver Corvette and cranked the engine. Maher ran up to the open car window.

"John. Will you stop a minute?"

Maher leaned down, his face even with Uribe's profile. Uribe stared straight ahead, still refusing to look Maher in the eye.

"I gotta go, Kevin. I gotta go."

Uribe pressed the accelerator, and the Vette almost catapulted down the street. Maher stared at the taillights until they disappeared into the night. *Please, John,* Maher thought, desperately hoping to float a telepathic message into the ether, *don't go running to Tia. Do whatever you want, but don't go running to Tia.*

WHEN SLAVANKI HAD EMPHASIZED THE IMPORTANCE OF IDENTIFYING suspects and for the various federal law enforcement bureaus to be in constant communication with each other, Maher wasn't paying much attention. Yet because of the open lines of communication among bureaus, a parallel U.S. Customs investigation of the Uribe family provided the DEA with a critical piece of information. Customs officials had bugged Maria Uribe's home and were in the process of taping conversations between Maria and her dealers. So when John Uribe burst into his aunt's house, the electronic ears of U.S. Customs were listening.

Customs officials first heard Uribe screaming in Spanish about the meeting he had with "Kevin." And then came the following exchange, also in Spanish:

MARIA: I knew he was a fucking cop.

URIBE: He's not a cop.

MARIA: I want that motherfucker dead.

URIBE (agitated): No! No! Please.

MARIA: He'll ruin our business. He'll take everything I own.

URIBE: No! Don't do it!

Then came the sound of a rotary phone being dialed. As the dial clicked around with each number, Uribe continued to plead with his aunt.

URIBE (crying): Please, Tia! Don't do this.

Tia ignored him. Click, click, click, click. Pause. Click, click, click, click. Pause. Finally, the last digit of the phone number was entered. There was a tense moment of silence, during which John Uribe could be heard crying, gasping for breath between sobs. Then Maria Uribe, speaking slowly and evenly into the receiver, ordered the immediate execution of Kevin Maher.

Chapter 13

"NORTH DAKOTA? HOW COME YOU GUYS ALWAYS WANT TO SEND PEOPLE to North Dakota?"

Slavanki leaned in on Maher.

"*South* Dakota?"

"You heard the tape," Maher countered. "Tia called it off."

In fact, Tia had relented. After she ordered the execution, Uribe continued to beg his aunt—for more than an hour—not to kill Maher. When sobbing didn't faze her, Uribe finally appealed to her sense of survival. Indeed, Tia possessed the keen instincts of a predatory animal. If she sniffed danger in the air, she moved off. And so, the emotion rung out him, Uribe changed the thrust of his argument.

URIBE: *You can't do this, Tia! It will only bring the DEA down on us!*
A long silence.
MARIA: *You promise me that you sever all ties with him, that you never speak to him again.*
URIBE: *I will, Tia. I will. I promise.*
MARIA: *If you see him on the street, you go the other way.*
URIBE: *Yes, Tia.*
MARIA: *And if you don't, I'll slaughter him and his family and send you back to Colombia.*
URIBE: *Okay, okay. I won't see him no more. Fuck him.* Fuck *him.*
Then the sound of the rotary phone being dialed.
URIBE: *Thank you, Tia. Thank you.*

199

A moment later, Maria Uribe could be heard withdrawing the contract.

"I'm not worried about that old bitch," Maher said derisively. "What am I going to do? Run away from some old grandma because she's shaking her cane at me? Fuck *her*."

Slavanki raised his eyebrows. Harkins was right: Maher *was* fearless.

"We'll let things cool down a little bit," Maher continued, "and then we'll go back to banging out dealers."

Slavanki recalled Harkins's *exact* words. "Kevin is the ultimate informant to the point of being reckless."

And this was as reckless as it gets.

MAHER'S ANXIETY ATTACKS CONTINUED, AND DURING THE MONTH OF MAY he had been off sick more than he was on the job. When he did show up, he was driving one of his three cars, all expensive: the Indy 500 replica, the Porsche, or Beth's Mercedes. Supervisor William French found Maher's vehicles highly unusual for someone on a railroad salary. Coworkers often told Maher of comments by French to the effect that Maher *must* be a drug dealer, otherwise he couldn't afford the high-priced automobiles. One day a coworker overheard French saying he was going to fire Maher. But Maher was not some blue-collar worker whose spirit had been dulled by long hours and the promise of a pension. Maher was a street kid, then an ex-convict, and now a cop without a badge. Each taught him a different form of settling scores, and he had evolved into a formidable hybrid of all three.

When Hector had gotten in his face for dropping keys on the marble table, Maher had reacted to the slight like a convict, but he had resolved it like a cop. And when John Uribe became a threat, Maher didn't wait for Uribe to come after him, he took the problem to Uribe. And now French had become a problem to Maher, a threat, just when Maher was trying to put his life back together. Maher owned a home. Had a family. And despite the potential income from the DEA, he didn't want to be a DEA informant forever. Maher's plan was to bank a lot of DEA money over the next year or so, then settle in as a good provider for his wife and "adopted" son. Which is why he needed a *real* job.

After simmering for a few days, Maher went to Academy Investigators, Inc., a private investigation firm in West Paterson, New Jersey. Upon handing over a $3,500 retainer, Maher told an investigator named Spinelli that he had observed his supervisor, William French, in recent weeks. According to Maher, French often disappeared from the job site for extended periods of time. And when French returned, he reeked of alcohol.

"I want you to follow him for a week," Maher said.

ON JUNE 4, 1984, MORE THAN FIVE YEARS AFTER THE BRUTAL MURDERS of Alice Molese, Marcia Ferrell, and Harold Ferrell, the long-awaited trial of Brian Molese got under way.

The man responsible for prosecuting Molese was Assistant District Attorney Dennis Calo. The New Jersey-born Calo was a graduate of Columbia University and received his law degree from New York University School of Law. In January 1977, after six months of private practice, Calo joined the Bergen County prosecutor's office. He was promoted to chief of homicide in May 1979, which was two months after the bloodbath at 24 Sanford Road. In April 1984 he was named first assistant prosecutor. Fewer than three months later, the thirty-six-year-old Calo found himself at the forefront of the Molese case, the prosecutor in what promised to be one of the most sensational murder trials in New Jersey history.

The media had already convicted Molese. Writing from within the walls of the Fourth Estate, journalists had issued a guilty verdict, and now the pressure was on Calo to deliver the same in a courtroom. Unfortunately, the case against Molese was almost entirely circumstantial. There were no witnesses to the crime, no weapons recovered, and no fingerprints. (Of course, even if Molese's fingerprints had been found at the scene, so what? It was *his* house.)

Molese had been arrogant throughout the entire investigation. He made weekly calls to Fair Lawn police headquarters to ask about the progress of the case. But his demeanor was taunting rather than inquisitive.

Molese's defense was of the "my word against yours" variety.

According to Molese, he and Alice were separated by the fall of 1978, and he had moved to an apartment in Greenwich Village. However, he was on speaking terms with his wife—they were trying to work things out—and so he did in fact visit 24 Sanford Road on Thursday night, March 22, 1979. Molese told police he spoke with Alice for a while, after which he sat with little Harold at the dining room table and played cards. Later in the evening, Molese related, Marcia Ferrell arrived home and he left, returning to Manhattan. Molese claimed that he stopped by a restaurant in the Village called Tiffany, had a grilled cheese sandwich, and then went back to his apartment, where he spent the rest of the night alone. The following evening, Molese said he drove to Fair Lawn with a friend named Larry Gallagher and made the grisly discovery. The motive must have been robbery, Molese speculated, because a number of valuable items were missing, including "a ring once owned by King Farouk."

When Fair Lawn police asked Molese to take a polygraph, he readily agreed. After flunking the lie detector test, Molese just shrugged. He was smart enough to know it wasn't admissible in court. And when police pressed him for an alibi for the night of March 22, he changed his original story. No, Molese suddenly remembered, he didn't stay home that night. He was with "a friend." Molese then produced a gay lover who swore he and Molese were together at a Village club called the Ninth Circle. But the story didn't check out. No one at the Ninth Circle—where Molese was a regular and therefore could be easily identified—recalled seeing Molese that evening.

In Calo's mind, it was clear that Molese was trying to accomplish three things with his statements to police.

1. *Neutralize his presence at 24 Sanford Road on the night of March 22.* Molese could have denied being at 24 Sanford Road on March 22. But what if the prosecution came up with a witness or witnesses who had seen him enter the house that evening? Following a denial, testimony placing Molese at the scene could be damaging. So Molese simply stated that he was at the house on March 22.

2. *Set the date of the murders as March 23.* By saying he was at 24 Sanford Road the evening of the twenty-second and by discovering the bodies on the twenty-third, Molese hoped to cre-

ate the impression that the homicides occurred on the twenty-third.

3. *Provide a motive for the killer or killers.* The extensive list of jewelry and silverware that Molese claimed was missing from the house was an attempt to indicate that robbery was the motive for the murders.

Despite what Calo theorized, how could the rookie prosecutor, in the absence of physical evidence, refute Molese's version of events? He first had to establish Molese's motive.

Calo set about to prove that Molese had two strong motives for killing his wife: hatred, and financial gain. The star witness in regard to Molese's animosity toward Alice would be Maher, who would testify about Molese's solicitations to kill "fat Alice" and describe how much Molese loathed her. And Calo had ferreted out other witnesses who would corroborate Maher's testimony. While proving that a man despised his wife was not enough to gain a murder conviction by itself, it was a beginning.

As for the financial gain half of the motive, that could be demonstrated by presenting the insurance documents in conjunction with evidence that Molese was deep in debt and that the house at 24 Sanford Road was about to be seized by the bank. Although being in debt and collecting on an insurance policy do not make someone a murderer, coupled with Molese's hatred for Alice, the financial motive gained substantial credibility. Still, not everyone who has a reason to commit murder actually does so. Therefore, Calo had to find a way to convince the jury that Molese didn't just wish Alice were dead, he also made his wish come true.

One incident that indicated Molese was serious about killing his wife involved Joseph "Mad Dog" Sullivan. Employees at a law firm where Molese worked as a paralegal in 1978 identified Mad Dog as the man who had stopped by the law office to pick up a set of keys to 24 Sanford Road. Armed with that bit of information, Calo could ask the panel of twelve men and women: Why would Molese give the keys to his wife's house to a notorious contract killer? The fact that Mad Dog was in possession of the keys wasn't definitive proof of anything, yet Calo felt it would have a powerful effect when presented in the right context.

Having established a clear motive, the next step was to tear apart Molese's story. As for his claim that he was at 24 Sanford Road until late evening on March 22, Calo had several witnesses—friends of Alice and Marcia—who would testify that after nine o'clock on that night, no one answered the phone. And as far as Molese's insistence that the house had been robbed, Calo had physical evidence: the sales receipts and pawn tickets that Maher had saved after he had disposed of Alice's possessions in 1975. While this proved that the items had not been stolen at the time of the murder, it didn't prove Molese killed Alice. Molese—an admitted arsonist and embezzler—could later claim he had intended to run an insurance scam and collect on the jewelry and silverware.

The strongest exhibit Calo had was a receipt of a different kind: a cash register receipt. Marcia Ferrell had a meeting at her attorney's office early on the evening of March 22 and then stopped off at a convenience store and bought some candy to take home to Harold. The receipt was time-stamped just after nine o'clock. What made this significant was the placement of Marcia's body. She was discovered in the foyer, still wearing her trench coat. And the bag of candy intended for Harold was next to her body. It seemed clear that Marcia was killed when she walked through the doorway on the night of March 22.

Another indication that the murders took place on the twenty-second and *not* the twenty-third came from Molese's own statement. Molese had said he was in the dining room playing cards with Harold. When police arrived on the scene, there were playing cards strewn all over the dining room. Since Alice's body was slumped in the corner of the dining room and since Harold's body was found just inside the back door—his throat slashed from behind—one could easily speculate that Harold witnessed an attack on Alice and tried to run away, scattering the playing cards as he jumped up from the table.

All these speculations made up the circumstantial case against Brian Molese. And so, on June 4, 1984, Dennis Calo stepped into a New Jersey courtroom with a potpourri of theories, a few scraps of evidence, and a strong belief that Brian Molese had murdered Alice Molese, Marcia Ferrell, and Harold Ferrell.

In his opening remarks, Calo dwelled on Molese's hatred for Alice and Molese's subsequent attempt to collect insurance proceeds.

"But Brian Molese's *real* motivation was not money," Calo insisted. "It was his hatred."

Calo described what he termed Molese's "true marital relationship" with Alice and pointed out that Molese lived an openly gay life. He told the jury that he would demonstrate that Molese had solicited a hit man to murder Alice. And he emphasized not only the brutality of the crimes but also the age of one of the victims: five-year-old Harold.

On the second day of the trial, Maher and Beth, who was scheduled to testify before Maher, entered the courthouse. As they were walking down the hall toward the courtroom, Molese was being brought in, bound in handcuffs and ankle shackles. When Molese saw Maher, he stopped suddenly, almost tripping on the chains around his feet. The look on Molese's face was one of horror.

Beth testified about the night Molese brutally beat Alice. Several female members of the jury winced as Beth described Alice's bruised face. But Beth's testimony was just a prelude to what was to come the following day when Maher took the stand.

For six hours, Maher held the jury rapt as he described how Molese solicited him to murder Alice, first as they sat in a cafeteria at Green Haven and then when he took Molese and Ronald Scofield to a New Jersey diner after Molese had pummeled Alice. Slowly and carefully, Maher reconstructed every detail of an incredible tale of intense hatred and unbounded greed.

Once, in the midst of painting a damning profile of a sociopath, Maher pointed to Molese and referred to him as "the baby-killer." This prompted an outbreak in the courtroom.

"Objection!" Molese's lawyer screamed.

"Sustained!" the judge bellowed, then admonished the jury: "Disregard that statement!"

But Maher knew that despite the judge's admonishment, the jury could never forget the phrase "baby-killer." In Maher's mind, Molese was convicted at that moment.

On cross-examination, Molese's lawyer did his best to rattle Maher, often posing complex multiple-part questions and then demanding a "yes or no answer." But Maher refused to answer yes or no to many of the questions. He often attempted to elaborate, usually directing his response not to Molese's lawyer, but to the jury.

"Just answer yes or no," Molese's lawyer bellowed the first time Maher went off on a tangent.

"But you don't understand," Maher protested. "When Molese came to me and—"

"Your Honor," the lawyer cut in, "please instruct the witness to answer yes or no."

"Just answer yes or no," the judge instructed.

Maher was chided by the judge a second time for offering an unsolicited explanation to one of the defense lawyer's questions. And then a third. Finally the judge lost his patience.

"Do that one more time and you're going to jail for contempt!" the judge warned Maher.

When the cross-examination was over and Maher stepped down from the witness box, he studied the jury, reading their faces one by one. Each furrowed countenance seemed to be saying the same thing: *guilty.*

ON THE SAME DAY THAT THE MOLESE TRIAL BEGAN, ACADEMY Investigators' Spinelli began shadowing William French. Each day, Spinelli would make entries in a diary, documenting French's movements. This information was being gathered for a report that would be titled *An Investigation Conducted by Investigator Spinelli . . . in Reference to Activities During Working Hours of One William French, New Jersey Transit Signal Supervisor.*

The first day of Spinelli's report was nothing if not thorough.

> Monday, June 4, 1984: At 5:45 A.M. this writer arrived at 162 North Road, Nutley, New Jersey, home of WILLIAM FRENCH, hereinafter referred to as the "Subject."
>
> The subject left Nutley around the same time, arriving at the Hoboken New Jersey Transit Terminal at 6:05 A.M.
>
> At 6:05 A.M., the subject parked his van at the terminal entrance and entered the terminal. . . . This writer sat outside the terminal to continue surveillance in case the subject should leave the terminal.

At 11:15 A.M., the subject left the terminal in Hoboken and later arrived at his home in Nutley, at 11:30 A.M.

At 11:30 A.M., the subject parked his van in his driveway next to his Cadillac, License Plate number 918-RAD.

At 12:30 P.M., the subject left his home in Nutley, driving his van in the opposite direction from work. The writer lost the subject due to traffic.

At 1:00 P.M., this writer returned to the terminal in Hoboken to see if the subject would return to work. This writer stayed at the terminal until 3:30 P.M. Subject did not return to the terminal that day. This writer called off surveillance for the day and returned to the office.

Subsequent entries were more damaging to French. Excerpts from those entries included:.

Tuesday, June 5, 1984: . . . At 9:15 A.M., subject left the terminal in Hoboken and stopped at a shopping center . . . 9:30 A.M., the subject . . . made a call from an outside phone booth . . . 9:50 A.M., the subject arrived in Nutley. . . . At 11:00 A.M. subject left his home . . . subject did not return to work. . . .

Wednesday, June 6, 1984: . . . at 11:00 A.M., subject is seen leaving terminal . . . at 1:10 P.M. subject and another employee . . . left train station . . . at 1:15 P.M., subject pulled into a bar called "Spanky's" on Broadway in Woodcliff Lakes, New Jersey . . . at 2:30 P.M., the subject and the other fellow left the bar, then this writer went passed [sic] them into the bar . . . and asked the bartender, whose name is Judy, what the subject and the other fellow had to drink. Judy said, the subject had three (3) Spritzers. . . .

Thursday, June 7, 1984: . . . at 9:40 A.M., the subject was seen leaving terminal . . . the subject arrived at his home in Nutley at 10:20 A.M. . . . at 1:10 P.M. . . . parked his van and proceeded on foot to a bar on the corner. The bar was called "For Pete's Sake." The subject then entered the bar through the back door, with this writer entering the bar through the front door . . . observed the subject having two (2) drinks which looked like Spritzers in a total of approximately 20 minutes. . . . At 3:30 P.M., the subject left the bar through the back door. . . . The subject had been in the bar for two hours and twenty minutes. . . .

Friday, June 8, 1984: . . . At 9:20 A.M., the subject left the terminal . . . this writer followed the subject and another employee to the entrance of Ramsey Golf Course and Country Club, arriving there at 11:25 A.M. . . . at 12:50 P.M., the subject and approximately 16 other men came out of the clubhouse and paired up with carts going in different directions onto the course . . . the fellow in the office said the game would probably continue for four and one-half hours (4 ¹/₂) so this writer just kept surveillance on the subject until 3:30 P.M. . . .

Drinking. Playing golf. Suddenly it wasn't Maher who appeared to have a problem. It was William French.

ON JUNE 8, MAHER AND BETH APPEARED IN DIVORCE COURT. THE JUDGE found that Beth had been abandoned due to Eschert's incarceration. The following Sunday, June 10, Maher and Beth were married by a justice of the peace. A week later they moved into their new home and added a new member to the family: a second German shepherd to keep Samantha company, a female they named Heidi. *This time,* Maher told himself as he walked around *his* house, *everything's going to be fine.*

THE MOLESE TRIAL CONTINUED THROUGH THE MONTH OF JUNE AS CALO— in the absence of hard evidence—produced a parade of witnesses.

Jerry Speigelman, a lawyer at the firm where Molese worked as a paralegal, confirmed that Molese despised Alice, adding that "he told me the only reason he married her was to build a credible parole plan." Speigelman said that in 1978, Molese told him he intended to have his wife killed and that he wanted to be out of town over Thanksgiving because "that's when the murders are going to take place." In addition, Molese had told Speigelman that he had hired "Mad Dog" Sullivan, "a real madman who was going to make a mess." And then, one day in September 1978, Mad Dog himself arrived at the law office to pick up keys to 24 Sanford Road.

(Calo opted not to call Mad Dog, an unindicted coconspirator in the case, as a witness. Mad Dog was probably not feeling cooperative. Since his arrest in 1982, he had been convicted of several homicides, and his earliest opportunity for parole would be the year 2094.)

Next on the stand was Suzette Holmes, a secretary at the law firm. She corroborated Speigelman's testimony.

Norman Nerl from the Provident pawn shop testified that Maher had indeed pawned an antique necklace Molese had listed as having been stolen.

Derek, one of Molese's gay lovers, told the court that Molese had shown up the morning of the twenty-third looking like he hadn't slept.

Larry Gallagher, who had been with Molese when the bodies were discovered, said Molese had found him in a bar and was persistent about driving to Fair Lawn the night of March 23.

GALLAGHER: *My car was in the shop and he insisted on loaning me* his *car, which was parked in Fair Lawn. I kept telling him I didn't need a car.*

CALO: *After you got to Fair Lawn, what happened?*

GALLAGHER: *He walked in the door and went right to the dining room where two of the bodies were.*

CALO: *Like he knew they were there?*

GALLAGHER: *Yes.*

On July 5, 1984, the jury found Brian Molese guilty of the three counts of first-degree murder.

It had been a decade since Molese sat in a cafeteria at Green Haven Prison, ranting on and on about "fat Alice." So when Maher heard the verdict, one might expect he would have been elated. Instead, he cried. Because Maher knew no matter how deep they locked Molese away in the dungeons of the penal system, it was too late to save Alice. Too late to save Marcia Ferrell. And too late for little Harold.

Chapter 14

MAHER'S BATTLE WITH WILLIAM FRENCH ENDED AS SWIFTLY AS A SUDDEN knockout in a boxing match. After receiving Spinelli's report in mid-June, Maher had instructed Spinelli to send copies of the report to both New Jersey Transit executive offices and the New Jersey Transit Police. New Jersey Transit had ruled that French should be "taken out of service" immediately pending further hearings. In September, French was terminated.

"That'll teach the bastard to fuck with *me*," Maher told a group of coworkers when news of French's dismissal spread through the ranks of railroad workers.

What Maher had done to French was the legal equivalent of what he had done to the inmate who had made a suggestive remark to him years ago at Rikers Island. At Rikers, Maher had delivered a vicious uppercut to the inmate's chin and had administered several bites to the inmate's face. One by one, the inmates who had witnessed Maher's attack diverted their eyes and moved off. Now it was Maher's coworkers who diverted their eyes. Nobody—at New Jersey Transit, at least—was ever going to fuck with Kevin Maher again.

His nemesis at New Jersey Transit disposed of, Maher settled into being a working man, husband, and father. It was such a comfortable feeling that he didn't miss the action of undercover work and began to wonder if it was worth it to rejoin the DEA.

Another part of Maher's life that held less appeal these days was drag racing. He sold his Corvette for $15,000 and bought a $48,000 Porsche. This left him without a vehicle capable of the quarter-mile dash at Connecting Highway. Yet the dichotomous nature of the two cars reflected the changing nature of Kevin Maher. The Porsche was engineered for the long run, the Vette for the short burst of speed.

In mid-September, Beth's job at *The Economist* required her to travel to London on business. Maher took the trip with her, partly because of his desire to rekindle romance in their marriage and partly because he was growing more suspicious. The nagging feeling that his wife was having an affair with coworker Richard O'Rourke would not go away. Maher was going to make sure that at least in London, Beth remained faithful.

The London trip did nothing to bring Maher and Beth closer together as Maher's underlying suspicion sabotaged any renewed emotion either of them felt. While Maher did not make spoken accusations during their stay in England, his eyes were more accusing than words. And, swirling amid the suspicion was the guilt Maher felt about his escapades with the "dopey bitches." Suspicion. Guilt. Like weeds on a lawn, they choked the roots of the relationship between Maher and Beth. And so they returned to New Jersey without rejuvenating their marriage.

While in London, Maher bought a pair of European-style halogen headlights for his Porsche. The headlights (illegal in the United States) were eight inches in circumference as opposed to the standard seven-inch U.S. seal beam, had twice the wattage, and illuminated a larger area. And since Maher often cranked the Porsche up to 150 an hour, he needed all the forward vision he could get.

Maher missed the social aspect of the weekends at Connecting Highway. So, one Friday night in late September, he decided to check out the drag races as a spectator, not a participant.

Maher parked his Porsche near a crowd of people who had gathered to watch the race. When he climbed out of the car he found himself face-to-face with John Uribe.

"Look, John," Maher said, "you were my friend. I wouldn't have locked you up."

After a tense moment, Uribe smiled. "I miss you, my friend. We had good times."

Uribe grabbed Maher and hugged him. Then he stepped back and inspected Maher's Porsche.

"What do you think of the Porsche compared to the Vette?" Uribe asked.

"As far as quality, ride, handling, there's no comparison," Maher said. "It may not take off like a Vette, but fuck that. When you pull up with a Vette, you just pull up. When you pull up with a Porsche, you *arrive.*"

Uribe took a slow walk around the Porsche.

"Wanna go for a ride?" Maher asked.

Maher and Uribe climbed into the Porsche. It was like old times. No mention was made of Tia. And not a word was said about their last meeting at Astoria Park. It was like it never happened.

"I've got some problems with my Vette," Uribe said at one point. "Will you take a look at it?"

"Sure," Maher said.

Uribe reached into his pocket and withdrew a plastic bag full of coke.

"A present for you," Uribe said.

The bond between them had been renewed and the tacit agreement once again defined. Maher would barter automotive repair for Uribe's cocaine.

COCAINE PERMEATED LIFE IN THE EIGHTIES. WHAT HAD STARTED OUT AS A recreational drug a decade earlier proved to be an addictive and destructive substance. Banks were corrupted trying to finance it, corporations were brought down by its debilitating effect on employees, even governments weren't immune to its poisonous reach. And while once it was confined to big cities, it seeped into the suburbs. So it wasn't unusual for Robert Colaneri to be battling the sale and distribution of the stuff even in the quiet little town of Carlstadt, New Jersey.

Colaneri had received his gold shield on January 1, 1985. As a detective, his objectives changed, and he set about cultivating informants. One informant—a two-time loser who was working off a burglary charge—had given Colaneri information about a dealer on Hackensack Street in Carlstadt. So Colaneri decided to set up a "controlled buy," a transaction in which an informant purchases cocaine from a dealer with cash provided by police. However, a controlled buy using an informant is tricky, especially when the informant is facing jail time. To ensure that the informant didn't plant drugs in the suspect's apartment, the informant was strip-searched and then kept under constant surveillance until the bust went down.

Colaneri stopped off at headquarters and picked up the informant. Then Colaneri, the informant, and several police units made their way to Hackensack Street.

"I saw him wrap coke up in tinfoil and put it in jelly jars in the refrigerator," the informant reminded Colaneri before he climbed out of the car and entered the apartment.

Ten minutes later, Colaneri and several cops burst into the dealer's apartment. As was planned, both suspect Charles Storniolo and the informant were arrested and charged with the distribution of a CDS, a controlled, dangerous substance. The cops went to the refrigerator and began digging out tinfoil packets from jelly jars and mayonnaise jars. The bust was a success. But then Colaneri noticed that the informant—who was handcuffed and sitting on the couch—was making faces and nodding toward a hallway. For the next few minutes, Colaneri and the informant played an impromptu game of "hot and cold." The informant would frown when Colaneri was "cold" and smile when Colaneri was "hot." Pretty soon, Colaneri was seizing coke from the medicine chest.

In addition to the cocaine, Colaneri stumbled on what he thought was an unexpected bonus: a cache of weapons. However, it turned out that Storniolo was an artisan, refinishing gun stocks. Storniolo produced the requisite paperwork that indicated that he didn't own the guns. The guns were not confiscated.

(Storniolo later pled out to possession, receiving a fine and two years' probation.)

And so it was that in 1985, Maher and Colaneri were both chasing after drug dealers, albeit from two different ends of the spectrum.

BY MARCH, MAHER'S ANXIETY ATTACKS HAD RESUMED WITH ALARMING frequency and were increasingly severe. So he once again applied for disability. Travelers Insurance, the insurance company representing New Jersey Transit, placed a condition on the disability payments: Maher was to see a psychiatrist twice a week. Dr. Peter Crane.

"These might not be anxiety attacks," declared Crane, who, as a psychiatrist, was also an M.D. "The chest pains you experience could have something to do with your heart."

Yet all cardiovascular tests had indicated Maher's heart was normal.

Crane studied Maher for a long beat. "Are you using cocaine?"

"I've stopped," Maher lied.

"You can die from cocaine, Kevin," Crane noted.

Maher had never before heard a doctor issue an admonition regarding the use of coke.

He's probably right, Maher thought. *I'm doing a lot of coke. I know it's terrible. I've got to stop.*

When Maher left the doctor's office, he threw the packet of cocaine he was carrying into the trash and vowed never to touch the stuff again. Then he stopped off at a pharmacy to fill a prescription for Xanax, which Crane had prescribed in an effort to combat the anxiety attacks. Thus Maher traded an illegal stimulant for a legal tranquilizer.

The Xanax worked its chemical magic almost immediately, and by May 1985 it had been two months since Maher had had an anxiety attack, the same period of time since he had snorted cocaine. Which meant he saw little of John Uribe, thus avoiding the offer of a "present."

During the last week of May it occurred to Maher that he had not spoken to Uribe for several days, which was odd. Even though they now saw each other infrequently, Uribe usually phoned at least once a day.

Maher dialed Uribe's home phone number. After several rings, someone answered. But instead of a greeting, Maher heard heavy breathing. And then the line went dead. Maher called back. The same thing happened. Heavy breathing. And then a click. The third time, Maher interrupted the heavy breathing.

"John? Is that you? *John? John!*"

Click. And a dead line.

Maher tried calling Uribe several times each day for the next two days. Sometimes there would be no answer. At other times it was the heavy breathing. Maher decided to drive into Manhattan and stop by Uribe's apartment. Something was definitely wrong.

Maher spoke to the doorman at the high-rise building on 22nd Street and Broadway. The building was more than thirty floors in height, and its base spanned the entire block between 22nd and 23rd streets.

"I'm here to see John Uribe," Maher told the doorman.

The doorman rang Uribe's apartment. But Uribe didn't answer the intercom.

"I haven't seen him for several days," the doorman said with a shrug.

"I better go upstairs and check on him," Maher said.

The doorman nodded. Maher took the elevator to the twenty-eighth floor and banged on Uribe's door.

"John! It's Kevin! Open the door!"

Nothing. Maher beat harder on the door.

"John! Goddamnit! It's Kevin! Open the fucking door!"

Maher heard the lock turn from the inside. The door opened slowly. Uribe—bags under his eyes and a week's worth of beard—peered out at Maher. Maher pushed into the apartment and shut the door behind him.

"John. I've been trying to call you for—"

Maher stopped in midsentence and looked at Uribe. He was standing there in his underwear, sweating profusely and trembling. Maher looked around the apartment. The floor, the coffee table, the couch, every piece of furniture was covered with a thin dusting of white cocaine residue. Then the stench hit Maher's nostrils. *It smells like the inside of a cocaine bag.* Maher looked at the windows. *No wonder it smells. The windows are all shut. And it's hot in here.*

Uribe walked to the center of the living room and sat cross-legged next to a bucket of sudsy water. Maher watched in astonishment as Uribe took a photograph, dipped it in the bucket of water, removed it, then rubbed it against his bare chest to remove the soap. Having done that, he placed the photograph on a stack of other photographs.

"John," Maher said softly, "what the fuck are you doing?"

"Washing pictures," Uribe said, as if it were normal.

Maher saw that Uribe had a stack of "dirty" photographs on one side of the bucket and a large stack of "clean" photographs on the other side. Some of the "clean" photographs on the bottom of the stack had dried and curled, indicating that Uribe had been "washing pictures" for quite a while.

Maher walked over and crouched next to Uribe.

"How long have you been doing this, John?"

Uribe didn't respond. He dipped another picture into the bucket of sudsy water and ground his teeth, moving his jaws from right to left. Then he began mumbling incoherently.

All Maher could do was stare. *What the fuck is happening to John?* And then Maher realized. *It's the cocaine. It's gotta be.*

Indeed, had a doctor examined Uribe he would have concluded that Uribe was in the midst of a cocaine-induced psychosis.

Suddenly Uribe's eyes flashed and his head snapped toward Maher.

"You're a fucking cop!" Uribe screamed. "Why did you come here? To arrest me?"

"John, I'm no fucking cop."

But Uribe seemed transported back in time to his confrontation with Maher in Astoria Park.

"Then why do you have these fucking people watching me?"

"*What* people, John?"

Uribe jumped up and ran to the window.

"You know I told my aunt about you!" Uribe shouted. "Did you tell *them* about *me?*"

Uribe pointed to a building across the street.

"Who, John? Tell me who?"

"The people in that building!" Uribe shouted. "They're looking in here with telescopes!"

Maher sighed.

"Come on, John. You're losing it, man. I'm getting you out of here."

Maher walked toward the bedroom to find something for Uribe to wear. As he passed the bathroom, he noticed a vinyl gym bag on the floor and opened it to see if there was something for Uribe to wear. In the gym bag he discovered an Ohoas triple beam scale, a sixty-four-ounce jar of baby laxative used to cut cocaine, one sealed kilo of cocaine, and one open kilo package, which was half empty.

When Maher returned to the living room, Uribe was holding the receiver to his ear and dialing a number.

"John!" Maher shouted, trying to wrest the phone from his hand. "Who the fuck are you calling?"

"My mother," Uribe said.

"In *Colombia?*"

Uribe's mother came on the line, and Uribe started chattering in Spanish. The mother began screaming so loudly Maher could hear her voice leaking out of the receiver. Although Maher didn't know the words, whatever it was, she repeated the same phrase over and over. Uribe hung up the receiver and ran into the bathroom. Maher chased after him.

"John! Will you fucking calm down?" Maher pleaded.

Uribe dove onto the floor and, kneeling in front of the toilet, began pouring the half kilo of cocaine into the bowl.

"John!" Maher howled.

Next came the flush, a $15,000 flush. Then Uribe pulled a knife out of the gym bag, picked up the full kilo of coke, and started to rip it open.

Maher grabbed Uribe by the shoulders and pulled him away from the toilet.

"John! For God's sake, stop it!"

Uribe struggled toward the toilet with the kilo. Maher ripped it out of his hands and dropped it back into the gym bag. They scuffled. Uribe, sweaty and slippery, not to mention big and strong, was difficult to hold on to. Managing to get between Uribe and the toilet, Maher tore out the float mechanism so Uribe couldn't follow up with a $22,000 flush. Then Maher grappled with Uribe, both falling to the floor. For the first time, Maher was face-to-face with a cocaine casualty. He held Uribe like a fallen comrade on a bloody battlefield.

Uribe was heaving, gasping for air.

"Calm down, John," Maher said again. "Everything's going to be all right. Everything's going to be fine."

Uribe's breathing became more even, and Maher released his hold on him. Maher stood up, then reached down and pulled Uribe to his feet. They walked into the kitchen, where Maher turned on a tap and filled a water glass.

"Drink this," Maher said as he handed the glass to Uribe.

Uribe, clearly dehydrated, gulped down the water. His eyes were dazed, focused on some faraway image.

Maher filled the glass a second time. And a third.

"Okay," Maher said. "Let's go find you some clothes."

Maher turned toward the bedroom. Uribe took off like a shot and ran into the bathroom.

Before Maher could react, Uribe emerged with the gym bag and ran to a window.

"John!" Maher yelled. "No!"

Uribe pushed open the window and, leaning his upper body all the way outside, heaved the gym bag into the air. Maher watched the gym bag disappear above the window and then drift past again on its way down.

Maher grabbed Uribe by the hair and pulled him inside the apartment. Then Maher returned to the window and peeked over the sill. The gym bag was at the end of its twenty-eight-story free fall. An instant later, it landed with a thud—right on top of a westbound city bus, stopped at a traffic light. As Maher stared down at the $22,000 gym bag, the light changed. And the bus rumbled down 23rd Street.

Maher stepped away from the window and started for the front door. *Now I've got to chase down the fucking bus*, Maher thought. But then Maher remembered something Slavanki had said: *Don't get caught with any coke by yourself. If you do, you're on your own.*

Maher looked at Uribe, who had crawled back to the window and was hanging halfway out again. *The fuckhead is going to jump. I can't leave him here.*

Maher ran to Uribe and jerked him back into the apartment. Uribe began crawling around on his hands and knees, using his fingertips to scrape cocaine residue off the floor. Scrape. Sniff. Scrape. Sniff. It was pathetic.

Maher managed to steer Uribe into the shower. The hot water seemed to revive him. Uribe got dressed and then left the apartment with Maher. They retrieved their cars from the garage: Maher's Porsche and Uribe's new BMW 318.

"Follow me to New Jersey, John," Maher said, adding: "We're going to take it real slow, all right?"

Uribe nodded.

The Porsche pulled out onto Broadway and the BMW fell in behind it. Maher glanced in the rearview mirror often, making sure the BMW was still there. All was well for a few minutes. But then Maher raised his eyes to check the rearview mirror. The BMW was not behind him. Suddenly the BMW exploded past the Porsche. And the chase was on.

Down Broadway. Across 14th Street. Up Third Avenue. Finally, in the East Sixties, Uribe's BMW became mired in traffic. Maher stopped his Porsche behind the BMW and leaned out the car window.

"John!" Maher shouted. "Pull the fuck over!"

Uribe turned the wheel of the BMW sharply and headed for the curb. But instead of pulling over, he gunned the engine and sent the BMW catapulting onto the sidewalk. The BMW traveled a few feet, then smashed into a canopy pole and stopped. Maher pulled to the curb and jumped out of the Porsche. The pole was bent around the front of the BMW, and the canvas was flapping in the wind. It might have been funny had it not been for the squad car that was inching along in traffic just opposite the destroyed canopy. Maher held his breath. But the cops were disinterested. The traffic light changed, and the squad car drove away.

Maher pulled Uribe out of the BMW and threw him into the Porsche.

"My car," Uribe whined. "What about my car?"

"Leave it," Maher said. "When we get to my house we'll report it stolen."

Maher locked the Porsche's doors. The search and rescue mission had been a success. Maher had his man. And he was bringing him in.

Uribe slept for hours on Maher's couch, waking late in the evening. Maher was sitting across from him.

"You crazy fuck," Maher said. "How much fucking blow were you doing?"

Uribe stared off for a long moment.

"She's a fucking whore," Uribe said quietly.

"*Who's* a fucking whore?" Maher asked.

"Laura."

Maher frowned. "Who is Laura?"

"I met her in Miami." Uribe smiled. "Tall. Long blond hair. *Beautiful.*"

Uribe's mood darkened. "Then I found out she's a whore."

Uribe explained how, on one of his runs to Miami to pick up cocaine, he met Laura at a party.

"You know how many dopey bitches I fuck," Uribe said. "But she was different."

Uribe went on with the story, insisting that Laura was not like the rest of the women he knew. According to Uribe, she had class, sophistication, poise, humor.

"One night," Uribe said, "I see her in a bar with some rich guy. And she tells me he's a *client.*"

Maher grimaced. Uribe continued.

"Then she tells me she's a 'call girl.' A fucking whore. And when I get pissed off, she tells me she gets five thousand a night. Like that makes it all right."

For the next five days, Maher and Beth nursed Uribe back to health. Each day, Maher would search Uribe for coke.

"I'm clean, man," Uribe would protest.

For the first time in years, Uribe stayed straight for five full days. Perhaps as compensation for the lost cocaine rush, he ate. And ate. And ate. His favorite food was Rocky Road ice cream, which he consumed by the gallon.

Finally Maher drove Uribe back into the city and dropped him at his apartment. Maher was drained from the experience. So was Beth.

"I've never seen anybody eat like that," Beth said with a sigh.

"That's the way John is," Maher observed.

Uribe did not practice moderation in anything. Sex. Drugs. *Or* food.

At 7:30 a.m. on December 2, Robert Colaneri had left Carlstadt police headquarters in an unmarked car and had gone to go pick up Deputy Chief John Occhiuzzo. A call came over the radio that a vault alarm had gone off at United Jersey Bank on Gotham Parkway and Route 120. Two units—Sergeant Herb Scheidewig and Patrolman Pat Cunningham—had been dispatched. When Scheidewig and Cunningham arrived, they started into the bank but stopped when they saw a man holding a gun to the head of the assistant bank manager, Dolores Nielsen. Nielsen had two sons—Tom and Chris—on the Carlstadt police force. Seeing the cops, the suspect released Nielsen, and she ran out of the bank. She told the cops that there were two suspects, both black males, and that there were several other employees still inside.

Before additional units could get to the bank, the suspects broke a window near the drive-in booth and fled. Just as Colaneri and Occhiuzzo arrived, one of the suspects was caught. The whereabouts of the second suspect was unknown. Colaneri assumed that he was still in the bank, so the building was secured and snipers were placed on rooftops. A command post was set up and telephone contact was attempted, but no one inside the bank answered the phone.

A short time later, a State Police helicopter arrived at the helipad in the Meadowlands Sports Complex. Colaneri was assigned the aerial surveillance.

Colaneri and a State Police pilot circled the marshes that make up much of the Meadowlands area of New Jersey. Then a call came over the helicopter radio that there was a report of a stolen car on Route 17 heading in the direction of Route 80. Colaneri and the pilot flew toward the reported stolen car. But they were unable to locate the vehicle and returned to the bank.

When Colaneri got back to the bank, cops stormed into the building. They found frightened hostages—including a woman who had been hiding in a toilet stall for the past two hours—but no suspects.

Later that afternoon, Colaneri dispatched Chris Nielsen to search the area to see if he could find potential evidence. As Nielsen trudged through the weeds and mud of the Meadowlands marsh, he almost stepped on someone. It turned out to be the suspect who had held a gun on his mother, Dolores. The suspect had been lying in the weeds for ten hours, apparently waiting for nightfall.

Both suspects—two-time losers Milton Rider and James Williams—were convicted and sentenced to twenty-five years to life.

* * *

WHILE COLANERI HAD TAKEN NOTICE OF MAHER AND HIS CORVETTE OVER the previous few months, Maher had registered Colaneri's face without realizing it. Maher walked into his house on the evening of December 3, 1985, plunked down beside Beth on the couch, and picked up the New York *Daily News*, which was lying on the coffee table.

"Wait a minute," Maher exclaimed when he saw the front page. "I've seen that guy somewhere."

The entire front page was a photograph of Colaneri and other officers at the scene of a bank robbery.

"Is that one of the cops you work with?" Beth asked.

"No," Maher answered, "but I've seen him riding around town in a Vette."

Maher studied Colaneri's picture.

"I *know* I've seen that guy *somewhere*," Maher said. "Absolutely. I have definitely seen him somewhere."

And so, on December 3, 1985, the convergent courses of CI Kevin Maher and Detective Bobby Colaneri edged a little closer.

MAHER SPENT THE MONTH OF DECEMBER DOING LITTLE MORE THAN getting ready for Christmas. Buying a tree. Shopping for presents. All the normal things a husband and father does as Santa Claus approaches.

Right after the first of the year, Maher sat down to watch television and happened upon a new show called *Miami Vice*. Maher was mesmerized. When he saw the fast cars, he exclaimed: I *drive fast cars!* When he saw the leggy bimbos banging everybody in sight, he chuckled: I *bang dopey bitches!* When he saw the cocaine, he shook his head: I *do coke!* And finally, when he saw an informant character, he was hit with a sudden realization: I *do that.* Indeed, to Maher, *Miami Vice* was not just a television show, it was his life. Or at least it used to be. Charged up by the action he saw on *Miami Vice*, Maher called Slavanki.

"Want to bang a dealer?" Maher asked.

In his travels, Maher had encountered a low-level dealer who lived on Parsons Boulevard in Queens. The dealer seemed wary of Maher, so Slavanki suggested that Maher take his time and "buy up." Buying up involved starting with small amounts—a gram, perhaps, or an ounce—and then making a series of incrementally larger purchases. But after a few weeks, Slavanki felt it was costing too much to "buy up" such an insignificant player. So they decided to take him off with half a kilo, which was where Maher was on the incremental ladder of volume.

Since the dealer didn't entirely trust Maher, he never allowed Maher in his apartment, and the transactions always took place in Maher's car. Maher would pull up in front of an apartment building on Parsons Boulevard and beep his horn. At the sound of the horn, the dealer would look out the window of his ground-floor apartment, then would leave the building and climb into Maher's car. (By looking out the window, of course, the dealer was showing Maher and the DEA exactly which apartment was his.)

On this particular night, the dealer slipped into the passenger seat of Maher's Mercedes with a half a kilo of coke. The price had been set at $15,000. (Since a whole kilo cost $22,000, the disproportionate price of a half kilo meant that even in the world of drug dealing, volume buying had its benefits.) The dealer handed Maher the half kilo, and—after administering the thumb-and-forefinger test to a sample—Maher handed the dealer $15,000 in cash. As was the routine, Maher would drive around the block while the dealer counted the money. (For some reason, the dealer felt more secure if the car was in motion.) While Maher drove, the dealer counted the money. Normally, he was amazingly fast.

"Two thousand, two thousand twenty, two thousand—oh, fuck!"

Maher glanced at the dealer: "What's wrong?"

"A fucking fifty!" the dealer squealed.

In fact, there *was* a fifty-dollar bill mixed into the twenties.

"What do you want from me?" Maher countered. "It's money, isn't it?"

"Yeah," the dealer said with a sigh. "But it fucks up my math."

The dealer jammed the fifty on the seat under his leg and resumed counting twenty-dollar bills. Off they went again around the block. A moment later . . .

"Another fucking fifty!"

The dealer placed that fifty-dollar bill under his leg as well and struggled to figure out where he left off in his counting.

Each fifty threw the dealer into such a confused state that it required a recount and another circle around the block. And each time, Maher would pass the DEA agents who were staked out at various locations. The agents frowned and shrugged as if to say: *What's going on?*

Finally the dealer placed a stack of twenties on the dashboard and picked up the pile of fifties on the seat. The counting was done, and Maher stopped in front of the apartment building on Parsons Boulevard. The dealer climbed out of the car. But instead of heading into his building, the dealer crossed the street and walked up to another man, who appeared to be a neighbor. After a brief, friendly exchange, the dealer walked *away* from the building, and the neighbor walked *toward* the building. DEA agents nabbed the dealer and also grabbed the neighbor. They found nothing on the neighbor except a key, which just happened to fit the dealer's apartment. In addition to the dealer and the neighbor, two women inside the apartment were arrested.

The case against the neighbor almost evaporated. When the neighbor's lawyer showed up at the DEA lockup, he asked what evidence existed to prove his client had anything to do with the dealer. The answer was: a key.

"Then there must be a lock on the dealer's door that the key will open," the lawyer noted smugly.

DEA agents rushed back to the apartment on Parsons Boulevard and found a hole where the lock used to be. Although the lawyer entered a motion that the charges be dismissed, the testimony of the DEA agents prevailed. The neighbor was convicted of conspiracy to distribute cocaine.

Maher was paid $12,000 for the four arrests, even though the two women were not charged. (They were, however, illegal aliens and were turned over to Immigration.)

A week later, someone told Maher about a dealer in Jackson Heights who had "some good shit." After a telephone introduction, Maher went to meet him. The dealer's apartment was dark, illuminated only by candles that were lined up on a bookshelf. *Who* is *this guy,* Maher wondered as he squinted toward the candles, *Dracula?* But on closer inspection Maher realized that each candle also had a picture of a child behind it.

"I have adopted these children," the dealer, who was Colombian, said as he rubbed the crucifix that hung from his neck on a gold chain. "I send in nine dollars a month for each of them."

The dealer waved his hand toward the candles.

"My sixty-two children," the dealer said softly. "They will not go to bed hungry tonight."

The dealer explained that he had watched "a thing on television" about starving children. Maher had seen the television appeals.

"I know about starving children," the dealer remarked. "In Colombia I have seen them for myself."

Maher became overwhelmed with emotion. He owned a Porsche and a Mercedes and a Camaro, he did thousands of dollars of cocaine in a month, and he had yet to send in his first nine dollars. After making a small buy, Maher fled the apartment.

Maybe it was the flickering candlelight or the sad little eyes of the children in the pictures or the crucifix around the dealer's neck. Whatever it was, Maher decided not to bang this dealer. He realized that actions and consequences did not always fall neatly to one side or another of the moral line.

For the next month, Maher had little success finding dealers worthy of DEA attention. As much as he hated to admit it, he needed Uribe. Uribe was the pipeline to major drug dealers. But right after he had sobered up at Maher's house, Uribe had gone to Miami. And as far as Maher knew, Uribe had not returned to New York.

It was as if thinking about Uribe conjured him up. Just as Maher had begun to wonder about him, Uribe reappeared at Connecting Highway one spring night.

"Hey, John," Maher said, "where the hell you been all this time?"

"Cooling out," Uribe answered.

Uribe told Maher he had made up with Laura, the $5,000-a-night call girl.

"I rented a big house in Miami with a pool and everything," Uribe said.

Uribe dug into his pocket and produced a bag of cocaine. He offered it to Maher.

"A present for you, my friend," Uribe said.

Maher hesitated. It had been months since he had done any coke.

"John," Maher said, "I stopped."

"A present for you," Uribe insisted.

Maher stared at the bag of cocaine. The white crystals glinted in the beam of a car's headlights, and the visual stimulus triggered a powerful craving in Maher's brain. Slowly, almost involuntarily, he reached out and took Uribe's present.

Chapter 15

DURING THE SUMMER OF 1985, MAHER CONTINUED TO IDENTIFY DEALERS for the DEA. He would ride with Uribe to a dealer's house, recording the address and phone number. Then he would give the information to Slavanki and Becker. But nothing seemed to happen after that.

"What's going on?" Maher asked Slavanki one day. "Nobody's getting busted."

Slavanki told Maher that he was opening case files and "ID-ing" the dealers. Busts would come as soon as the files were complete.

"All we want you to do for now," Slavanki said, "is continue to identify dealers."

In mid-August, Slavanki gave Maher $3,000, payment for information Maher supplied on a dealer named Julio. Maher was happy to get the money, to see that *something* was going on, yet nothing about the bust made any sense. Julio was a low-level dealer, something Maher had made a point of telling Slavanki.

"Why'd you bust Julio?" Maher asked Slavanki.

Slavanki didn't respond. So Maher decided to check into Julio's bust on his own. He drove into Queens and spoke to one of Julio's friends. The friend said "cops" armed with a search warrant had burst into Julio's apartment and discovered cocaine and cash.

"Cops?" Maher asked, frowning.

"Yeah," the friend said. "NYPD detectives."

"Are you sure?" Maher pressed.

"You don't think Julio knows what a fucking NYPD detective badge looks like?"

Maher shook his head. *NYPD?* Julio's friend related how the "cops" had threatened to impound Julio's BMW if he didn't cooperate, a threat Maher knew well. It was a DEA ploy designed to "flip" a suspect.

The incident sounded to Maher less like an NYPD bust than it did a DEA raid. Plus Maher couldn't help but wonder why the DEA would be paying him for an NYPD bust.

By now Maher had solid sources inside the NYPD, so he dialed a number and asked two simple questions: *Did the NYPD exercise a search warrant at such-and-such an address on such-and-such a date? And did the NYPD lock up a dealer named Julio?* The answer was no on both counts.

Maher hung up the receiver. *So what about the badges? Of course!* Maher thought. *The bogus badges were used to conceal DEA involvement and make the big dealers believe the DEA had not invaded the territory.* As Slavanki had intimated, the DEA investigation was in the intelligence-gathering, *not* the enforcement phase.

SEPTEMBER BROUGHT WITH IT THE HINT OF WINTER. ON A COOL EVENING, much cooler than one might expect this early in the season, Maher and Uribe were cruising along in Maher's Porsche.

"Why don't you come to Florida with me tomorrow?" Uribe asked. "I've got to pick up a few kilos."

Early the next morning, Maher met with Slavanki.

"Just identify the dealers," Slavanki insisted.

Maher thought about that for a moment.

"I don't mind identifying them," Maher said. "But I don't get paid until you bust them."

Slavanki knew what Maher was asking.

"We'll pay your expenses," Slavanki offered.

"Expenses." It was ambiguous enough a word. But at least Maher would be on a paid assignment, which made him feel more like a cop than an informant. Besides, the *real* money would come later, when the DEA finally pulled the trigger. Thus Maher's territory increased. New York. And now Florida.

Maher drove home and told Beth he was going to Miami. She

didn't offer any protest. *What's she so happy about?* Maher wondered. *What's she going to be doing while I'm in Florida? Fucking Richard?* The thought gnawed at him all the way to Uribe's apartment.

Uribe climbed into the Porsche, and they were off to Miami.

"You know how much cheaper a kilo is if I buy it in Miami and bring it back to New York myself?" Uribe asked.

"No, John. How much cheaper?"

"I save eight thousand dollars a kilo," Uribe said. *"Eight thousand dollars."*

"That's great, John," Maher acknowledged.

Maher made Miami in an incredible sixteen hours, stopping only briefly for gas.

Although Uribe had rented a house, he held his "parties" at a hotel, either the Fontainebleau or the Mayfair. This trip, Uribe had opted for the Mayfair.

Maher and Uribe checked into a large suite, and then they headed over to a dealer's house in Miami Beach. When the dealer opened the front door, he was not happy to see a stranger.

"He has to wait outside," the dealer insisted.

Uribe started to protest. Maher stopped him.

"It's okay, John," Maher said.

While Uribe and the dealer conducted their business, Maher strolled to a Mercedes that was parked in the driveway. Maher knew that a dealer's car was like his second home. So, making sure no one was watching from the house, Maher slid into the passenger seat and opened the glove compartment. It was full of credit card receipts for gas and oil. Maher took one of the receipts and stuffed it in his pocket. *The dumb fuck won't miss one receipt.* Then Maher jotted down the dealer's address and the license plate number. One more DD "identified."

The next dealer was more trusting. Maher stood to the side as the dealer counted the money Uribe had brought and Uribe tested the cocaine he was buying. The six-figure transaction took fewer than five minutes.

"It's time to party," Uribe said as they climbed into Maher's Porsche.

When Maher and Uribe arrived back at the hotel suite, there were two girls waiting for them.

"Pick one," Uribe smiled. "Or take them both."

The girls sashayed into the bedroom, peeling off clothes as they walked. Maher followed.

The next morning, Maher and Uribe left the suite together and stopped by Uribe's Florida home. It was a spectacular place. Three bedrooms, with a white marble entrance, a sauna, every amenity one could want. The residence sat on a landscaped half acre. And, of course, there was a large swimming pool.

When Maher met Laura, he could understand Uribe's insecurity about her. She was five-foot-eight, with hair the color of sunshine. Her eyes were ocean blue. But she was not the fresh-scrubbed, All-American girl in a Florida orange juice commercial. Laura exuded sex, oozed sensuality like a Vermont maple tree oozes sap in autumn. She could have been the poster girl for a porn palace.

After spending the night at the house, Maher left Uribe in Miami and drove back to New York alone.

"When are you going to start busting these guys?" Maher asked as he handed Slavanki data on four more dealers.

"Soon," Slavanki answered. "Very soon."

For the next several months, Maher made frequent trips to Miami. Essentially Maher had begun playing the role of Uribe's courier, bringing large sums of cash to Florida to pay for the drugs. Another service Maher provided was that of occasional chauffeur, swinging by Miami International Airport to pick up one of Uribe's dealers. However, this was rare, since most dealers refused to fly in and out of Miami. And with good reason.

As with any port of entry—particularly a southern one—the airport was well staffed with U.S. Customs officials. But all Customs officials did not wear uniforms and examine baggage. Many were in plainclothes and wandered through the terminal "profiling."

"Profiling" is an iffy practice. For example, a cop spots a black man in a white neighborhood. The cop decides, based solely on the man's race, that he fits the profile of a burglar. That is a form of "profiling." It is not only racist, it is blatantly illegal and in violation of federal civil rights laws.

In the case of Miami International Airport, however, U.S. Customs officials could profile anyone arriving or departing from the airport. And anyone they felt fit the profile of a drug dealer—Colombian, expensive clothes, etc.—was stopped and questioned. The difference between a neighborhood and an airport was its access. While a neighborhood was a public place, an airport was a "secured area." Thus profiling was considered a legal means of maintaining airport security.

Fortunately for Maher, being a cash courier and part-time livery driver was the extent of his duties for Uribe. Uribe never asked Maher to transport cocaine.

On each subsequent foray to Florida, Maher "identified" three or four dealers. *When the DEA hits these fucking guys*, Maher thought, *I'm going to be filthy fucking rich.*

Another aspect of each successive trip was Uribe's attempt to top himself in the party category. Three women. Then four. Then five. Once, Maher had six women in bed with him at the same time.

Unlimited supply of cocaine. Willing nymphs by the half dozen. What more could Maher ask for? The answer always came crashing down on him when the cocaine wore off.

Beth.

DESPITE THE FACT THAT HE WAS TAKING INFIDELITY INTO THE BIG LEAGUES, a longing came through it all. There was still a part of him that ached for the feeling he had when he first held Beth in his arms. Maher wanted desperately to get back there, so desperately that he asked Beth to come with him to see his psychiatrist, Dr. Crane.

"Maybe we can work this out," Maher said.

The look on Beth's face wasn't hopeful. Still, she consented to seeing Dr. Crane.

So, in addition to his required visits to Dr. Crane mandated by New Jersey Transit, Maher added another session each week for him and Beth. Week after week, they would discuss their marriage. And almost every week, the session came down to one issue.

"I don't trust her," Maher would say.

"Why not?" Dr. Crane would ask. "Do you have a reason not to trust her?"

Maher would then reiterate that he thought Beth was having an affair. Beth would deny it. And they were back where they started. Sadly, the marriage appeared to be over, although neither of them wanted to admit it.

On one solo visit, Maher broke down and cried.

"I love her, Dr. Crane," Maher said, sobbing. "I love her so much."

Of course, if that were true, what about the coke whores? The answer was not simple. The operative word in the phrase "coke whores" was "coke." Cocaine had turned these women into little more than prostitutes. And while Maher's libido might have driven him at first, cocaine had rendered him incapable of stopping the pursuit of pleasure. It had made *him* the moral equivalent of a whore.

By the end of 1985, Maher had identified more than fifty Miami coke dealers and slept with at least that many "dopey bitches." And Beth wasn't slipping away anymore.

She was gone.

In February 1986, Maher's anxiety attacks resumed. But rather than stop using coke—something he was physically unable to do—he underwent a heart catheterization. Purple dye was shot into his veins, and he watched a television monitor along with the doctor. The dye moved through Maher's circulatory system unimpeded.

"I see no blockage," the doctor told Maher. "Everything seems fine."

New Jersey Transit was notified by Travelers Insurance that Maher was fit to report to work, and in early March Maher received a certified letter to that effect.

If Maher went back to work he wouldn't be able to make the trips to Miami, so there was a choice to be made. But Maher found the choice an easy one: He would return to the job. Even coked up, he knew the *Miami Vice* life he was living was a fantasy. Besides, he had identified so many dealers, he felt like a stockbroker who had acquired a large portfolio. Eventually the DEA would get around to making busts, and when they did, the dividends Maher would receive would be enormous. So he decided he would "retire" his imaginary badge once again.

Any hope of saving his marriage, however, seemed remote. He knew his marriage was little more than a facade. He and

Beth had not made love for months, the passion squelched by infidelity. A year earlier, he had begun to avoid sleeping with her. Often, when the coke wore off, he feared he might have caught a venereal disease from one of the women. So he would make an excuse and stay up long after Beth had gone upstairs. Only when Maher was certain she was asleep would he join her in bed.

The return to New Jersey Transit was less difficult than Maher thought it would be. He didn't miss the parties at the Mayfair and the Fontainebleau; rather, he felt relieved to have a reason to break away from the insanity of it all. But his return to work was not entirely painless. Beth was now making $75,000 a year. Maher was still at the same railroad job he held when they first met. His sense of self-worth as measured against his wife suffered from the comparison.

Over the next three months, Maher worked diligently at his job, dramatically lowered his cocaine intake, and began to emerge from the fog of the previous year. He felt good again, and actually was hopeful about the future. But on July 1, 1986, something thwarted Maher's sense of well-being. A weed killer used by New Jersey Transit on the railroad tracks splashed into his eyes.

The irritation caused by the chemicals in the weed killer led to infection in both eyes. New Jersey Transit's response was to order Maher to wear protective goggles. Maher protested, citing all the same reasons he offered the first time the goggles became an issue. New Jersey Transit stood firm. So Maher took a leave of absence while the dispute was turned over to union arbitrators.

Maher grew despondent during the weeks the arbitration process dragged on. *It seems like every time I try to have a normal life, something happens to fuck it up.* But there was another thing that always seemed to happen whenever Maher was spun out of his quest for normalcy: John Uribe would reappear with his "presents" and his promise of wild parties. August 1986 was no exception.

"Too bad about your job, man," Uribe said, showing up at Maher's house unexpectedly one afternoon. Then, holding out a bag of cocaine: "A present for you, my friend."

"I thought you were in Miami," Maher said as he snorted a little coke.

"Let's go back there right now," Uribe said, his voice hyper. "Come on, Kevin. Let's go to Miami."

Maher shrugged. "Why not?"

Sixteen hours later, at eight o'clock the following evening, Maher, exhausted from the long drive, slowed his Porsche to a stop in front of the Mayfair. A short elevator ride, and Maher was back at one of Uribe's parties.

Maher looked around the suite. He recognized eight dealers. And coke whores were everywhere. Black. White. Blond. Brunette. Tall. Short. Maher smiled. He'd have a few drinks and a couple of snorts. As Maher made his way to the makeshift bar that was set up on a side table, he turned and looked right into a pair of incredible brown eyes.

She was brunette. Long, perfectly shaped legs poked out of her leather hot pants just as provocatively as her braless breasts strained against her low-cut blouse. She was sitting in a huge leather chair with her left leg over an arm of the chair and her right leg thrust straight out and to the right side. Maher could see she wasn't wearing panties. As he stood there gaping, she slowly kicked her left leg, flipping a high-heel shoe up and down on her toe.

"I'm Beverly," she said sweetly. "Beverly Merrill."

Maher collected himself. "I'm Kevin Maher."

Beverly smiled. *"You're* Kevin Maher?"

"Yes," Maher said, frowning.

Beverly laughed. "John's told me all about you. You're the guy who had six girls at one time."

Maher didn't know what to say. What *could* he say?

Maher and Beverly looked at each other. Maher was thinking: *She's beautiful. I hope she's not just another coke whore.*

Suddenly Maher felt a hand on his elbow. It was Uribe.

"Kevin. I need to talk to you for a minute."

"I'll be right back," Maher told Beverly as Uribe led him away.

"I'll be here," Beverly said seductively.

Maher and Uribe stopped in a corner of the suite.

"Man," Maher said, looking over Uribe's shoulder at Beverly, "she's *hot!*"

"Yeah," Uribe said, "but I want to warn you."

Maher's heart dropped.

"Be careful what you tell her," Uribe continued. "She just got busted for extortion, kidnapping, and possession. She's out on ten thousand dollars bail."

Maher smiled. He had expected to hear worse.

Uribe noticed Maher's grin. "Didn't you hear me?"

"Yeah, John, I heard you." Maher turned and stared at Uribe. "What happened?"

"Some rich kid from Buffalo owed a dealer twenty-five thousand. The kid kept saying he didn't have the money. But the DD knew the father was some rich old fuck, so the DD grabbed the kid. Beat the shit out of him for three days. Didn't feed him. Kept telling the kid that if his father didn't send money, he was going to kill him."

"What did Beverly have to do with it?" Maher asked, already making excuses for her.

"She was *there*, man," Uribe said with a sigh. "She was there through the whole fucking thing. She was partying with the DD for a month straight."

"How'd they get busted?"

"They took the kid to a pay phone and made him call his father. They told the old man, send money now. So the old man wired money Western Union."

"*Real* smart," Maher said with a laugh. "The old fuck called the cops. Right?"

"Yeah. The FBI followed the DD and Beverly back to the house. Then the cops burst into the place, firing."

Uribe paused.

"They killed three German shepherd puppies," Uribe said with a sigh, his voice dripping with disgust. "Fucking cops shot three puppies. They didn't have to do that."

Maher and Uribe stood in silent vigil for a moment. Then they both stared at Beverly.

"Don't get me wrong," Uribe said. "Maybe she's a good girl. But she's out on bail, man. Facing time. That's why I told you to be careful. The feds are going to try and turn her, I know they are."

Maher smiled again. *No, John. The* feds *aren't going to turn her, I am.*

"Listen," Uribe said, "I've got to do a little business. Come with me."

Maher hesitated and looked at Beverly.

"She can come, too," Uribe said.

Maher, Beverly, and Uribe went downstairs.

"Can I drive the Porsche?" Uribe asked as the valet pulled up with the car.

"Yeah, John," Maher replied, laughing. "You can drive the Porsche."

Uribe got behind the wheel, and Maher got into the passenger seat. Beverly slid onto Maher's lap.

Uribe sped through the streets of Miami, ultimately whipping the Porsche into the parking lot of a club in Coconut Grove.

"Look, baby," Uribe said, "me and Kevin have a little business. We'll pick you up later."

Beverly shrugged and got out of the car. Uribe sped away.

"You like her, huh?" Uribe said.

Maher didn't respond.

Uribe concluded a quick cocaine transaction, then stopped back at the club to pick up Beverly. Then the three of them returned to the Mayfair.

A few snorts and a couple of drinks later, Maher and Beverly were in bed. The sex was explosive. When it was over, Maher held Beverly in his arms and had the strangest thought: *This is a good person. She has no morals, but she's a good person.*

Maher and Beverly emerged from the bedroom at about 2:00 A.M. Uribe was gone.

"Where's John?" Maher asked one of the dealers.

"He went out," was all the dealer knew.

An hour later, the phone rang. Maher let it ring several times, unsure whether he should answer it. Finally he grabbed the receiver.

"Hello?"

"Hey, Kevin!"

It was Uribe on a cellular phone.

"Kevin. Listen."

Maher heard a whooshing sound.

"John? What is that?"

Uribe laughed. "That's what it sounds like when you hold a

cellular phone out the window of a Porsche going a hundred and ten."

"*What* Porsche?" Maher demanded.

"*Your* Porsche," Uribe answered.

"How did you get my fucking Porsche?" Maher screamed.

"The valet parking guy gave me the key," Uribe answered.

Maher howled. "John! Goddamnit! You bring my Porsche back right now!"

Uribe laughed.

"John! You got one hour to get my Porsche back here!"

Click. Uribe hung up.

An hour passed. Uribe did not return.

Maher and Beverly stayed up the rest of the night, talking.

"I can help you," Maher said at one point. "I work with the FBI."

Beverly was stunned, and her body language changed. She edged away from Maher.

"I can *help* you," Maher repeated. "Trust me."

Beverly moved back near Maher and placed her arms around him. *I'm in love,* Maher thought as he lost himself in her embrace. *I'm fucking in love.*

The next morning, Uribe called.

"Don't go near the car," Maher warned him. "Leave it parked."

The tone of Maher's voice shocked Uribe.

"Sure, man. I won't touch the fucking thing."

"Where the fuck are you?" Maher demanded.

Uribe gave Maher an address on Biscayne Boulevard.

Maher and Beverly took a cab from the Mayfair to Beverly's apartment, picked up Beverly's 1979 Cadillac El Dorado, and then drove to Biscayne Boulevard to meet Uribe.

Maher walked around the Porsche, kneeling down often to look under the body.

"Brake dust on the fucking wheels," Maher said with a sigh, disgusted. "I bet you burned out my brake rotors."

Maher, Uribe, and Beverly climbed into the Porsche and drove to a nearby garage. Eleven hundred dollars later—a $600 brake job and a $500 pair of Perelli tires—and the Porsche was as good as new.

The next day, in an effort to keep Uribe away from his

Porsche, Maher took Uribe to a car rental agency that special-ized in exotic cars.

"Let's get a Lamborghini," Uribe suggested.

"How much for the Lamborghini?" Maher asked a clerk.

"A thousand a day and a dollar a mile," the clerk answered.

Maher smiled. At 150 miles per hour, the dollar a mile would cost more than the rental charge.

"Okay," Maher said, "we'll take it."

Because Uribe was careful never to leave a paper trail of any sort, Maher whipped out his own American Express card and charged a $5,000 deposit. *What do I care?* Maher mused. *The DEA is paying my "expenses."*

Later that night, coked out of his mind, Maher steered the Lamborghini into the parking lot of a club just a little too fast, hit the curb, and did a three-sixty. Maher laughed. Uribe didn't. Something was wrong. Uribe's head was pushed down onto his shoulder.

"John? You all right?"

"Wait a minute," Uribe said. "You fucked something up."

"What's wrong with your neck?" Maher asked.

"I don't fit too good anymore in this seat. Did I grow?"

Maher jumped out of the Lamborghini, got down on his hands and knees, and looked under the car. The curb had hit the Lamborghini just under the passenger seat and pushed the frame up about four inches.

"Fuck! The frame is bent."

Uribe climbed out of the car. "Maybe they won't notice it when we take it back."

"I hope not," Maher said. "Or there goes five fucking grand."

Maher found Beverly inside the club, and they wound up spending their third consecutive night together. With each glance, each kiss, each embrace, each passionate union, he was getting more and more hooked.

The next morning, Maher and Uribe returned the Lambor-ghini. No one at the car rental agency bothered to check the frame. The clerk gave Maher the American Express receipt with the five-thousand-dollar deposit, and Maher tore the receipt into pieces.

"That comes to seventeen hundred dollars," the clerk said as he handed Maher the rental charge to sign. "A thousand for the day and seven hundred miles at a dollar a mile."

Maher climbed into his Porsche, dropped Uribe off at his house, and headed north to New York. It was the first time he had left Miami reluctantly, the first time he had a reason to stay.

Beverly.

AS HE ALWAYS DID UPON HIS RETURN TO NEW YORK, MAHER STOPPED BY DEA Group 43 and handed off the information he had accumulated in Florida. Slavanki mentioned matter-of-factly that the DEA had conducted raids in New York. He handed Maher a payment of $18,000 in cash.

"Who'd you hit?" Maher asked as he flipped through the money.

"You're better off not knowing," Slavanki responded.

"When are you going to start busting the dealers I been giving you in Florida?" Maher pressed.

"You're better off not knowing," Slavanki said again.

Maher shrugged. Then: "By the way, I need you to help me with something."

Maher discussed Beverly's situation with Slavanki, insisting she was merely at the wrong place at the wrong time. Maher also bent the truth a little about one of the dealers.

"Beverly Merrill was instrumental in helping me identify that dealer," Maher fibbed, picking one at random.

"Okay," Slavanki said with a sigh. "Let me see what I can do."

WHILE MAHER WAS BUSY BOUNCING BACK AND FORTH TO FLORIDA, BETH was taking "business trips" as well. With Richard. Beth also was beginning to develop a passion for golf. Richard was a golfer.

At the end of September, Maher traded his '84 Porsche for an '86 model. The price was $54,000. Maher got $30,000 for the trade-in on his old car and laid out $24,000 in cash. The day after buying the new car, Maher hit the road for Florida.

During the month of October, Maher made five trips to Miami. He and Beverly partied with Uribe on a grand scale, renting expensive cars. A Ferrari one trip. A Lotus Turbo Esprit the next. They rented speedboats. They rented lavish hotel suites. They rented an entire lifestyle. About the only thing Maher and Uribe bought were guns.

Maher chose two weapons for himself: a .25-caliber Berretta, which was basically a small "pocket gun"; and a nickel-plated, five-shot Smith & Wesson .38, essentially a "detective gun." Uribe opted for an Uzi, which was the weapon of choice for terrorists.

The transaction was almost as easy as buying a suit. All Maher had to do was produce a Florida driver's license. Then he gave his American Express card to the clerk.

Of course it wasn't Maher's money. Part of his arrangement with the DEA regarding "expenses" was that the DEA paid his Amex bill.

After a 3 day waiting period, Maher and Uribe picked up the guns and drove to a machine shop where Uribe knew a gun expert. Uribe paid the man $500 to make the Uzi fully automatic. By nightfall, Uribe was carrying a very powerful assault weapon.

"YOU DID *WHAT?*" SLAVANKI SCREAMED INTO THE PHONE WHEN MAHER called from Miami. "You bought Uribe an Uzi?!"

There was a long beat of silence, during which it probably occurred to Slavanki that the DEA had just bought a drug dealer an assault weapon. Slavanki was furious.

"Uribe didn't have enough cash on him," Maher explained, "and I was standing there with my American Express."

Maher pointed out that he made sure Uribe registered the gun in his own name.

Slavanki was not soothed. So Maher attempted to deflect Slavanki's anger with a little humor.

"Look at it this way," Maher said. "If anything happens, at least we have the serial number."

It was a joke, of course, but it hit at the core of the DEA conundrum. Federal drug enforcement was an extraordinarily nasty business and it demanded a plan that was equally nasty, even if it meant allowing dealers with assault weapons to operate freely. While an NYPD sting might last for weeks, the DEA was forced to think in terms of years. And while the NYPD's objective was to battle crime within the boundaries of New York City, the DEA's mandate was to stop drug trafficking on a nationwide scale.

Over the ensuing months DEA officials knew that there would be a host of cocaine casualties, deaths that could be prevented by arresting dealers as soon as they were identified. Yet, by taking short-term action, DEA efforts would suffer in the long term. The DEA wanted the generals, not the foot soldiers.

Even Maher was nothing more than a soldier to the DEA. Or, perhaps more accurately, a fighter pilot. He would fly his missions to Miami and return with surveillance information. Slavanki and Becker most certainly had reservations about using Maher and permitting dealers like Uribe to roam around with an Uzi, but these reservations were offset by an overriding objective: stop drug trafficking. The objective was noble even if the methods were sometimes not so savory.

The conversation turned to Beverly. Somehow Slavanki had managed to work out a deal for her on the condition that she plead guilty to extortion, which carried a five-year sentence. When Maher protested, Slavanki explained that in federal court you cannot cop out with a stipulation of no time. Unlike state courts, where the whole deal, including the sentence, is worked out in advance, federal pleas require a bit of faith. The accused agrees to plead guilty *without* any guarantees. Then, *after* the plea, the federal court decides whether jail time is warranted.

At Maher's urging, Beverly agreed to plead guilty to extortion. Prior to entering the plea, she met with a probation officer. She did not make a good impression. At the November trial, the probation officer stood in court and recommended "half custodial and half noncustodial." In other words, he felt Beverly should serve two and a half years.

Beverly squirmed as the judge looked at the U.S. attorney and asked if he had anything to say before sentence was passed.

"We have nothing to say, Your Honor," the U.S. attorney said.

This made Beverly even more nervous. But Maher understood enough about courtroom procedure to know there was an unwritten rule between U.S. attorneys and judges. Had the U.S. attorney wanted Beverly to serve time, he would have said so.

By saying nothing, it was a signal to the judge that the prosecution preferred a sentence with no incarceration.

"Beverly Merrill," the judge proclaimed, "you are sentenced to five years' probation."

Maher and Beverly hugged tightly. She stared into Maher's eyes in the dreamy way someone would regard a hero.

Maher and Beverly left the courtroom and went to Beverly's apartment, where she packed. Maher had arranged for Beverly to serve her probation in New York. And he had arranged a place for her to live: with two go-go dancers in Queens. The way Maher looked at it, this got Beverly out of Miami, where she was likely to fuck somebody; and in New York, Beverly didn't know any dealers. In fact, she didn't know anybody, which suited Maher fine. Even better, Maher's dancer friends could keep an eye on her.

And so it was that Maher found himself in New York on a crisp November night in 1986, with several new acquisitions. A nasty coke habit. A sexy but morally questionable girlfriend. A mean, jealous streak. And a gun.

It was not the most stable combination of elements.

Chapter 16

MAHER INTRODUCED BEVERLY TO GO-GO DANCERS CARMEN AND SARA. Not only did the two girls seem to take an instant liking to their new roommate, they also were happy to fill the third bedroom of the large apartment, thus lowering their monthly share of rent. Of course, to pay her share of the rent, Beverly would have to get a job.

"I was a dancer in Miami," Beverly said.

"We can get you into Gallagher's," Carmen assured her. "They're looking for dancers."

Gallagher's was a strip joint on Queens Boulevard in Woodside, a favorite hangout for coke dealers. At first Maher thought it was a good idea. He could identify dealers while he watched Beverly dance. But then, a week later, he saw her onstage. And suddenly it wasn't such a good idea at all.

For her debut at Gallagher's, Beverly emerged in bra and G-string, her beautiful body exposed for all to see. With each seductive pose, Maher could feel blood rushing to his head. And each time she cast her gaze into the audience and stared at a man, Maher felt a rush of anger. He hung around all night—through all three of her performances—and then ushered her out of the club.

THANKSGIVING AND CHRISTMAS AT THE MAHER HOUSE WERE UNHAPPY occasions. Neither Maher nor Beth could walk away, yet both wanted to be somewhere else. For Beth, it was a romantic allure

243

that tugged at her. But for Maher, every minute away from Beverly drove him crazy. *What is she doing right now? Is she* fucking *somebody?* And so, on most nights, he would rush to Gallagher's, where the anguish increased. When Beverly seemed overly friendly to the club owner, Maher imagined that she was granting him sexual favors. And when Beverly became the featured dancer after the first of the year, Maher saw that as proof of his suspicions. *You don't become the featured dancer at Gallagher's making six hundred a night unless you're fucking* somebody. Additional "confirmation" came when the club owner arranged for Beverly to move into an apartment of her own on Cross Bay Boulevard.

"The owner's friend owns the video store in the building," Beverly said. "He gave me a good deal. Four hundred a month."

Four hundred a month and what else? Maher thought, seething.

OVER THE NEXT TWO MONTHS MAHER SHUTTLED BACK AND FORTH TO Florida five times. Each trip, he found that Uribe's mind had deteriorated a little more and his psychosis appeared to have returned, as was demonstrated one bizarre night in early March.

Maher and a rich kid from the Hamptons named Herman—who was one of Uribe's regular customers, especially during the summer season, when he needed party favors—were staying at Uribe's stash house. Uribe had rented the apartment under a false name expressly for the purpose of storing cocaine. Maher had claimed the bedroom. And Herman was sacked out on the couch. In the middle of the night, Uribe burst into the apartment, brandishing his Uzi.

"The fucking bitch!" he roared. "The fucking bitch!"

Herman cowered under a blanket. Maher jolted out of a sound sleep and ran out of the bedroom.

"What's the matter, John?" Maher asked.

Uribe, wild-eyed and perspiring, ranted and raved about a fight he had just had with Laura. Then he ran into the bedroom and called her. The argument continued via phone for fifteen minutes. No word was vile enough for the way Uribe felt about

Laura. Finally Uribe stomped into the living room, holding a cordless phone.

"She hung up on me!" Uribe howled, then squeezed the trigger on the Uzi and fired a round into the floor.

Herman began to quiver and grabbed a couch pillow, holding it in front of him like a shield. Maher looked at Uribe, stared at the gun, and decided he had to do something before Uribe accidentally killed himself or Herman.

"Hey, John," Maher said with a laugh, "you're scaring Herman."

Uribe frowned as he peered at the diminutive Herman, who was shaking violently.

"You think a couch pillow will stop a nine-millimeter Uzi?" Maher asked.

Herman whimpered. Uribe couldn't help it. He started laughing. And Maher took advantage of the opportunity. He snatched the Uzi away from the larger, stronger Uribe.

"All right, John," Maher said. "Calm the fuck down!"

Herman locked himself in the bedroom while Maher talked to Uribe. An hour later, Uribe left.

"He's gone, Herman," Maher yelled through the bedroom door. "You can come out now."

Herman emerged and went back to the couch. Maher crawled back into bed.

That's what women can do to you, Maher concluded as he stared at the ceiling, unable to sleep. *They can get you crazy. They can get you killed.*

But it hadn't been Laura's fault. Uribe *was* full of coke. And he *was* holding a gun. It didn't occur to Maher that he was doing a lot of coke, owned two guns, and Beverly was making *him* crazy.

WHILE MOST IRISHMEN STAY UP ALL NIGHT ON ST. PATRICK'S DAY, Maher got a jump on the celebration. At eleven in the morning on March 17, 1987, he had already been up for more than twenty-four hours. He was on a cocaine binge, and as he watched Beverly get dressed to head to Gallagher's, his mood grew dark. *I know she's fucking the owner.* Maher patted his jacket. He was carrying his .25-caliber Berretta.

"You're not going to Gallagher's," Maher said with a growl. "You're not working there anymore."

"Yes, I am," Beverly said defiantly as she stuffed the last of her work clothes into a gym bag.

"No, you're not."

"Watch me," Beverly said and then strutted out the door.

Beverly climbed into her 1979 Oldsmobile Cutlass, and Maher got into his Porsche. He followed closely behind her. When they arrived at Gallagher's, Beverly ran inside. Maher walked in a moment later and caught a glimpse of Beverly hurrying down the stairs to the dressing room. Maher headed for the stairs and started down after her. But there was a large obstacle in his way: Eddie, the 350-pound bouncer. Maher tried to push Eddie aside. It was like trying to move the *QE II*.

"Get the fuck out of here, you little punk," Eddie said as he shoved Maher back out of the stairwell, pinning him against a wall.

Maher maneuvered his hand to his waistband and pulled out the Berretta. He pointed the gun at Eddie's temple and tried to get his left arm around Eddie's huge girth so he could reach the slide mechanism that would load the chamber with a bullet. But because of Eddie's waist size, Maher's right hand, which was holding the Berretta, could not make contact with his left hand.

"Get off me!" Maher screamed.

"Fuck you," Eddie responded, unaware there was a gun to the side of his head.

Someone yelled, "Eddie, he's got a gun!"

Eddie turned slowly and found himself staring down the barrel of the Berretta. He slowly backed off.

"Everybody get down!" Maher ranted. "Everybody get down!"

Eddie, the waiters, the busboys, *everybody* got on the floor.

"First one to get up buys it!" Maher shouted.

Hearing the commotion, Beverly came upstairs.

"You're crazy!" Beverly screamed, then looked at the people on the floor. "He's crazy."

Maher sneered at Beverly. "Whore!"

Then Maher stormed out the door.

"I'm calling the cops," Eddie said as he heaved himself into a standing position. He headed for the phone.

"Don't do it, Eddie," Beverly yelled. "You don't want to fuck with him."

"I'll fuck with him," Eddie huffed. "The little punk."

Eddie picked up the receiver.

"Eddie," Beverly continued, "you don't understand. He works with the fucking FBI and the DEA. It won't do any good to call the cops."

Eddie slowly placed the receiver back onto the cradle.

Later that night, Maher showed up at Beverly's apartment. Incredibly, she let him in. Even more incredibly, she wasn't angry.

"You shouldn't have done that, Kevin," she said with a smile.

Beverly laughed. Maher laughed. Then they tore each other's clothes off.

MAHER CONTINUED HIS TRIPS TO MIAMI. BY NOW IT HAD BECOME A routine. But in mid-April something unusual happened. There was a DEA raid on one of the dealers Maher had identified. In May, there were two more. When Maher asked about the raids, Slavanki and Becker were tight-lipped. They paid him his bounty and told him to continue making the trips. But Maher sensed that D day was coming, and it frightened him. When he returned home from a Florida run at the end of May, he studied his doorstep. There in large black numbers was 30. Maher thought about removing the numbers, but instead he went to a hardware store and bought a number 4. The house number became 34. He reasoned that if one of the dealers managed to get his address, they wouldn't be able to find the house.

The sporadic DEA raids in Miami continued through May, June, and July. Since they were all dealers who in some way were associated with Uribe, Uribe earned the nickname "Black Cloud."

"What the fuck is going on?" Uribe wondered aloud as he and Maher sped along the Inland Waterway.

"I don't know, John," Maher said with a shrug.

The only reason the drug community didn't suspect Uribe of being an informant was because it was *his* coke that was being seized. And while it would seem that he would naturally suspect that Maher—an admitted FBI informant—had something to do with all the busts, Uribe never showed any suspicion. In Maher's mind, there were two reasons why Uribe was so trusting: (1) He had told Uribe that he was an FBI informant only because he was testifying against a "baby-killer." (2) Uribe had not been busted. Thus Uribe's logic told him that Maher was honest for leveling with him at Astoria Park that night and that Maher couldn't be a DEA informant; otherwise, Maher would have already locked him up.

By now, Uribe had accumulated two Uzis, the one Maher bought for him and a stolen 9mm with a thirty-two-round clip.

"Will you take this gun back to New York for me?" Uribe asked. "There's too much heat down here to be carrying a hot piece."

"Sure, John," Maher assented, then thought: *I bet the ATF never got a weapon away from a dealer this easy.* Maher had added another weapon to his arsenal.

In late August, simultaneous raids from New York to Miami netted carloads of cocaine, suitcases of cash, and dozens of dealers. One dealer had not been arrested: John Uribe. The DEA had kept its word to Maher, and that made him feel even more like part of the law enforcement community. Honor among cops.

Maher, who was in New York when the raids went down, spoke with Slavanki and was told that the DEA owed him $126,000, an amount that far exceeded any single payment the Justice Department had ever made to an informant.

The first thing Maher did with the money was get a new 1987 Porsche, for $61,000. He added special $4,000 seats, a $5,000 cellular phone system, an $8,000 stereo, $4,000 BBS wheels and tires, and a $3,000 high-performance exhaust, among other enhancements. By time he was finished, he had spent more than $80,000.

As autumn moved in, Maher was ready to retire his imaginary badge once again. He had proved himself, and for Maher that was the most important thing. *I could've been a cop. I could've been a federal agent. I could've been anything I wanted to be if hadn't stolen that Roadrunner.*

But what now? Maher believed he still loved Beth. Then there was Beverly. He loved her, too, didn't he? Or was he just obsessed? And what about children? Maher longed to have a child of his own, but Beth was staunch in her refusal to get pregnant. Yet when he daydreamed about starting a family with Beverly, he realized that Beverly wasn't mother material. *Was* she? Maher became so confused by it all that he did the only thing he thought would help him reach a conclusion: He bought an ounce of coke. Which is how he wound up one mild September night at Gallagher's. High. And carrying an Uzi. Only this time, the police were called. When Maher chose to challenge the cops, a scuffle ensued. He was arrested and charged with assaulting a police officer.

Maher realized he was in real trouble when he asked a lieutenant from the 108th Precinct to call Slavanki.

"The DEA will straighten this shit out," Maher insisted.

But when the lieutenant got Slavanki on the phone, it wasn't much of a conversation.

"The DEA has no jurisdiction here," the lieutenant told Slavanki. "And I'll tell you this: *Nobody* hits one of my cops."

A hour after Maher was brought to the precinct, Beth showed up. She looked weary, sick of all the trouble, tired of the struggle. Here she was, a top executive at a respected publication, and she was visiting her husband in jail.

"Excuse me, Mrs. Maher," the lieutenant said, "I think you should know what brought all this about. Your husband has a girlfriend. A stripper named Beverly."

"You motherfucker!" Maher screamed.

Maher drew in his breath and was about to hurl a flurry of insults at the lieutenant. But then Maher looked at Beth. She was hurt. Devastated. Maher slumped in the cell. The charade of a marriage was over.

Beth walked to the bars of the holding cell.

"Look, Beth," Maher began. "I—"

"You're hurt," Beth said, not wanting to hear some lame excuse.

"We're transferring him to a hospital," an officer remarked.

After the briefest of conversations with Beth, Maher was taken to a hospital and placed under police guard. For the next day and a half, he was treated for the injuries he sustained during the melee.

An officer named Bell, officially the arresting officer, entered the hospital room. The first thing Maher did was apologize.

"I'm sorry, officer," Maher sighed. "The woman got me crazy."

Bell was not impressed. He went over the charges with Maher—three assaults on a police officer—and proceeded to take down Maher's version of events. When the statement was completed, Bell commented on a Marine tattoo that was on Maher's arm.

"I was in the Marines, too," Bell said.

Maher then launched into one of his DEA stories. From the look on Bell's face, Maher could see that he didn't believe it. So Maher called Slavanki and handed the receiver to Bell. After a five-minute conversation with Slavanki, Bell handed the receiver back to Maher and left the room.

"Okay, Agent Slavanki," Maher said, "how do I get out of this?"

Slavanki explained that there was nothing the DEA could do. Maher was charged with a serious offense, and it was up to the NYPD how the case was resolved.

Maher panicked. Then he remembered the Vincent Caldera incident from 1983. The players were major league. A U.S. congressman. A high-ranking law enforcement official. He had promised Caldera he wouldn't do anything, but that was because Caldera was an NYPD cop at the time and Caldera merely wanted his job back. Caldera had since left the force and was working for Metro Dade County police in Florida. Maher felt he had no choice. This was a big case, big enough to get the attention of the Internal Affairs Division of the NYPD. Handing IAD the Caldera case was his only hope. Still, it bothered Maher that he was bartering a deal. Maher hadn't traded information for help in mitigating a charge since the rug guy he gave Doherty more than a decade before. But then, Maher had never been in this much trouble before either.

Then next day Maher was shuttled off to court, where bail was set.

"Bail is four thousand," the judge said. "Cash."

Beth was there with the money.

When Maher returned home, he and Beth talked honestly. Maher was contrite about his indiscretion with Beverly.

"I'm glad it's out in the open. I'm glad it's over. All I can say is—"

Beth cut him off.

"That's the past, Kevin," Beth said sternly. "We have to talk about the future."

After hours of apologies, tears, and even a little laughter, Maher and Beth agreed to try one last time to make the marriage work.

"But you have to be a good boy," Beth insisted. "No more coke, no more guns, and no more women."

"I'll be a good boy," Maher said. "I swear."

However, even as they tried to tell themselves this was a second chance, they both knew it was an ending, not a beginning, a temporary truce until the terms of surrender could be hammered out.

A couple of days later there was another ending in Maher's life. The arbiters at New Jersey Transit had reached a decision. On September 21, 1987, Maher was officially terminated. To Maher, it was a bitter conclusion to a dispute he felt certain would be settled in his favor. After all, the weed killer had caused the conjunctivitis, and he couldn't help the fact that wearing goggles rendered him virtually blind. Maher retained a lawyer. He wasn't going down without a fight.

THE LAST WEEK OF SEPTEMBER, AT FOUR O'CLOCK IN THE MORNING, Maher was awaked by the ringing of the phone. He grabbed the receiver.

"Hello?"

Instead of a response, Maher heard a grinding sound. An unmistakable gnashing of teeth. Uribe. And Uribe only ground his teeth when he was coked up.

"John?"

"You fuck," Uribe said with a growl. "You're history, and so is everybody in that house."

Click.

Maher bolted upright. Beth stirred.

"Who was that?" Beth asked.

"Uribe," Maher said, offering no further explanation.

Maher remained awake the balance of the night. *Where was Uribe calling from? Miami? New Jersey?*

At nine sharp, Maher called the DEA. Becker answered the phone. Maher told Becker about the phone call from Uribe and speculated that Uribe probably put two and two together after the DEA raids and had come up with Maher.

"Don't mention Dakota," Maher said. "North *or* South. I'm going after him."

Maher didn't want to lock up Uribe, but he figured he didn't have much choice. Uribe's coke habit made him dangerous.

Becker contacted an agent in Florida to verify Uribe's address. Uribe had been arrested on a domestic violence charge for a fight he had with Laura. According to the arrest report, Uribe was now living in Coconut Grove.

Maher called Beth at *The Economist* and told her he had to go to Miami. She wasn't pleased.

"This is the last trip," Maher said. "I *swear.*"

Within an hour, Maher was speeding toward Florida, arriving the following afternoon in Coconut Grove. Maher found Uribe's house. Located down a dead-end street, it was even bigger than the previous one. As Maher peered toward the house, Uribe appeared at the huge picture window that overlooked the front lawn. Before Maher could get the car turned around, Uribe was out of the house. Maher jumped from the car and looked Uribe over. He didn't appear to be armed.

"How did you find me?" Uribe demanded.

"It's on your arrest record," Maher said. "From when you beat the shit out of Laura."

Maher and Uribe studied each other for a long beat. Maher could hear Uribe thinking: *The fuck is a cop.*

Maher smiled. "You fuck! You call me up and threaten me? What the fuck is up with that?"

"That wasn't me," Uribe countered.

Maher's smiled broadened. *Of course it was you. No one else grinds his teeth like that.*

"John," Maher said, "you think I set up the DDs? You think it was me? Then what are you doing standing there? Why aren't you locked up?"

Uribe fought back a smile.

"Come in," Uribe said. "I have a present for you, my friend."

As they walked toward the house, Uribe asked: "What are you doing in Florida?"

"I'm down here to meet a DD I know and buy a kilo," Maher answered.

Uribe reacted. Maher smiled.

"What?" Maher said. "You think you're the only DD in town?"

Uribe seemed convinced that Maher was planning a buy. Now Maher would offer to make the buy from Uribe. Would Uribe take the bait?

"Hey," Maher said, "I don't care where I get the kilo. Why don't you sell it to me?"

Uribe hesitated for a moment.

"Okay," Uribe finally said. "Maybe tomorrow."

The following day, Becker flew into Miami. Maher and Becker met with the DEA Florida Region group supervisor and outlined a plan.

"I'll get him to sell me a kilo," Maher said.

But the group supervisor was not so keen on the idea.

"Busting him for a key is a throw-out case," the group supervisor said.

The difficulty was that there already was an active warrant on Uribe for dozens of charges.

"Any defense lawyer will use that," the group supervisor noted. "The lawyer's bound to say to a judge: why didn't they arrest him all these years? Why did they accumulate all these charges?"

The answer, of course, was Maher's deal: Don't lock up Uribe.

It was decided that the obvious solution was to exercise the active warrant and forget about the one-kilo buy. Maher's job was to make sure Uribe was in the house when the DEA arrived.

The next afternoon, Maher met Becker near Uribe's house. There were DEA agents, detectives from the Florida Department of Law Enforcement, and cops from the Coconut Grove Police Department. Twenty in all, each wearing bulletproof vests and hood masks. *They look like terrorists*, Maher thought. The cops and agents were armed with Mac 10 automatic rifles equipped with a ten-inch silencer. It was the most fearsome display of law enforcement power Maher had ever seen.

Maher drove the short distance to Uribe's house and knocked on the door. A few seconds later, Uribe appeared.

"Hey, Kevin. What's up?"

"Just checking to see if you're going to be home. I've got to make a little run. But I'll be back in an hour."

"I'll be here," Uribe said.

Maher walked to his Porsche, climbed behind the wheel, and drove slowly down the street. Two vans and three radio cars sped past him. Maher stopped the car and rolled down the window. Seconds later he heard the raid begin.

"Police!"

"DEA!"

"Don't move!"

"FBI!"

Maher laughed to himself. FBI. There were no FBI agents in the group. But the DEA often shouted "FBI!" because it had a harder sound. If someone didn't know the acronym DEA, they certainly understood FBI.

Maher slammed the Porsche into first gear and headed back to New York.

WITH THE TRIAL ON HIS ASSAULT CHARGES APPROACHING, MAHER contacted the IAD and told the Vincent Caldera story. Skeptical at first, the IAD became convinced after checking Maher's references: Doherty, DeBellis, Slavanki. The only obstacle now was Officer Bell, the arresting officer in the case against Maher. If Bell would withdraw the complaint, the charges would be dropped. Bell agreed, and the case was dismissed. Maher went undercover for the IAD.

But Caldera refused to cooperate. So, despite an overwhelming amount of evidence gathered by Maher, there were no arrests. It appeared the incident was being "swept," a term used by cops as a shorthand for "swept under the rug." And at a level this high, no one could stop the broom from doing its work.

Still, for Maher the Caldera case had served his purpose. He avoided a jail sentence. And gained another opportunity to get his life straightened out. To that end, Maher kept his promise to Beth. He stopped using coke. Cold turkey. Actually, it was Wild

Turkey, which is how Maher got past the withdrawal symptoms. He drank heavily. And once again, he merely switched drugs.

In January 1988 there were hopeful signs that New Jersey Transit might settle the dispute. But the signs were misleading. So on January 27, Maher's attorney, Randi Doner—from the law firm of Sanford/Oxfeld—filed a $2 million lawsuit charging New Jersey Transit with wrongful dismissal, handicap discrimination, and violation of the whistle blower statute. A flurry of motions followed. By March it was clear that the railroad would contest. Doner's assessment was that the dispute could take years before it even got to the courts.

Maher grew more anxious. His safety net, the railroad job, was a thing of the past.

"GUESS WHAT," DETECTIVE FRANK DELPRETE HAD TOLD MAHER ONE DAY when the two of them ran into each other on the street. "Your buddy's dead."

"Who?" Maher had asked.

"Brian Molese," DelPrete had answered. "I just heard he died in prison of AIDS."

The death of Brian Molese provided a punctuation mark to Maher's career as an informant. Much had begun at 24 Sanford Road. So now that Maher's cop persona no longer existed, it seemed fitting that Molese no longer existed as well.

Seventeen years ago, when he stole the Roadrunner and took the cops on a chase to the Catskills, it was evident that Maher was an excitement junkie. And his sources of excitement took many forms. Uribe and Beverly were two. Each, in his or her own way, had always given Maher that needed fix of risk and adventure. But following Maher's outburst at Gallagher's, Beverly had quit her job and left her apartment. No one knew where to find her. And Uribe was locked up.

No undercover work. No Beverly. No Uribe. No excitement. So Maher looked to his wife to ease the craving. *At least I still have Beth,* Maher told himself. But on a hot and humid night in June 1988, he destroyed that, too.

Maher and Beth had just finished dinner when Beth mentioned something she had to do at the office.

"Like I was telling Richard—" Beth began.

But before she finished her sentence, Maher jumped up from the table. He couldn't bear the way she said the name "Richard."

"I'm going out for a while," Maher said, and then walked out the door.

For the next six hours, Maher stopped at bar after bar. By the time he staggered home at 3:00 A.M., he was mean drunk.

Maher entered the bedroom and turned on a light. Beth was awake. She gave Maher a dirty look, then rolled over, facing away from him. Infuriated, Maher reached under the bed and emerged with his Smith & Wesson.

"Hey, bitch!" Maher screamed.

Beth turned around. Her eyes widened when she saw the gun.

"When I catch you and that motherfucker O'Rourke," Maher said with a sneer, pulling the slide back to eject a bullet, "I'm going to blow his fucking brains out."

Maher took the bullet and, using the lead tip, wrote in large letters across the wall: Richard O'Rourke.

Maher staggered over to the side of the bed and looked down at Beth, who was lying on her back. He held the bullet a couple of feet above her face.

"The *next* time you see one of these coming at you . . ."

Maher dropped the bullet on Beth's forehead.

". . . it'll be coming at you a lot faster."

Chapter 17

Maher—still brandishing his Smith & Wesson—charged out of the room. Beth slowly got out of bed, collected her son, Bobby, and slipped out of the house. She drove to the police station and arranged for an order of protection against Maher. The cops returned home with her.

"So where the fuck am I supposed to go now?" Maher raged at one of the cops.

"Wherever you go," the cop stated evenly, "it better not be here."

Maher climbed in his car and thought about his options. *I'll go to Mike Bellzano's house,* Maher decided. Maher had met Bellzano, who lived nearby in Rutherford, because Bellzano's children often played with little Bobby.

Maher cranked up the engine and tore out of the driveway. Just as he was about to turn a corner, he glanced in the rear-view mirror and caught a glimpse of the squad car in front of his house. The realization of what had just happened—what he had done to Beth—sobered Maher a little. *What the fuck did I do this time?!*

Maher drove to Bellzano's house and banged on the door. A couple minutes later, a sleepy-eyed Bellzano appeared.

"Kevin," Bellzano said, "what's going on?"

"Beth threw me out," Maher answered.

When Maher checked his bank account the next day, he found he was low on cash. The Porsche, the improvements to the Porsche, the nights out on the town buying drinks for the house, had depleted the DEA windfall.

For the next two days, Maher laid on Bellzano's couch, listless, depressed. Bellzano called Beth.

"He's a wreck," Bellzano said. "I think he needs to go into drug rehab."

Beth didn't want to hear about Maher's problems, much less deal with them.

"Okay," Beth said with a sigh, "I'll sign whatever insurance papers you need to check him in."

Bellzano took Maher to a place called The Harbor, which was in Hoboken. Cost for a twenty-eight-day drug rehabilitation program: $22,000. As Beth had said she would do, she signed the insurance papers. She also signed another set of papers: She filed for divorce.

After only a week at The Harbor, Maher walked out. He wound up back on Bellzano's couch. A few days later, Maher's cellular phone rang. His hands shook as he fumbled for the send button. *Please let this be Beth.*

"Hello, Kevin," a female voice said. "Do you know who this is?"

It was Beverly.

COCAINE AND PASSION, ENDLESS WEEKS OF DELIRIOUS PLEASURE. MAHER and Beverly floated into the charcoal days of autumn. By October, Maher had moved into Beverly's Brooklyn apartment.

"You know, Kevin," Beverly said one night, "I've been with probably a thousand guys and I've never felt this way about any of them."

Maher looked at her in disbelief. A thousand *guys?*

Maybe it was the cocaine. Maybe Maher had just gone crazy. Whatever it was, Kevin Maher and Beverly Merrill were united in matrimony on October 20, 1988. Of course, there was a small problem with the union. Maher was still married to Beth.

Maher and Beverly found a place to live in Elmwood Park, New Jersey, a nice, spacious apartment in a two-family house on Grove Street. This required that Beverly's parole be transferred from New York to New Jersey. But that was easy, since

Maher had accumulated so many contacts in law enforcement he could have worked a deal for Jack the Ripper.

Beverly supported both of them with the money she made from dancing, which ranged upward to $3,000 a week. They lived the high life, never worrying about saving for the future. That's because they had their future already set.

"I'm going to win the case against the railroad and get two million dollars," Maher would tell Beverly.

But the case dragged on. Motions and countermotions. Postponement after postponement. Deposition after deposition. Clearly, it was going to be a very long time before Maher would see a cent from New Jersey Transit, if in fact he saw anything at all.

ALTHOUGH BETH WAS NO LONGER SPEAKING TO MAHER, HER SON, BOBBY, missed the man who had been his father for thirteen years. So, on November 19, 1988, which was Bobby's eighteenth birthday, Maher took his "son" out to celebrate.

"Who was my father?" Bobby asked suddenly.

Maher took a breath. Beth had never told Bobby the truth about his biological father.

"I'm your father now, Bobby."

"I mean my *real* father."

Maher was stung.

"Your father's name is Robert Eschert."

"Where is he?"

A million lies zapped across Maher's mind.

"Your father is in prison," Maher said.

"Why?"

Maher hesitated. Then he explained—as gently as one could relate such a thing—that Robert Eschert was a killer. A murderer.

"I put him away," Maher added.

Bobby looked away. Not verbally, not with a facial expression, not in any way.

"I know where he is," Maher told Bobby. "If you want to see him, I'll go there with you."

Bobby looked away. Apparently he wasn't quite ready to deal with his father. And, despite his bravado, neither was Maher.

*   *   *

FROM THE MOMENT MAHER AND BEVERLY HAD TIED THE KNOT, THEY began trying to have a baby. But a couple of months later, when Beverly had not conceived, they resorted to an unorthodox method of fertility enhancement. Beverly would stand on her head for several minutes, having heard how this would make sure that all the sperm reached the egg.

"How much longer?" Beverly would ask, her legs sticking straight up toward the ceiling.

"Two more minutes," Maher would say, checking his watch.

It was a happy time for Maher. Beverly seemed devoted. And she *was* going to have his baby. But then in spring 1989, that old sick feeling returned. *Beverly is fucking around. I know it.*

One night in April, when jealous thoughts wouldn't leave him, he tried to drink it away. He got drunk and waded into a bar fight with three bouncers at a place called The Bench in Carlstadt. He was arrested and thrown in a holding tank to dry out.

The next morning, a Carlstadt detective sergeant arrived for work. He read Maher's arrest report. Drunk and disorderly. Assault, because he shoved a cop. Then the detective walked to the holding cell and looked in at Maher, who was sprawled across the narrow bed. His face was badly bruised.

"What the hell happened to you?" Detective Sergeant Bobby Colaneri asked.

"I showed those fucking bouncers," Maher said with a laugh, grimacing because it hurt to smile. "I rammed my face into their fists a few times."

And so it was that on April 12, 1989, the parallel paths of Kevin Maher and Bobby Colaneri had converged at long last.

Maher and Colaneri sized each other up from opposite sides of the bars.

"What'd you give the cop a hard time for?" Colaneri asked.

"I was drunk and stupid," Maher replied. "I didn't have anything against the cop. It was that fucking bouncer."

Maher stood and walked to the cell door. "I want to apologize to the cop. I like cops. I *work* with cops."

Maher launched into his undercover stories, mentioning that he had worked with FBI agent Bob DeBellis.

"I know Bob DeBellis," Colaneri noted.

Then Maher started talking about the Molese trial and prosecutor Dennis Calo.

"I know Dennis Calo, too," Colaneri said.

For the next two hours, Maher spun a series of complex tales that ran from murders to bank robberies to DEA drug busts. He told Colaneri how he had posed as a hit man. And he confessed the troubles he was having with Beverly.

In turn, Colaneri talked about his own life. The many close calls with the law when he was younger, the hostage crisis at the bank, his marriage to Patti.

Maher and Colaneri related like old friends. And, in a way, they were. Each lived a sort of mirror image of the other's life.

Colaneri asked Maher if he wanted to file countercharges against the bouncer, a strategy Colaneri had come to expect whenever two guys got into a fight. Maher declined to file charges, and this made Colaneri like him more. *He's from the old school. He takes his lumps.*

After contacting DeBellis and Calo to confirm that Maher was who he said he was and not a potential flight risk, Colaneri called a judge and arranged to have Maher released ROR (released on his own recognizance).

Once again, Maher had made a friend in law enforcement, one who could help him out of a fix. But this time, Maher had gained more than a police contact, more than a father figure like Doherty. He had encountered someone his own age, someone who had the same hopes and fears.

THE FEELING THAT BEVERLY WAS CHEATING ON HIM PERSISTED. ALTHOUGH he knew it would be futile to accuse her of infidelity, Maher couldn't help himself.

"You're fucking somebody!" Maher screamed one night.

"I am not!" Beverly countered.

The argument escalated. Beverly called the police. And once again Maher was ejected from his home.

Maher went directly to a bar, where he ran into Eric Jann, whose father owned Jann's Deli in Wood-Ridge. As it happened, there was a vacant apartment over the deli, and Maher moved in that night.

On May 24, 1989, a final decree of divorce was recorded by the Superior Court of New Jersey in Bergen County. Beth was now his ex-wife. And at least Maher was no longer a bigamist.

Maher ran to Beverly, but she was not receptive. She informed Maher that she had contacted a lawyer and was planning to file for divorce. *Two divorces on the same day*, Maher thought. *What's wrong with me?*

Maher and Beverly argued for an hour and then, like a flash fire, wound up in bed. Despite the brief flare of passion, Beverly told Maher she wasn't ready for him to move back in.

Once a week, sometimes twice, Maher would stop by and see Beverly. He didn't feel like a husband. He felt like an alley cat, sneaking in to get a piece of something that wasn't his. He was infuriated by the thought. Often he would accuse Beverly of having a lover, which would result in another screaming match.

Maher decided he should stop the accusations and look at the situation like it was a case. He would get proof, then confront Beverly with irrefutable evidence.

On the next visit to his estranged wife's apartment, he waited until she went into the bathroom, and then he quickly removed the plastic case from the handset of the cordless phone that was on the bedside table. He jotted down the dip switch settings that control the frequency over which the remote phone operated and put the handset back together.

Maher then bought a cordless phone. He opened the handset of the new phone and set the dip switches so that they matched the settings on Beverly's phone. Maher added two more items to his makeshift surveillance kit: a suction microphone and a small tape recorder. When he was done, he wound up with his own ingenious phone tap.

Later that night, Maher parked his car on the street behind the house—the bedroom was in the rear of the apartment—and found that he was well within range of the base unit on Beverly's phone. The tap paid off immediately. When Maher punched on the talk button, he found himself in the middle of a conversation between Beverly and the tenant in the downstairs apartment.

"Do we have time for a quickie?" the tenant asked. "Meet me in the laundry room."

"He's not here," Beverly said, her voice dripping invitation. "Why don't you come up to the apartment?"

"But I like fucking you on the washing machine," the tenant said.

They both laughed.

"Okay," Beverly consented. "I'll meet you in the laundry room in fifteen minutes."

Maher pressed the off button on the handset and fell back against the car seat. *She's fucking the guy downstairs?* Before Maher could catch his breath, he heard the phone ring. He clicked on his handset. It was the landlord.

"I miss you," the landlord whined. "Can you stop by on your way to work?"

"Sure, baby," Beverly responded. "Tomorrow night."

Then Beverly's lawyer called. And a bar owner. Maher was shaking. Was the phone ever going to stop ringing?

This time it wasn't anger he felt, it was resignation. Maher walked to the front door. Beverly was surprised to see him.

"Not tonight, Kevin. I have to do laundry."

"I know," Maher said.

Beverly looked at him quizzically. "You know I have to do laundry?"

"I know a lot of things," Maher said. "Like I know you're fucking the guy downstairs."

"Get out of here!" Beverly shrieked, "or I'm calling the cops."

"And you're fucking your lawyer," Maher continued, *"and* you're fucking the landlord."

"You're crazy!" Beverly shouted. "Get out!"

Maher reached into his pocket and took out the tape recorder. He pressed play. Beverly's mouth dropped open. When the tape finished, Maher turned and walked away.

The next night, the anger set in. Maher stopped by Shaker's, a bar in Carlstadt where Beverly had started dancing under the name "Danielle."

"Where's Danielle?" Maher asked a waitress.

"She has the night off," the waitress replied. "Who are you?"

"I'm her husband."

"Husband? I didn't know she had a husband. I know she has a boyfriend."

Maher's nostrils flared. "What boyfriend?"

The waitress started to walk away.

"Who is the fucking boyfriend?" Maher demanded as he pulled a handful of hundred-dollar bills from his pocket, money he had earmarked for a coke buy.

"I don't think I should . . ."

"One," Maher said as he placed a hundred on the table.

The waitress's interest was piqued.

"Two." Maher counted a second hundred. "Three. Four."

Maher held the fifth hundred in the air. "At some point, I'm going to stop counting. If you tell me the name of the boyfriend, you can have the money on the table. But when I stop counting, you get nothing, even if you tell me."

Maher lowered the hundred slowly.

"Five."

The waitress swallowed.

"Six."

"Al," the waitress blurted out. "Al Harris."

Maher slid the money toward the waitress but kept his hand on top of the stack of bills.

"Where does he work?"

"Bennigan's. In Saddle Brook."

Maher lifted his hand and walked out. He headed home and picked up his Smith & Wesson 9mm.

When Maher arrived at Bennigan's, three bouncers guarded the front door of the popular Irish bar. Maher swept past them like they weren't there. Once inside, he looked at the bartender. *That's gotta be Al,* Maher thought.

Al walked from behind the bar and started across the restaurant. Maher intercepted him.

"Your name Al?"

Al nodded.

"My name is Kevin Maher and I want to talk to you."

"Look, I'm busy," Al said.

"It's about Danielle."

Al thought it over for a minute, then led Maher to a booth. They sat face to face.

"Danielle," Maher stated evenly, "is my wife."

"Hey," Al said with a growl, "let me tell you something right now—"

"No," Maher said as he slid his Smith & Wesson from his waistband and jammed it in Al's crotch. "You're not going to tell *me* shit, motherfucker. *I'm* going to tell *you*."

Al looked down in horror at the nickel-plated barrel pressed into his genitals. His expression drew the attention of a bouncer.

"You got problems here?" the bouncer asked Al.

Maher pressed the gun harder into Al's crotch.

"No," Al squeaked. "Leave us alone."

The bouncer backed off.

"Now," Maher said, "this gun is a lie detector. I'm going to ask you questions, and the fucking minute I think you're lying to me, I'm going to blow your balls off."

Maher stared at the terrified Al for a long, tense moment.

"Do you know Danielle?" Maher asked.

Al nodded. "I didn't know she was married."

Maher applied more pressure with the barrel of the gun.

"Boom!" Maher said. "That's one lie. The next boom you hear is coming from my Smith & Wesson."

Al trembled slightly.

"Where did you meet her?" Maher demanded.

"She came in here with one of her girlfriends."

"How long have you been fucking her?"

"Since May."

Maher grimaced. That was a month before he and Beverly separated.

"Did you use a condom?"

Al hesitated.

"Did you use a condom?" Maher asked with a snarl, jamming the gun hard into Al's crotch.

"No."

"Did you fuck her in my bed?"

"Yes."

Maher pulled the gun away. He reached in his pocket and pulled out a hundred-dollar bill, dropping it on the table.

"Don't get up from the booth until I'm out the door," Maher said.

Al nodded.

And then Maher, tears clouding his eyes, stumbled out of the bar.

* * *

IN MID-JULY BEVERLY STOPPED BY MAHER'S APARTMENT. MAHER WAS coked out of his mind.

"I miss you so much," she said.

"Whore!" Maher replied. "You're nothing but a fucking whore!"

Beverly began to cry.

"I'm sorry, I'm so sorry," Beverly said, sobbing. "I need you. I want you to come back home."

"Are you crazy?" Maher shouted. "Come back to *you?* I can't face people here. I don't know who the hell you fucked."

Beverly walked over and put her arms around Maher's waist. He pushed her away. She did it again. He pushed her away. A third attempt. A third rejection. A long stare. Dead silence. The next thing Maher knew, he was in bed.

Incredibly, they decided to get back together.

As Maher was packing to leave the apartment over Jann's Deli, Eric Jann told Maher he was moving to Scotsdale, Arizona.

"Here's my number," Jann said. "Give me a call sometime."

Again living with Beverly, Maher tried his best to put her promiscuity behind him. But every man he saw in the neighborhood gave him pause. *Did she fuck* him, *too?* Maher decided that he and Beverly should move. Someplace where they didn't know anyone, someplace far away.

At the end of July, Maher and Beverly rented a place in Tobihanna, Pennsylvania, deep in the Poconos. Beverly got a job dancing at Satin Dolls in Hackensack. Each night, Maher would take her there in his Porsche—the normal two hour drive translated to an hour and twenty-minutes with Maher behind the wheel—and he would pick her up eight hours later. It seemed to work for a while. Perhaps Beverly had really changed her ways. Or perhaps Maher had resigned himself just to look the other way.

IN AUGUST, AS MAHER'S COURT DATE IN CARLSTADT FOR DISORDERLY conduct and assault was approaching, Colaneri arranged for Maher to meet with Dave Smith, the arresting officer from the bar fight. Maher apologized, and Smith agreed to drop the charges. The case against Maher would be dismissed.

As Colaneri was showing Maher out of the squad room, Maher turned to him and said:

"I want to repay you for what you've done."

"You don't owe me anything, Kevin."

But Maher was insistent.

"Give me a case. I'll help you solve it."

Colaneri shrugged. "Well, we're getting killed with car radio thefts."

"I'll find out who's stealing the radios and get back to you."

Colaneri laughed. "Knock yourself out."

Two weeks later, Colaneri wasn't laughing. Maher appeared at Carlstadt police headquarters. He handed Colaneri a piece of paper.

"Here's the guy who's stealing the radios."

Colaneri looked at the piece of paper. It had a name, address, phone number, and license plate number.

"How'd you manage to find this out?" Colaneri asked.

"Easy," Maher said, then explained how he did it. "I just went out and told all my contacts in the neighborhood that I wanted to buy car radios. Bingo."

Armed with the information provided by Maher, Colaneri obtained a search warrant and raided the address. The Carlstadt police recovered dozens of radios. Then, like so many of Maher's cases, it escalated. The raid led to information that pointed to a corrupt police official in a large New Jersey town. Despite the evidence, however, the case was not pursued.

While Maher was happy that he repaid Colaneri, he was also disillusioned. First the Caldera case and now this. Two straight cases involving police corruption "swept."

By November it had become clear that Beverly had not reformed. And Maher could no longer look the other way. Following a horrendous argument, Maher packed his bags and left their home in the Poconos.

As Maher sped south over the twisty roads that led out of the mountains, he was thinking: *I gotta get as far away as I can get.* Maher remembered that Eric Jann was in Arizona. Maher called Jann, who was happy to hear that Maher was thinking about heading to Scotsdale.

"I was looking for a roommate," Jann said.

"I'm on my way," Maher replied.

IN SCOTSDALE MAHER MOVED INTO JANN'S APARTMENT, WHICH WAS located in what Maher referred to as a "fancy yuppie complex." There were tennis courts, a pool, all the amenities.

In January 1990 Maher flew back to New Jersey for a hearing on his railroad case. No sooner did he return to Arizona than he was informed by his attorney that the railroad had scheduled *another* hearing two weeks later. In February the railroad demanded two more hearings. While they had slowed down the process when Maher was living locally in New Jersey, they were speeding it up now that he was in Arizona, and it was a hardship for him to attend the hearings.

In February Maher moved to Hasbrouck Heights, New Jersey. His money dwindling, he began drinking heavily. There *was* the Porsche, which could probably be sold for $60,000. But Maher decided he couldn't sell the Porsche. He knew that, the way he handled money, he would blow that money in a couple of months. No matter what, he had to hang on to it. It was more than a car now, it was also his financial lifeline.

ON THE MORNING OF JUNE 20, 1990, COLANERI, SPORTING A BEARD AND long hair *and* wearing an earring, walked up to a cinder block garage in the back of a warehouse, glanced at a sign that read "Bimini Auto Detailers," took out a key, and let himself in. It was the first day of an undercover operation aimed at a stolen car ring. Colaneri had spent the past few weeks setting up the sting. *This is a perfect job for Kevin,* Colaneri told himself as he worked on the plan. However, as far as Colaneri knew, Maher was still in Arizona.

Colaneri and two undercover investigators from the Bergen County prosecutor's office—Ken Nass and Rich Barbato—had decided on the sting when two men who were associated with car thieves had been arrested on other charges. Deals were made, freedom in return for "referrals" to Bimini Auto Detailers.

The money for the sting came via NATB—the National Auto Theft Bureau—which was funded by insurance companies. The initial investment, $10,000, was used to build offices inside the garage and equip those offices with hidden video and audio equipment. A video camera was positioned so it was pointed at Colaneri's desk. Still cameras were placed behind nude pictures of women.

"That's how we'll get the close-ups," Colaneri said with a laugh, knowing the men would wander over to get a good look at the centerfolds.

Business cards were printed. Colaneri's said Robert Schultz, which was the name of his deceased brother-in-law. And then Bimini Auto Detailers opened its doors. Before long, the cars started rolling in.

Since Colaneri and the two Bergen County investigators often went in and out of the secret video room, Colaneri had to have a way to keep from being surprised by the car thieves. One day, when two guys showed up unexpectedly, Colaneri became furious.

"*Never* show up here unannounced!" Colaneri shouted.

"Why not?" one of them asked.

"The other people we're dealing with don't want to know you," Colaneri barked. "And *you* don't want to know them."

Colaneri went on to say that "we guarantee all our customers the same confidentiality."

The two guys bought it. In fact, so did all the car thieves. Bimini Auto Detailers was able to conduct transactions in an orderly fashion—and, of course, reduce the risk of being detected as an undercover law enforcement operation.

Although the sting was aimed at an auto theft ring specializing in Cadillacs and BMWs, Colaneri could not specify a make or model because it might be construed as entrapment if he "ordered up": So thieves were told that Bimini wanted only "luxury cars, expensive cars." Since Colaneri was working on a tight budget, he offered $500 a car. When one thief saw Colaneri with a wad of money—actually flash money used not for spending, but to impress the thieves—the thief complained about the "low price." Colaneri silenced him with: "Hey! It's a half-hour work for you."

One of the things that the sting demonstrated was just how ingenious some thieves could be. A Bimini customer got his hands on a T-Shirt from Brogan Cadillac. He slipped onto the Brogan lot and, when an old lady drove her car in for service, he smiled and said, "I'll take that for you, ma'am." In fact, he did take it. All the way to Bimini Auto Detailers. Another thief, wearing a shirt from Park Cadillac, stood at the rear of a car-carrier tractor-trailer truck and watched the brand-new imports being unloaded. "I'll take that one into the garage," he offered. The driver handed him the keys, and the Cadillac was off to Bimini.

The biggest problem Colaneri had was not getting cars but identifying the people who stole them. All transactions were, of course, in cash, and most of the thieves only went by their first name or a nickname. So Colaneri always did two things. First, he would ask the thieves to sit across the desk from him when he paid them, making sure the transaction was caught by the video camera. And then, at some point, Colaneri would motion toward one of the centerfolds and say:

"Hey, look at the tits on that one."

The thieves always obliged. They'd walk up to the centerfold and stare at her breasts.

Click! Another portrait.

By October, Bimini Auto Detailers had received forty-two cars—all luxury models—several guns, and a stash of counterfeit titles and bogus license plates. And all the thieves except one had been identified. The operation a success, it was time to shut down. But how could they begin the arrests without tipping off other suspects? The solution was simple.

Colaneri spread the word that Bimini had "tagged" the cars— that is, changed the Vehicle Identification Numbers to render them salable—and now needed people to drive the altered autos to Ohio.

"You get five hundred dollars," Colaneri told the thieves, "and when we get to Ohio there'll be a big party. Drugs. Hookers. And we'll give you a bus ticket back to Jersey."

On October 5, 1990, a twenty-foot box truck was parked outside Bimini Auto Detailers, as was a windowless van. Inside the truck was a SWAT team, and inside the van was a canine unit, just in case one of the suspects made a run for it.

The trap set, the thieves were given staggered pickup times, and a passenger van was dispatched to collect five or six of them at a time. Waiting in front of their homes and clutching overnight bags, the thieves eagerly bounded onto the van.

When the van returned to Bimini Auto Detailers, the thieves disembarked and filed into the garage to see Colaneri. After greeting them, Colaneri uttered the magic phrase—"Oh, we're going to have a great time in Ohio!"—which was a signal for the cops to jump from the truck and burst in. A few minutes later, the passenger van was off on another roundup.

One of the van runs even netted the only suspect Colaneri had been unable to identify. The suspect had been told about the Ohio trip from another thief.

"I heard about the party," the unidentified suspect said to Colaneri. "Can I drive a car to Ohio? I can use the money."

"Sure," Colaneri said, and then: "Oh, we're going to have a great time in Ohio!"

In came the cops.

"What about the party?" one of the thieves asked as he was being led away.

Colaneri was pleased with the Bimini sting. Still, he couldn't help but feel that he might have done better if Maher were around. *Kevin could have collected a lot of money on this one,* Colaneri mused.

MAHER SPENT THE AUTUMN OF 1990 IN CONSTANT EMOTIONAL postmortems. He felt lost. Adrift. Then one day at the end of October, the phone rang.

"You want to have lunch?" a voice asked.

It was Jim Doherty.

The timing was perfect. Doherty's fatherly presence always had an uplifting effect on Maher.

"Sure," Maher said. "I've got a lot to tell you."

"And *I've* got a lot to tell *you,*" Doherty said.

The previous March, Doherty had returned to law enforcement as an investigator at the Suffolk County district attorney's office.

The next day, Maher and Doherty met for lunch at a diner in Queens.

"How'd you wind up in Suffolk County?" Maher asked.

Doherty explained that after ten frustrating years as a federal investigator, and feeling decidedly not well suited for the Defense Department's procedures, he heard about a test being given by the Suffolk County DA's office for the position of investigator.

"I did great on the written exam," Doherty related. "But then they told me I had to have a *physical* exam. So I go in and see the doctor and the doctor says, 'You're sixty pounds overweight. We're gonna have to fail you. You won't be qualified when we call you.' "

"*You* should've called *me*," Maher said with a laugh. "I know a guy who would have taken the physical for you."

Doherty shook his head and then continued the story.

"Anyway, I knew it was going to be a while before they staffed the position, so I figured I had plenty of time to lose the weight."

"How much did you weigh?" Maher wanted to know.

"Two hundred and seventy pounds," Doherty reluctantly responded.

"Two hundred and seventy pounds!" Maher howled with laughter.

"Hey," Doherty said, frowning. "It's not *that* funny."

When Maher got his laughter under control, Doherty picked up the story.

"Eight months later, I was called in for another physical. Guess what I weighed?"

"What?"

"Two hundred and twelve pounds."

"You lost fifty-eight pounds in *eight months?*" Maher reacted.

"Yep," Doherty said. "So then the doctor says, 'You pass.' And I say, 'Are you *sure* I pass?' And the doctor says, 'Yeah. You pass.' So I say to the doctor, 'Do you know where I'm going now?' And the doctor asks, 'Where?' "

Doherty smiled at Maher for a few seconds.

"Where?" Maher pressed, taking the bait. "Where did you go?"

"I went to the Pancake House," Doherty responded. "I had

three fried eggs, orange juice, toast, a stack of pancakes, sausage, *and* bacon."

Maher and Doherty had a good laugh.

"So," Doherty asked, "what's been happening with you? You still doing the same shit?"

Two hours and three cocktails later, Maher finally wound down.

"Now I'm back living in New Jersey," Maher said, then added, "I'm fucked up."

Doherty reassured Maher. "It'll all work out."

"Yeah," Maher said with a sigh. "I guess it will. I'm looking for a job."

"Now that I'm back in the business," Doherty said, "if you hear of anything out my way, give me a call."

"I don't mean *that* kind of job," Maher countered. "I'm not doing the CI thing anymore. I'm looking for a *real* job."

A real job was the best thing for Maher, and Doherty knew it. On the other hand, Doherty also knew that Maher seemed incapable of steering clear of trouble. Sometimes cases just seemed to drop into Maher's lap.

"I hope you find a good job," Doherty said. "I'll check around out here if you want me to."

"That'd be great, Jimmy," Maher said.

Jimmy. Until then, Maher had always been more formal. *Sergeant Doherty.* But on this day in late October 1990, Maher was not a CI and Doherty was not a cop. They were, simply, friends.

IN NOVEMBER 1990, A MINOR MIRACLE OCCURRED. MAHER'S LAWSUIT against New Jersey Transit embodied two different complaints— one that charged the railroad and a codefendant, Asplum Tree Company, with the unsafe use of a toxic weed killer, and the other that pertained to Maher's wrongful termination. While the wrongful termination segment of the suit was bogged down, the chemical part of the suit had proceeded. A judge ordered New Jersey Transit and Asplum Tree Company to compensate Maher for his pain and suffering. Each company was to pay Maher $25,000. So, although Maher's $2 million wrongful termination suit was still pending and would be undecided for some time, he had money again: $50,000—or, more accurately,

$33,000, after Maher's attorney deducted $17,000, which represented the standard one-third contingency fee.

Immediately after the settlement, the possibility of a "real job" arose when one of Maher's childhood buddies, Mark Pasquale, mentioned he needed a partner for a small car dealership in Queens, at 40–45 Crescent Street in Long Island City. It was called M.A.P. Auto Sales, which stood for Mark Anthony Pasquale. Maher invested $10,000 in M.A.P. and, to be close to his new venture, moved from New Jersey to Astoria, Queens, renting an apartment at the corner of 49th Street and 20th Avenue.

Ownership in M.A.P. made Maher feel anchored. Now with a business to build, Maher found a purpose. He once again vowed he would stop snorting coke.

The first time Maher had tried to stop, he really believed he could do it. But now, the *second* time would be more difficult because he knew from experience he couldn't. But while Maher had made a conscious decision to break the chains of his coke habit, there was more than willpower alone to keep him clean. Maher was a businessman now, and he had more important things to do with his money. Maher needed the balance of the money from the lawsuit—which was now $15,000—to buy cars at auction. The cars would be placed into inventory, and once M.A.P. sold the cars, Maher got his money back plus a profit.

Unlike Maher the informant, Maher the part owner in M.A.P. Auto Sales stayed off coke and kept to himself. It was the most sedate period Maher ever spent. The only excitement in his life was the once-a-day sighting of Bill Cosby. Cosby—who taped his television comedy *The Cosby Show* at Kaufman Astoria Studios in Queens, would head back to Manhattan at the end of the day via the 59th Street Bridge. Since the main entrance to the bridge was a street that passed in front of M.A.P. Auto Sales, Maher and Pasquale would watch for Cosby each evening and wave when he rode by.

AT THE MANHATTAN DA'S OFFICE, MAHER'S RETIREMENT DID NOT GO unnoticed, which is why Harkins called Doherty one day in early 1991.

"What the hell ever happened to Kevin?" Harkins asked.

"He's still around," Doherty said.

"He's been awfully quiet lately," Harkins noted.

Doherty laughed. "Yeah. But you know Kevin. Something's bound to happen sooner or later."

Just then, Maher was listening to the radio when he heard about a daring, broad-daylight holdup. A gang of thugs had ambushed a jeweler on a Midtown street, pumping twelve rounds into his Range Rover. They killed the jeweler and made off with $250,000 in precious gems.

A couple of hours after the news broadcast, one of Maher's associates in the car business (we'll call him Sammy), who was a used car broker, walked into M.A.P. Auto Sales. Sammy had an expression of horror on his face.

"Sammy!" Maher said when he saw him. "Are you okay?"

Sammy nervously looked around to make sure no one was listening.

"I just saw a guy get killed," Sammy said, his voice cracking.

"Who?" Maher asked.

"A jeweler," Sammy croaked. "A bunch of Chinese guys killed him. It's all over the news."

Maher felt a rush. He was back in the game.

Chapter 18

Maher took Sammy into the office and calmed him down.

"Okay, Sammy," Maher said. "Tell me what happened."

"I was driving a cab," Sammy began, "right behind a Range Rover. This BMW pulled up and these Chinese guys in the BMW started shooting."

"You get a look at their faces?"

"Yeah."

Maher went to a phone and called Harkins.

"You know the robbery in Manhattan," Maher said, "the one that happened a few hours ago?"

"Robberies happen every few minutes," Harkins noted.

"The one where the jeweler was killed and they got away with two hundred and fifty thousand?"

"Yeah," Harkins said, now interested.

"Well, I've got a witness."

"Can I talk to him?" Harkins asked.

"I don't know if he'll talk to you," Maher said. "But I'll see what I can do."

Sammy adamantly refused to speak with the police. Maher called Harkins again.

"He won't come forward," Maher reported to Harkins. "He's scared. I'll have to work on him."

Maher convinced Sammy to call 577-TIPS, the confidential hot line set up by police.

"You don't have to give them your name," Maher explained. "They'll assign you a number."

Sammy hesitated.

"You'll get a thousand dollars, Sammy," Maher said. "Couldn't you use a thousand dollars?"

But when Maher told Harkins that Sammy had agreed to make the call, Harkins said that the detective who was handling the case was against it.

"He feels that if Sammy calls, it might taint his testimony. The detective wants to handle Sammy himself."

Maher got Sammy to agree to meet with the detective. At the precinct, Sammy wondered aloud why he couldn't just call.

"That way," Sammy said, "I get paid and I don't have to give my name."

The detective promised Sammy he would make sure he was paid for his help and that his name would remain secret. Maher had to promise Sammy he would stick with him through the process. So Maher walked Sammy through the entire ordeal, from picking a suspect out of a photo lineup to Sammy testifying before the grand jury. The suspect was indicted.

But Sammy wasn't paid.

"I don't want to taint your testimony," the detective said.

Sammy was furious. And Maher was disgusted.

"If he lied to me about money," Sammy speculated, "he could be lying to me about keeping my name out of it. No way I'm testifying at the trial."

"I don't blame you," Maher said. "Fuck them."

Considering that Sammy was the sole witness to a vicious crime, it might have been prudent to make the promised payment. Instead, it looked like the prosecution had lost a witness. Or, more to the point, they *had* lost a witness, unless Maher could turn Sammy back around, which meant Maher now wielded power in a major homicide case. This time Maher would ask for money. And it would be a hell of a lot more than the $1,000 that would have made Sammy happy.

At the end of March 1991 Maher was in a strip joint in Queens called Pussycat. Just like in a Western, two men walked in. One of them gave Maher a challenging look. Although Maher didn't recognize him at that point, the man was the owner of another bar with whom Maher had gotten into a fistfight several months earlier.

"What the fuck are you looking at?" Maher slurred.

A bouncer intervened. The man glared at Maher and then walked out.

A few minutes after the man left, Maher remembered where he had seen him before.

"I know who that prick is," Maher told the bartender. "He owns a bar down the street."

Maher shoved off the bar stool, sauntered outside, climbed into his Porsche, and drove off to the other bar. Just as he was making a U-turn in front of the place, a Chevy S-10 Blazer rammed the driver's door of the Porsche. The window shattered, and hundreds of small chunks of glass rained inside the car. Maher glared at the driver of the Blazer and realized that the collision had not been an accident. The driver of the Blazer was the owner of the bar.

Maher looked through the windshield and, to his horror, saw another Blazer, this one a full-size model with monster wheels. The monster Blazer pulled in front of the Porsche. Now the Porsche could not go forward, so Maher reached for the shifter and pushed it from drive toward reverse. But the shifter wouldn't go past neutral. A piece of glass had lodged in the shifting mechanism.

As Maher was trying to force the shifter into reverse, one of the bar owner's cronies jumped from the S-10 Blazer and ran to the passenger side of the Porsche. The crony tried to open the Porsche's door but it was locked. Instinctively, Maher reached to his waistband for his gun. But instead of a gun, his hand wrapped around a beeper. Maher ripped the beeper from his waist and, holding it like he would a weapon, pointed it at the crony. Since it was dark—and since Maher kept his hand in constant motion—it was a convincing act. The panicked crony ran.

"He's got a gun!" the crony screamed.

At that point, another one of the bar owner's cronies stepped from the darkness and fired two shots at the Porsche. The bullets pierced the front left fender. *Maybe pulling a beeper wasn't such a good idea*, Maher thought. Instead of waiting for more shots in his direction, Maher "power-braked" the Porsche—held his foot on the brake while jamming the accelerator to the floor—then slid his foot off the brake. The Porsche catapulted head-on into the front of the monster Blazer and began pushing it backward.

Another two shots. One round hit the rim of the rear left tire, and one round hit the tire itself, which instantly deflated. Maher kept his foot on the accelerator and turned the steering wheel until he cleared the front of the Blazer. The Porsche screeched away, the two Blazers in pursuit.

Maher sped toward the upper level of the 59th Street Bridge, taking a sharp right turn onto the ramp. But the Porsche was traveling too fast, and it spun out. The monster Blazer hit the front of the Porsche—which was now facing the wrong way on the ramp—springing the hood. Since the mangled hood was blocking his vision, Maher stuck his head out the window and hit the accelerator, speeding back down the entrance ramp in the wrong direction. Even with a flat tire, he managed to lose the two Blazers.

The Porsche, Maher's financial safety net, was totaled. In April Maher received a check for $39,000 from the insurance company, well below market value. Maher bought a $34,000 1991 Corvette and pocketed $5,000, which he added to the pool of funds he used to buy cars at auction for M.A.P. Auto Sales.

M.A.P. was doing well. But then something happened that Maher could never have anticipated. New York City began repairs on the 59th Street Bridge. Traffic was diverted away from the entrance to the bridge, and the street that ran past M.A.P. no longer had a steady flow of potential customers. Before long, the area around the car dealership looked so much like a ghost town you could almost see tumbleweed blowing down the street.

"They'll finish the construction soon," Maher assured his partner, Mark Pasquale.

They didn't. By August 1991, plummeting sales forced M.A.P. to fold. Maher and Pasquale wholesaled the remaining cars on the lot, each netting $15,000.

As Maher and Pasquale were closing out the operation, a New York City cop stopped by M.A.P. The cop told Maher he had to find a home for his dog. Maher offered to take the dog, an eighteen-month-old German shepherd named Zena.

Maher and Zena moved back to New Jersey.

In February 1992 Maher spent an afternoon drinking with a friend on Long Island, then headed back to Jersey. As usual, Maher exceeded the speed limit by about forty miles an hour. He was pulled over and given a Breathalyzer test by a state trooper using a portable device. Maher registered .09. (A reading of 1.0 indicates intoxication.)

"I'm taking you in," the trooper said.

Maher protested. "I blew point zero nine."

"I'm taking you in," the trooper said again.

At the State Police barracks, the Breathalyzer showed 1.0, indicating Maher was legally drunk. Maher was charged with DWI—driving while intoxicated. He was held overnight and then released.

As serious as a DWI was, Maher wasn't worried. He had been charged in Suffolk County. And his friend Jim Doherty worked in the Suffolk County district attorney's office. When Maher got back home to New Jersey, he called Doherty.

"Of all the fucking crimes you could have committed," Doherty bristled, "you committed the *worst* one."

Doherty went on to say that because of MADD (Mothers Against Drunk Driving) and "all these other antidrinking groups" there was pressure from the top not to let anybody plead out on a DWI.

"I'll do the best I can for you." Doherty said with a sigh, adding, "I'll tell somebody all you did for me in the past. But you've got a tough road here."

When Maher hung up the receiver, he felt nervous. Doherty didn't sound hopeful. And Maher knew that he could get up to one year in jail for a DWI conviction.

The heart is a resilient muscle, a fact Maher proved when he walked into the Z Bar in Greenwich Village in March 1992. As Maher surveyed the room, his eyes locked on a pretty brunette.

He walked over to her and started a conversation. Her name was Mary Catherine Williams.

"I'm an actress," Mary Catherine said. "I've been in three movies." She rattled off the titles of the films. "You see any of them?"

"All of them," Maher lied. "They were great."

"I have an idea for a screenplay," she said.

"What is it?"

"It's about my life. About a homecoming queen from North Carolina."

"You were a homecoming queen?"

"Yes. You think it will make a good movie?"

"Absolutely," Maher reacted.

"For now my father is sending me money," Mary Catherine said. "But as soon as I get my screenplay written, I'm going to pay him back. Of course, I'm up for a lot of parts in big movies. All I need is one break. Just one good part. You know what I mean?"

Maher nodded.

"What do you do?" Mary Catherine asked.

"It's a long story."

"You in a hurry to go somewhere?"

Maher laughed. "No."

A couple hours later, they left the bar. Maher dropped her off at her apartment and soared to New Jersey. The next day Maher called her, and they met again that night.

"You want a hit?" Mary Catherine asked as she pulled out a small amount of coke.

Maher shrugged. He hadn't done any coke for months. One hit was no big deal.

They went to Maher's apartment, sniffed coke, and made love. The next morning, Maher woke up and looked beside him at Mary Catherine. She was so beautiful, so angelic. This wasn't Beth, the wife of a Mafia hit man. This wasn't Beverly, a coke whore. This was different.

For the next week, Maher and Mary Catherine were inseparable. They talked for hours, mostly about dreams.

"I'm going to turn my idea into a movie and be rich and famous," Mary Catherine would say.

"I'm going to win my lawsuit against the railroad and get two million dollars," Maher would say.

WHILE MAHER WAS ROMANCING MARY CATHERINE, DOHERTY HAD BEEN dealing with Maher's DWI problem. He called Harkins and explained the fix Maher had gotten himself into. But Maher had beaten Doherty to it. He had already spoken to Harkins.

"We've got a problem here, Jim," Harkins said. "Kevin, as usual, has stumbled onto something. He's got a guy who was a witness to a Chinese gang robbery, and the witness is the only one who can identify the robbers. Kevin is the only one who knows the whereabouts of the witness. The witness is scared, but Kevin says he can deliver him."

It was a moral dilemma. Squash a DWI. Or let a murderer go free.

"Look at it this way," Doherty pointed out. "Kevin swears he blew a zero point nine on the portable Breathalyzer. And he blew a one point zero at the station. That's right on the edge."

Harkins laughed: "That's just like Kevin. Right on the edge."

"Tommy," Doherty said, "can you write a letter or get the DA to write a letter about what Kevin has done for the Manhattan DA's office?"

Harkins sighed. "I wish this wasn't a Dee Wee."

"Yeah," Doherty agreed. "Me, too."

Harkins spoke with Manhattan assistant district attorney Deborah Gelb about writing a letter to the Suffolk County DA's office. She agreed to do it.

On April 10, 1992, Gelb sent a two-page memo to Robert Creighton, chief investigator for the Suffolk County district attorney's office. After introducing herself and explaining the relationship between Maher and the Manhattan DA's office, Gelb wrote:

> He has had a seventeen year special rapport and record of cooperation with one of our Senior Detectives, Thomas Harkins, which began in 1975 with our Detective and a Senior Investigator on your staff, who was Supervisor of Detectives then, James Doherty.
>
> Kevin's history of cooperation is remarkable in that

only on the initial contact with him did he request any help from us back in 1975. Since then and only through his direct involvement were we able to make arrests, prevent serious injuries or death and obtain convictions in the following types of cases:

Gelb listed four cases on which Maher had aided the Manhattan DA's office. Then, noting that Maher's actions were "at great personal risk to himself and owing nothing to this office," she concluded by writing:

Kevin has a matter pending in your jurisdiction. . . . The foregoing information is provided to you for the purpose of assisting you and the Court in determining the ultimate disposition of the pending case and I hope you and the court will take it into consideration.

Courtesy copies of the letter went to Harkins and Doherty.

As a result of the intervention by the Manhattan DA's office, Maher was allowed to plead the DWI down to a misdemeanor. He was fined $275, lost his driver's license for ninety days, and was required to attend Alcoholics Anonymous meetings.

Appreciative of Harkins's effort, Maher did everything he could to convince Sammy to testify at the trial. But Sammy steadfastly refused. The case against the Chinese gang charged with the jeweler's homicide was dismissed.

MAY AND JUNE WERE HAPPY MONTHS FOR MAHER. HIS RELATIONSHIP with Mary Catherine had resonance. But there was something mitigating against a happy ending.

Cocaine.

By July, Maher was doing almost as much coke as he used to do during the Uribe days. And Mary Catherine's consumption of the insidious white crystal shocked even Maher. She would snort twenty-four hours a day for three days, then sleep motionless for an entire day and night. When she woke up, she'd start the process again.

"Mary Catherine," Maher said one night as concern about her condition grew, "you're doing too much coke."

"No, I'm not," she protested.

"Yes, you are," Maher insisted. "We *both* are."

The sad and predictable scenario of drug abuse began to play out. Mary Catherine—who had been living with a roommate in an East Side apartment—was told by the roommate that she had to leave.

Maher called the roommate, hoping to change her mind.

"Look," the roommate said, "I've been putting up with her shit for a year. I can't deal with it anymore."

The roommate explained that every time it seemed like Mary Catherine had gotten herself under control she would go on another coke binge.

Maher knew the pattern well. He recognized it in his own life. He finally understood what thousands of "occasional" coke users had found out much too late: Snorting coke could never be an occasional indulgence. It was powerful stuff. As destructive as a bullet. As addictive as heroin.

Maher summoned up all his inner strength. *I ain't doing that shit no more,* he told himself. Twice he had stopped for months. This time he told himself he would stop for good. And he would help Mary Catherine stop as well.

Maher asked Mary Catherine if she wanted to move in with him while she looked for a place to live, but she said she had already rented an apartment.

"I met this guy," Mary Catherine said. "Joe Leo. He owns some apartments on Ninth Street."

Maher didn't like the sound of it. And when he saw Mary Catherine's new apartment a few nights later, he didn't like the look of it.

At one time, 439 East 9th Street housed two retail stores. But the owner of the building had converted the two storefronts into living spaces. The narrow front door of the building led into a hallway. There were two interior doors downstairs, one on either side of the hall, which opened into two adjacent storefronts. At the top of a set of stairs was a third apartment.

Mary Catherine's apartment was the one on the left. The single window on the street was blocked by a steel gate. There was no bathtub or shower, just a sink and a toilet. It was stark and cold. The only flicker of warmth in the place was provided by a candle Mary Catherine had placed on a tin TV stand. Next to the candle was a picture of Jesus. Rosary beads were draped over the frame. There was a small pillow in front of the TV stand, where Mary Catherine would kneel and pray.

"It's just until I get the screenplay done," Mary Catherine said. "Or until I get a big part."

Maher looked around the room. There was a crack vial on the coffee table. And a crack pipe.

"You're not smoking crack?" Maher said with a gasp.

"Sometimes," she said matter-of-factly. "It's cheaper than coke."

"Don't do that shit!" Maher shouted.

"Don't tell me what to fucking do!" she screamed. "If you're going to tell me what to do, just get out!"

Maher turned and left the apartment. As he headed for his car, he crossed 10th Street, which was crawling with whores. *A stroll. Mary Catherine lives a block away from a hooker stroll.* Maher felt a wave of nausea. Drugs. Whores.

Déjà vu.

ALTHOUGH PREOCCUPIED WITH MARY CATHERINE'S CONDITION, MAHER had another problem: He had run out of money. So Maher sold his Corvette for $22,000, bought a 1966 Cadillac Coupe De Ville with 18,000 miles on it for $7,000, and netted $15,000 out of the transaction. Maher wouldn't have had to sell his Corvette if he could have held out another month. In mid-July 1992 Maher's wrongful termination lawsuit against New Jersey finally found its way onto a court calendar. Following two days of court proceedings, New Jersey Transit offered a settlement: $85,000 in back pay, but no punitive damages. Although Maher's attorney was willing to continue, Maher was not. Beth had obtained a judgment for half of any punitive damages awarded, and Maher didn't want Richard O'Rourke to enjoy any of the money from the lawsuit. With back pay, Beth was entitled to only a small amount: $2,500.

After deducting $2,500 for Beth and $23,000 for the attorney, Maher wound up with a little under $60,000. The first thing he did when he got his check was drive to the Harbor Hoboken and talk to a counselor about Mary Catherine. Maher said he wanted to place her in the twenty-eight-day program.

"Does she have insurance?" was the first thing out of the counselor's mouth.

"No," Maher replied.

"Then the payment will have to be in cash or certified check. Twenty-two thousand. In advance."

The Harbor wasn't a charity, it was a business run by businessmen.

The counselor explained that The Harbor wouldn't accept Mary Catherine until she had undergone a complete physical. Maher would first have to check Mary Catherine into a hospital. The Harbor would pick her up from there.

Maher raced through the Lincoln Tunnel and headed to Mary Catherine's apartment. She had "big eyes." ("Big eyes," a street term, referred to the bulging eyeballs, dilated pupils, and permanently raised eyebrows of someone on a cocaine high.)

"Let's go," Maher said.

"Go where?" Mary Catherine asked.

"To a hospital."

Mary Catherine frowned. "Why? Are you sick?"

"No. *You* are."

"What are you talking about?" Mary Catherine asked, sneering.

"I'm going to put you in a drug program called The Harbor. Twenty-eight days."

Mary Catherine laughed derisively. "Oh, yeah? And who's paying for this?"

"*I* am," Maher said.

Tears formed in Mary Catherine's eyes. Knowing he had struck an emotional chord, Maher now sought to seal the deal with a professional incentive.

"Look," Maher said, "no one's going to give you a part in a movie when you're in this kind of shape. And you can't write a screenplay when you're crazed out of your mind. You go to The Harbor. Sober up."

Mary Catherine walked over and hugged Maher tightly.

"Okay, Kevin. I'll go."

Maher rocked her in his arms for a long time. Then:

"All right, Mary Catherine, pack your stuff."

"Not today, Kevin. Tomorrow."

Maher knew that, for an addict, tomorrow never comes.

"No," Maher insisted. "You come with me right now."

"I can't, Kevin. I have to tell people I'm going away or something. I can't just disappear."

"You come with me right now!" Maher said firmly.

"Tomorrow, Kevin. Just let me get myself together, okay? Tomorrow. I promise."

Maher drew in a breath. Mary Catherine smiled.

"I'm meeting this screenwriter later on. Then I'll come back here and get a good night's sleep. Tomorrow we'll go to the hospital. Okay?"

Reluctantly, Maher left.

When Maher returned the following day, Mary Catherine had "big eyes" again. Naturally, she said she couldn't go to the hospital right then. There were things to do.

"Tomorrow, Kevin. I'll go with you tomorrow."

Maher spotted a crack pipe on the floor next to the couch. It enraged him. He walked over and crushed the glass stem with his foot.

"Who do you think you are?" she screamed.

"I'm somebody who fucking cares about you!" Maher shouted back.

"Who the fuck asked you to care about me?" Mary Catherine bellowed.

Maher walked over to the coffee table and picked up an address book. It was open to a page filled with names. John. Barry. Lou. Vinny. First names only. Never a last name. Maher knew all too well what that meant.

"You turning tricks now to support your fucking habit?"

Mary Catherine stomped over and ripped the address book out of his hands.

"What I do is *my* fucking business. Now get out of here!"

Maher walked out of the apartment. It was September, and a hint of winter was in the air. He stood on 9th Street and closed his eyes, then spun back toward the apartment and started for the door. Something stopped him. And then, as much as it hurt him to do it, he walked away.

Over the next few days, Maher came to terms with himself. With Beth, he had felt obligation. With Beverly, lust. But what he had once felt for Mary Catherine had been free of obligation, seasoned, not permeated, with desire. But the Mary Catherine of 439 East 9th Street was not the Mary Catherine of those first days and weeks. He couldn't love Mary Catherine blindly; the emotional cost was too high. For he didn't just see Mary Catherine's decline when he looked at her, he saw something even more terrifying: his own precarious hold on sobriety. When he faced Mary Catherine soul to soul, it was like looking in a mirror. So, just as he was learning to love himself again, he would learn to love Mary Catherine in a different way. Not as an object but as a person. Not as a lover but as a friend.

Over the next few weeks, Maher stopped by 9th Street often. He would bring Mary Catherine food and small presents. Sometimes she was sober. Maher hung on to the memories of those meetings. Sometimes she was incoherent from the crack and Maher would hold her, talk her down.

When Mary Catherine wasn't home, Maher would stop in to see Joe Leo, the owner of the building. Leo—who had inherited the building from his father—lived in an upstairs apartment. He was about forty, tall and lanky with dark brown hair. His favorite saying—actually, his only saying—was "there's nothing like sex, drugs, and rock and roll."

Sometimes, when Maher left the 9th Street storefront and headed for his car, he would stop for a moment and watch the hookers parading on the corner of 10th Street. Mary Catherine, whom Maher had once loved, still did love, had become a whore. She now openly entertained johns at her home. It cut Maher each time he saw some man shuffle into the storefront. But what could he do?

There was a pimp, of course. Peter. A stocky black man with a pleasing disposition and a slick patter. Peter's presence made the hookers feel safe. And the hookers made Peter a lot of money.

One afternoon in September 1992, Maher was in the apartment of Alicia Wittington, an exotic dancer who lived across the hall from Mary Catherine. Maher heard a scream. He recognized the tortured howl as Mary Catherine's.

Maher ran into the hall. He pounded on Mary Catherine's door. There was silence.

"Open the door!" Maher yelled, pounding harder.

More silence.

Maher began kicking the door: "Open the fucking door!"

Finally, the door cracked open a few inches. A man peeked

out. His eyes, which were magnified by a pair of thick glasses, were cold and emotionless.

"What the fuck's going on?" Maher said. Maher recognized the man. He was one of Mary Catherine's regular johns. Although the man was large and hulking, he was strangely withdrawn. Maher always referred to him as "the nerd."

"She took a hit of crack, that's all," the nerd said.

Maher peered into the apartment. He could see the entire space, but he couldn't see Mary Catherine.

"Where's Mary?" Maher yelled. "Where's Mary?"

"Calm down," the nerd said.

Maher grabbed the nerd's shirt and shouldered his way into the apartment. Sitting behind the door was Mary Catherine. She was nude from the waist down. Her face was white, and her lips were purple. She was trying to say something but couldn't speak.

"I told you," the nerd said. "She just took a big hit of crack."

Maher studied the nerd for a beat, then looked at Mary Catherine. There was terror in her eyes. Something wasn't right.

"He choked me," Mary Catherine squeaked. "He tried to kill me."

Maher saw a flash of red. He drew back his fist and hit the nerd as hard as he had ever hit anyone before. The nerd's glasses flew off his face, and he crumpled to his knees.

"You sick motherfucker!" Maher screamed. He grabbed the nerd by his hair and dragged him to the front door, walking him along on his knees. Then Maher pushed open the door and kicked him out. The nerd tumbled onto the sidewalk.

Maher returned to Mary Catherine's apartment and made her drink a glass of water. As soon as she regained full consciousness, she started looking around.

"Where's my stem?" Mary Catherine moaned.

Maher spotted the stem, or crack pipe. He picked it up.

"Here's your fucking stem," Maher said.

He threw the pipe on the floor and crushed it. This sent Mary Catherine into a frenzy. She began pounding on Maher's chest.

"Get out! Get the fuck out! Leave me alone!"

"Hey! I just saved your fucking life!"

"Fuck you! Get out of my apartment!"

Maher walked over and ripped a mirror off the wall. He held it in front of Mary Catherine's face.

"Look at yourself! Look!"

Mary Catherine turned away. Maher stared at her for a moment, shook his head, and then returned to Alicia's apartment.

"What's going on?"

"She had a fight with a john. I threw him out."

The intercom buzzer went off. Maher bounded into the hall. The nerd was standing outside. Figuring that the nerd had gone somewhere and picked up a gun or a knife and was coming back to seek revenge, Maher rushed at the door like a charging bull. In seconds, he had the nerd by the shirt.

"No, no, no," the nerd whined. "Please don't hit me."

"What the fuck do you want?"

"My glasses."

Maher scowled.

"Please," the nerd begged. "I've got to drive back to Long Island."

Maher turned to go to Mary Catherine's apartment. Holding the glasses, Mary Catherine stepped into the hall. She walked around Maher and went outside with the nerd. Then they started down the street.

"You're not going with *him*, are you?" Maher shouted. "He just tried to fucking choke you to death."

Mary Catherine didn't respond. She and the nerd disappeared around the corner. But Maher wasn't surprised. He knew why Mary Catherine followed the nerd. The nerd had something she was willing to be strangled for.

Crack.

THE THIRD DAY AFTER THE INCIDENT, MAHER FOUND MARY CATHERINE sober. She was standing outside, engaged in a lively discussion with Peter the pimp.

"You come live with me at my house in Westchester. I'll clean you up, baby. There are lots of rich fuckers in Westchester. We'll make a fortune. We'll hire a screenwriter. I'll be your manager."

Peter bantered away.

Maher and Mary Catherine walked into her apartment, and Maher renewed his offer to pay for her stay at The Harbor.

"It's only a matter of time," Maher pleaded. "If I hadn't been there, you'd be dead. Now let's go. Now."

"Tomorrow," Mary Catherine said, her sweet smile softening her drug-ravaged features. "I'll go there tomorrow."

Maher thought about calling Mary Catherine's parents. *But who would they believe? Me? Or their daughter?*

Maher showed up again at 439 East 9th Street the next day. He was going to grab Mary Catherine and say, *You said you would come with me tomorrow. This is tomorrow.*

But Mary Catherine wasn't home. Alicia had no idea where she was. Neither did Leo. Another day went by. And another. No Mary Catherine.

"Oh, she probably hooked up with some rich guy," Leo said. "Don't worry, she'll be back."

But two weeks later, she still wasn't there. Maher was frantic. And now Leo had a different take on the situation.

"She probably ran off," Leo said. And then: "I got somebody to rent the apartment."

"You can't do that, Joe," Maher said.

"Look, Kevin," Leo countered. "I been through this shit before. They just up and leave. She ain't coming back. And I got to make a living."

"But she left all her stuff."

"They always do," Leo said.

"You can't just throw her stuff in the street."

"What do you want me to do?"

"I'll take it," Maher said. "When she shows up, tell her I have her stuff."

Maher filled two large leaf bags with Mary Catherine's clothes and personal belongings. As he stuffed the things into the plastic bags, he felt numb. Beth. Beverly. And now, Mary Catherine.

MARY CATHERINE'S DISAPPEARANCE SENT MAHER INTO A DEPRESSION. HE stayed home virtually around the clock. *What if she calls? I need to be here.* Every time the phone would ring, Maher's stomach churned. But it was never Mary Catherine. October turned to November. Still no Mary Catherine.

By December he was out of money again. *Where the fuck did it all go?* Maher wondered. To live, he traded the mint-condition 1966 Cadillac for $4,000 in cash and a 1984 Nissan. By the end of the month, the $4,000 was gone, too, and Maher went on welfare. It was an embarrassing ordeal. The welfare office was in the same building as the Carlstadt police headquarters, and the "welfare couch," as Maher called it, was in a hall area through which Carlstadt police officers had to pass to reach the detective bureau. Once in a while, Colaneri would walk through. Maher didn't want Colaneri to see him. Whenever he saw Colaneri approaching, Maher would hide around a corner until Colaneri was gone.

On Christmas Eve 1992 Maher stared out his window and watched as couples strolled under sparkling Christmas lights. Everyone seemed happy except him. He had no one to love. No family to turn to. His father was dead. His mother had moved to California the previous summer. And he was estranged from his sister. Suddenly his mind flashed with disjointed images and emotions.

Poor little Harold.

Poor Alice and Marcia.

I lost Beth.

I cheated on Beth. If I was a good husband she wouldn't have gone to someone else.

I miss my son, Bobby.

Beverly hurt me so much. How could we hurt each other like that?

Mary Catherine is missing.

At 3:00 A.M., Maher walked into the bathroom and stared at himself in the mirror. *I look like shit.* He reeled with self-hatred. *All the bad things that happened in my life I did to myself. I fucked up.*

Maher stumbled into the bedroom and retrieved his Smith & Wesson 9mm. He returned to the bathroom and climbed into the bathtub. *This way,* he thought as he leaned back against the cold porcelain, *I won't mess up the floor. The blood will run down the drain.*

Maher put the barrel of the gun in his mouth. Then he closed his eyes, curled his finger around the trigger, and slowly began to squeeze.

Chapter 19

MAHER FELT THE TRIGGER BEGIN TO YIELD AGAINST THE PRESSURE OF HIS finger. Since the Smith & Wesson was a double-action weapon, the trigger mechanism would go through *two* steps before firing. First the hammer would cock, and then, as the trigger passed the halfway point, the hammer would drop against the round.

Maher held his breath and pressed the trigger harder. The hammer was positioned for the deadly click.

Maher continued applying pressure, and he braced for the bullet. Suddenly his eyes popped open as the distant memory of his Catholic upbringing moved to the forefront of his psyche. *I could go to hell for doing this!*

Maher placed the gun on the floor and climbed out of the tub. He collected a phone book and a cordless phone and got back into the tub. He looked up the number of St. Joseph's Church in East Rutherford, New Jersey, and dialed. After several rings a man answered.

"St. Joseph's. Father Daly speaking."

Father Daly sounded sleepy. Of course, it *was* three o'clock in the morning.

"Sorry to wake you, Father."

"That's quite all right."

After a long pause, Maher said: "Father Daly, my name is Kevin."

"My name is Kevin, too," Father Daly responded.

"I'm depressed," Maher stated somberly. "And I'm contemplating ending my life."

293

"Nothing could be that bad."

"Father, you have no idea."

Father Daly waited for Maher to continue. *Now what do I say?* Maher wondered.

"I want you to hear my confession before I do this," Maher finally said. "I don't want to go to hell."

"If you kill yourself," Father Daly said sternly, "you *will* go to hell."

"Unless I get absolution."

Father Daly laughed. "So you're trying to get absolution *before* you commit the sin?"

Maher, ever the player, was trying to work a deal with the priest. As if the priest was a cop and God was a judge.

"It doesn't work that way, Kevin," Father Daly said. "Besides, there *is* no absolution for suicide."

"You're sure there's nothing we can do here?" Maher asked.

"I'm sure," Father Daly responded. "If you commit suicide, you won't be able to be buried in a Catholic cemetery."

Maher tossed Father Daly's statement around in his mind. *I hadn't thought of that. So if I kill myself, where* would *I be buried?*

"You'll burn in hell," Father Daly added.

Neither of them spoke for at least a minute. Finally Father Daly said, "Kevin, why don't you tell me why you want to kill yourself."

"It's a long story, Father. My life is totally fucked up."

"I've got plenty of time, Kevin."

Three hours later—after the car chase, the FBI, the DEA, Uribe, Beth, Beverly, and the missing Mary Catherine—Father Daly probably wished there *was* an absolution for suicide. But his patience paid off. At the end of the telephone conversation, Maher promised Father Daly he wouldn't kill himself. Then Maher hung up the receiver and began to cry. *What am I going to do? I have to do something to turn my life around.*

EARLY IN JANUARY, MAHER WAS SITTING ON THE WELFARE COUCH, daydreaming. He didn't hear Colaneri's footsteps coming up the stairs.

"What the hell happened to you?" Colaneri asked when he saw Maher slouched outside the welfare office.

The last time Colaneri saw Maher, Maher was driving a $100,000 Porsche. He had a swagger about him then, the cocksure attitude of a winner. Now Maher looked defeated.

"I'm going through a hard time," Maher said.

"I can see that," Colaneri noted, then thought: *I've seen homeless people who looked less alone than he does.*

"Look," Colaneri said finally, "when you get done, stop into the office."

After picking up his welfare check for $75, Maher walked across the hall and spent an hour hanging out with Colaneri. The next day Maher was back again. And the next. It gave Maher a place to go, a reason to get out of bed in the morning. Once in a while, Colaneri would "loan" him $20. A month later, Colaneri invited Maher to come over to his house.

"My wife, Patti, will cook you a good meal," Colaneri said.

And so Maher became part of the Colaneri family. Patti's reaction, however, was mixed. At first she, too, was taken by Maher. But by February she grew suspicious of Maher's motives.

"I think he's using you," Patti said one night.

"Come on, Patti," Colaneri countered. "He's just a troubled kid."

"He's not a kid," Patti pointed out. "He's older than you are."

"By four months," Colaneri noted.

Yet in many ways Maher seemed much younger than Colaneri. Perhaps Maher's four years in prison—which robbed him of an adolescence—could account for the fact that part of him never grew up. As for Colaneri, maybe the presence of a wife and kids so early in his life forced him into an escalated process of maturity. Whatever the reasons, it was true. Colaneri, four months younger than Maher, was the *older* brother.

Eventually Patti warmed to Maher again and made an effort to understand him. She came to the conclusion that while he was jaded in some ways, in other ways he seemed almost innocent.

The more time Maher and Colaneri spent together, the more Colaneri felt comfortable playing the role of big brother.

"You shouldn't be doing coke," Colaneri said one day.

Maher laughed. "Coke?! What are you talking about? I don't do coke anymore."

Colaneri stared at Maher. Maher quickly diverted his eyes.

"You gonna lie to me now?" Colaneri asked. "I'm trying to help you, and you lie to me?"

"Sometimes I take a hit," Maher admitted.

"And where do you get the money to buy it?" Colaneri demanded.

"I get a gram sometimes. It only costs—"

"I didn't ask you what it costs," Colaneri cut in. "I asked you where you get the money."

Maher didn't respond.

"You use your welfare money to buy cocaine?" Colaneri pressed. "Or do you use the money I loan you?"

Maher took a deep breath.

"It's hard, Bobby. It's hard to stop."

"You want to be my friend?" Colaneri asked.

"Sure I do," Maher responded.

"Okay. Then stop that shit."

Maher knew that the pain of withdrawal could not possibly hurt more than losing Colaneri's friendship.

"Okay, Bobby. I'll stop."

And this time Maher felt certain he would succeed.

A few days later, Colaneri turned his attention to Maher's alcoholism.

"I'm not an alcoholic," Maher protested.

"Then why do you get drunk every time we go out?" Colaneri asked.

Maher had a million excuses. Colaneri listened to Maher's rationalizations, sitting patiently while Maher explained all the events in his life that made him drink the way he did. Prison. Beth. Beverly. Mary Catherine. Ultimately, Maher talked himself out.

"You through?" Colaneri asked.

Maher nodded.

"Good," Colaneri said. "Because everything you just told me is bullshit. You've got to stop making excuses and quit drinking so much."

From that day on, Maher drank less, especially whenever he was around Colaneri. Colaneri's faith in him had become more important than drugs.

And then there was Maher's temper. One day Maher was

driving and Colaneri was a passenger. A pickup truck darted in front of Maher, cutting him off. Infuriated, Maher blasted his horn and raced up beside the truck, screaming and making obscene gestures at the driver. Then Maher jammed his foot on the accelerator and sped away.

Colaneri glared at Maher.

"Kevin, you've got to stop that shit."

"He cut me off," Maher protested. "The dumb fuck just cut right in front of me."

"Oh, yeah? Well, let me tell you about a homicide from several years ago."

"What's that got to do with anything?" Maher asked, already calming down.

"December '85," Colaneri began, "I was paged at home around eleven o'clock at night. My partner, Mike Barbire, was working that night and he was called to the scene of a stabbing on Paterson Plank Road, near the entrance to Brendan Byrne Arena. A white male named Vasile had been knifed in the chest. You know how he wound up getting stabbed?"

"How?"

"I'll tell you how," Colaneri said. "Vasile was riding with a friend—they had just left the hockey game—and they were merging into traffic when a pickup truck cut them off."

Colaneri looked over his shoulder through Maher's rear window.

"Just like that truck back there cut you off," Colaneri noted.

Maher shrugged, not giving Colaneri anything.

Colaneri continued, "The driver of the car Vasile was in and the driver of the truck, who was a white male, exchanged words. Vasile gets out of the passenger seat and goes over to say something to the driver of the pickup. The driver stabs Vasile in the chest. But Vasile doesn't go down right away. He walks over and gets back in the passenger side of the car. The pickup truck takes off. Vasile's friend now sees that Vasile is bleeding profusely and drives up Washington Avenue to the Executive Motor Inn. That's when I arrived."

Colaneri paused, allowing the story to sink in.

"The blood was unbelievable," Colaneri added.

Maher and Colaneri rode along in silence for a long time.

"You catch the guy?" Maher finally asked.

"Vasile's friend couldn't remember the license plate number of the truck. He wasn't even sure what kind of truck it was. Could have been a Toyota, he said. Or a Chevy Blazer. The only thing he was certain about was that it was white. We even hypnotized the guy, hoping that would bring something out of his subconscious."

Colaneri shook his head.

"Nothing."

"You catch the fucking guy?" Maher asked again, his voice showing some impatience.

"It's the toughest kind of homicide to figure out," Colaneri said. "No connection between the people. And we don't even know for sure if the driver of the pickup was at the hockey game. He could have been down the road at the Barge Club."

Maher was taking all this in.

"You met Bobby Rehberg," Colaneri said. "Bergen County homicide squad."

Maher nodded. "Yeah. He worked on the Molese case."

"That's right. And Bobby worked with me on the Vasile homicide."

Colaneri took a deep breath. "We never solved it. The case is still open." Then: "A real shame. A young guy dying for no reason. And it all started over something like you just did."

Day after day, Colaneri counseled Maher. He continued to loan him money on occasion and even found Maher work—as a dispatcher for a local trucking company.

Maher felt indebted to Colaneri and often wished he could find a way to repay his kindness. In May 1993, Maher found the perfect opportunity.

Maher had gone into Manhattan one night and stopped by The Z Bar, the place where he had met Mary Catherine. Although he didn't hold out much hope—serendipity had only brought him trouble in the past—Maher half believed he would walk in and see Mary Catherine sitting at the bar.

Maher walked in. Mary Catherine was not there.

But Maher did see a familiar face, that of Lewis Klein. Klein had been a regular at 439 East 9th Street. He was a coke dealer.

"Hey, Kevin," Klein said. "Long time no see."

"Hello, Lewis," Maher said flatly.

Maher wasn't pleased to see Klein. Klein had been one of Mary Catherine's main suppliers of crack.

"What are you up to?" Maher asked, trying not to sound too interested.

"Same old thing," Klein said.

"Dealing?" Maher noted.

"Yeah," Klein responded.

"What about you?" Klein asked Maher.

"Nothing much. I'm living over in Jersey. Got a job with a trucking company."

"Jersey," Klein exclaimed. "I've been over to Jersey a lot. Fort Lee."

"What's going on in Fort Lee?" Maher wanted to know.

"I got customers over there," Klein said. "I do about five thousand a week in business in Jersey."

Maher looked at Klein with disdain. *And how many other Mary Catherines are you fucking up over there?* Maher knew that blaming a drug dealer was like blaming the gun if you shot yourself. Still, Maher felt Klein's crack cocaine was the reason he had lost Mary Catherine. Maher didn't care about the fact that if Klein hadn't sold crack to Mary Catherine, somebody else would have. *Klein* had supplied Mary Catherine with crack, *not* somebody else. And Klein was standing right there in front of him. *Why don't you put a bull's-eye on your chest, motherfucker,* Maher thought, laughing to himself. *'Cause I'm going to bang you out.* And at that moment, Maher decided he would pin on his imaginary badge one more time.

"Listen, Lewis," Maher said as he leaned in on Klein, "I know a guy over in Carlstadt who wants some coke."

"You *know* the guy?" Klein asked.

"That's what I just said, isn't it?" Maher snapped.

"Okay," Klein agreed. "When?"

"I'll have to get back to you."

Klein gave Maher his beeper number and his address, a sleazy hotel on Times Square.

The following morning, Maher stopped by the Carlstadt police headquarters and found Colaneri at his desk.

"Hey, Bobby," Maher said, "I got one for you."

"Got one what?" Colaneri wanted to know.

"A DD," Maher said. "He's transporting shit from New York to New Jersey."

"Is that right?" Colaneri asked with a smile.

"Yeah. I told him I had a new customer for him."

"Well," Colaneri said, "bring him on over."

Maher and Colaneri worked out the details of the sting. The entrapment issue would not be a factor because Klein had previously transported cocaine to New Jersey.

"Pull off Route Seventeen onto Paterson Plank Road," Colaneri instructed. "Just drive like you always do. And speed up when you go past Tenth Street. I'll have a patrol car waiting to pull you over."

At eleven-thirty that night, Maher picked up Klein in Times Square. Klein showed Maher an "eight ball," which was a small packet of crack.

"This what your guy wants?" Klein asked.

"That's it," Maher answered with a smile.

Maher followed the course he and Colaneri had mapped out. As Maher exited Route 17 and zoomed past 10th Street, a patrol car, lights flashing and sirens blaring, pulled him over.

"License and registration," Sergeant Dave Smith said in a monotone.

"I don't have a valid license," Maher responded, following the script.

"Step out of the car," Smith demanded.

Smith slapped handcuffs on Maher's wrist. Then Smith asked Klein for some identification. Klein could not produce any and was arrested.

At Carlstadt police headquarters, Klein was searched. All he had on him was a crack pipe. Even though a computer check turned up priors on Klein in Fort Lee, in the absence of an appreciable amount of cocaine, Klein could only be charged with "possession of drug paraphernalia." He was released ROR.

This made everyone angry, especially Maher. On the way back into the city, Maher asked Klein what he did with the drugs.

"I had the shit stuck in the back of my belt," Klein said.

Since Klein's hands were cuffed behind his back, he was able to work his fingers under his belt and remove the tiny packet of crack cocaine.

"I slipped it out of my belt," Klein explained, "and stuffed it into the seat of the police car."

Maher dropped Klein at his hotel and raced back across the Hudson River to Carlstadt. Maher and Smith searched the patrol car. Sure enough, stuffed between the cushions of the backseat was an "eight ball."

"Don't worry," Maher told Smith, "I'll get the bastard for this."

The next day, Maher again met Klein in Times Square.

"My friend Barry still wants to make a buy," Maher told Klein. "Only he doesn't want an eight ball, he wants an ounce of cocaine."

Klein's eyes lit up. An ounce would bring a nice profit.

Soon, Maher and Klein were back on Route 17. Klein kept glancing at the speedometer.

"Stay under the fucking speed limit, will you?" Klein pleaded.

Maher glided the car off Route 17 and drove to a hotel where an undercover Carlstadt police detective was waiting.

This time Klein was caught with a significant amount of cocaine and was charged with far more serious crimes than possession of drug paraphernalia.

The Carlstadt police had quite a few laughs over the drug dealer Colaneri and the fact that Maher had been arrested *twice* in twelve hours.

As summer arrived, Maher bore little resemblance to the person who sat in a bathtub with a gun in his mouth. He had not done coke for months. He had brought his drinking under control. He was content, looking forward instead of backward, and it appeared Maher finally had everything under control. His drug habit. His emotions. With Colaneri's help, his life had been transformed. But then, on July 14, 1993, something happened to upset his carefully constructed yet fragile existence.

Maher had his television tuned to *A Current Affair*, and although he wasn't paying attention to the show, a woman's face flashed on the screen. He snapped his head around. *It can't be! It fucking can't be!*

But it was. The woman on Maher's television screen was Mary Catherine Williams.

A Current Affair was doing a promo for the next day's program. According to the promo, Mary Catherine Williams was believed to be one of the victims of the most notorious serial killer in New York State history: Joel Rifkin.

Maher picked up the phone receiver and called Doherty. Doherty wasn't home. After a mostly sleepless night, Maher reached Doherty at his office the following morning.

"You been reading about the guy the State Police picked up?" Maher asked.

"Oh, yeah," Doherty replied. "The one they found with the dead body in a truck. Joel Rifkin."

"I saw a thing on *A Current Affair*," Maher said, sighing. "They believe Rifkin killed this girl I used to date. Mary Catherine Williams."

Maher began to cry. Doherty tried to comfort him.

"That's too bad, Kevin. I'm sorry."

"I loved her," Maher confided.

Doherty listened sympathetically as Maher reminisced about Mary Catherine.

"I have her address book in my closet," Maher said at one point.

"You have her address book?!" Doherty almost jumped through the receiver. "Get it out and bring it to the phone!"

Maher raced to the closet and dug around until he found Mary Catherine's address book. He returned to the phone.

"Okay, Jimmy. I've got it."

"Turn to the R section," Doherty said. "See if Rifkin is listed."

Maher opened the address book. In addition to the names and phone numbers, Mary Catherine had written sideways notes to herself in large block letters. Sometimes she jotted down a quote from the Bible. This made Maher recall her little TV altar stand with the picture of Jesus. Tears filled his eyes, and he could barely see the pages as he flipped to the R section.

"There's nothing here, Jimmy."

"Try the J section," Doherty suggested. "Maybe she just used first names."

Maher turned to the 'J' section and found an entry: J. R. There were two phone numbers.

"Jimmy," Maher said as he looked at the phone numbers, "what are the first three digits in Rifkin's telephone number?"

Since the Rifkin case was so prominent, Doherty, as did many other law enforcement officers, had a case file on his desk that detailed the serial killings. Doherty opened the folder and checked for Rifkin's phone number.

"Four-eight-one," Doherty said.

Maher finished the number. "Four-one-six-four."

"Bingo," Doherty almost shouted. "That's a hit."

It was Rifkin's unlisted phone number.

Maher read the second number listed beside J. R. It was Rifkin's mother's number.

"Don't lose that book," Doherty said.

The following morning, Doherty followed police protocol and called the New York State Police, the lead agency in the Rifkin investigation.

"I have information that looks like it is relative to Joel Rifkin," Doherty told a trooper who answered the phone.

"We'll get back to you," the trooper said.

Click.

Doherty stared at the receiver in disbelief. He had found the tone of the trooper's voice unacceptably dismissive. Doherty's instincts told him that working with the New York State Police was not going to be pleasant.

Later that day, Maher bought a *Daily News* to see if there was anything about Mary Catherine in the paper. Since the moment Rifkin had been arrested two weeks earlier and subsequently confessed to seventeen murders, there had been an enormous amount of media interest. Everywhere you turned—radio, television, magazines, newspapers—there were stories about the infamous murderer.

Maher leafed through the pages of the newspaper. There was a large picture of Joel Rifkin staring out from the page.

Until now, the only photos Maher had seen of Rifkin were snapped after he had been taken into custody. In those pictures, Rifkin was always covering his face with his arm or pulling the hood of his prison garb down to obscure his features. But this was a posed portrait of Rifkin, a smiling face that belied the horror he was capable of inflicting.

Maher studied the photo in disbelief. *Joel Rifkin,* the caption said. But Maher didn't know him as Joel Rifkin. Maher had always referred to him with a derisive nickname.

The nerd.

The man in the photo was the same man Maher had caught choking Mary Catherine Williams that horrifying day on 9th Street.

Chapter 20

MAHER CALLED DOHERTY IMMEDIATELY.

"Joel Rifkin," Maher said, out of breath. "I *know* him."

"You're full of shit," Doherty reacted.

"It's the guy I beat up in the apartment," Maher insisted.

Maher then explained how he had come face-to-face with Rifkin. How Rifkin had choked Mary Catherine one day on 9th Street and how he had punched Rifkin in the face.

As Doherty listened to the story, he knew Maher was providing him with a crucial piece of information, especially in view of what had occurred since Rifkin had been arrested on June 28 for the murder of Tiffany Bresciani, the twenty-two-year-old woman who was found in the back of his truck.

When Rifkin was interrogated by the New York State Police shortly after his arrest, he confessed to seventeen murders before a lawyer showed up and stopped him. Now the lawyer was claiming that his client may not have been read the Miranda rights prior to the confessions. Should that kind of challenge succeed, the seventeen confessions would be inadmissible and, in that event, seventeen homicide cases could be damaged beyond legal repair.

Significantly, Mary Catherine Williams was *not* one of the women Rifkin had admitted killing. She had been included in the list of Rifkin's possible victims because her credit card had been found at Rifkin's house.

Since the State Police had a name on a credit card but no body, law enforcement agencies around the New York area were contacted to see if they had an unidentified female corpse. Police in Yorktown Heights, a village in Westchester County, reported that a badly decomposed body had been discovered in a wooded area on December 21, 1992. Via dental records, the body was positively identified as that of Mary Catherine Williams.

The fact that Mary Catherine Williams had been murdered was no longer in question. As to who killed her, there was much speculation in law enforcement circles that she may have been Rifkin victim number eighteen and, had Rifkin's lawyer not stopped him, he would have confessed to Mary Catherine Williams's murder as well.

Now Doherty had someone who could place Rifkin and Mary Catherine Williams together, providing a chain of association between them. Coupled with the credit card found at Rifkin's house, Maher's testimony could be a powerful factor in the successful prosecution of Joel Rifkin for at least one homicide.

Doherty called the State Police again and upped the ante.

"I have a *witness* who can link Rifkin to a murder victim," Doherty stated. "And that witness is *extremely reliable.*"

Doherty got the same response.

"We'll get back to you," a trooper stated.

Doherty couldn't believe it. *What the fuck* is *it with these guys?*

ON SATURDAY, JULY 17, AS DOHERTY WAS IN THE MIDDLE OF HOSTING A baby shower for his daughter-in-law, a senior investigator with State Police called to say he would like to take Maher's statement that afternoon. Doherty was not overly thrilled—all of his sons and daughters (except a son who was in the Navy) were gathered at the house.

Doherty rendezvoused with Maher at State Police barracks in Farmingdale. They were greeted by the supervisor of Troop L, who took Maher's statement:

> On Thursday, July 15, 1993, I contacted Suffolk County Detective Investigator James J. Doherty to advise him that I knew Mary Catherine Williams, that she was the girl I would visit on 9th Street, and that I was in possession of her address book. . . . On Friday,

July 16, 1993, I saw a picture of Joel Rifkin on page 3 of the New York *Daily News*. I recognized him to be a person who would come to the 9th Street apartment to have sex with Mary Williams. On a day in mid-September, in the early evening, I was in the first floor apartment with a girl named Alicia Wittington. I heard a scream from Mary Catherine Williams's apartment.

The written statement then described how Maher intervened and threw the man out. The statement went on:

The man is the person identified in the July 16, 1993, *Daily News* photo as Joel Rifkin. In the prior four months, Joel Rifkin was a frequent visitor to the 9th Street apartment to have sex with prostitutes.

"Thank you," the supervisor said in a monotone when he finished taking Maher's statement.

Maher and Doherty looked at each other. *Is this guy taking a statement on a stolen car radio or a homicide?*

Driving away from the barracks, Maher and Doherty discussed the fact that Mary Catherine's body was discovered in Yorktown Heights rather than in one of the boroughs of New York City or on Long Island, like the rest of Rifkin's victims.

"Yeah," Doherty concluded, "it seems strange he would dump one of the bodies fifty-five miles away from the city out in Westchester County."

Maher was startled. "Westchester County?"

"Yeah. That's where Yorktown Heights is. In Westchester County."

Maher grew animated. "Jimmy! There was a pimp hanging around Ninth Street! Peter B. The last day I saw Mary Catherine alive, Peter B. was trying to get her to move into his house. In *Westchester County!*"

MAHER AND DOHERTY DROVE TO WESTCHESTER COUNTY. THE YORKTOWN Heights Police Department, using a facial reconstruction computer program and, based on the bone structure and characteristics of the skull, had generated a likeness of Mary Catherine

Williams. When Maher saw the computer-generated image, he began to tremble.

"That's her," Maher stated.

Doherty frowned. "Kevin, that's a computer *approximation* of what the deceased *may* have looked like."

"That's her!" Maher shouted, tears in his eyes.

Upon returning to Manhattan, Maher went to see Joe Leo on 9th Street and found out that Peter B.'s house was about five minutes away from where Mary Catherine's body had been discovered. Although there was no hard evidence to link the death of Mary Catherine Williams to Peter B.—or Joel Rifkin, for that matter—Maher was convinced that both of them were responsible. And he was determined to prove it.

NOTHING HAPPENED IN THE HOMICIDE INVESTIGATION INTO MARY Catherine Williams's death until a steamy morning in mid-August when Doherty received a disturbing call from the State Police supervisor who had taken Maher's statement in July.

"Detective Doherty," the supervisor said, "we'd like you to supply Kevin Maher again."

"Sure," Doherty replied. "What's this all about?"

"You don't have to be here," the supervisor remarked, avoiding Doherty's question. "We only need Maher."

Doherty didn't hesitate with a response: "*I* don't go, *he* don't go."

"Have it your way," the supervisor said.

On August 19, Doherty and his partner, Joe Daley, met Maher at the State Police barracks. Maher was ebullient.

"That bastard Rifkin is going to pay for Mary Catherine's murder," Maher exclaimed. "And I'm going to give them that pimp, too."

But Doherty had serious reservations about the reason the State Police had requested a second statement from Maher. While he didn't know exactly what was going on at State Police barracks, over the years Doherty had learned to read nuances in someone's voice. Having interrogated hundreds of suspects, Doherty had developed an ability to distinguish between the truth and a lie. He trusted his powers of observation more than he trusted a polygraph. So, as Doherty headed into State Police barracks on this summer afternoon, he replayed his conversation with the supervisor in his head. Doherty was certain the supervisor was hiding something. And whatever it was, it wasn't good.

The moment Maher, Doherty, and Daley entered the barracks, one trooper stepped up to Maher and led him down a hallway. A second trooper steered Doherty and Daly back into the vestibule.

"Can you wait here, please?" the trooper said.

Doherty was indignant. "What do you mean, can we *wait?*"

"I'm asking you to wait here, Detective," the Trooper asserted. The tone of his voice, his demeanor, everything about him seemed to say: *Detective Doherty, this is not the Suffolk County district attorney's office. This is the State Police barracks.*

"And I'm asking you what's going on," Doherty fired back.

"We're going to give Kevin Maher a polygraph," the trooper answered.

"Why?" Doherty was stunned.

"Because we don't believe his story," the trooper said. "We think he might be an accessory."

Doherty felt sick to his stomach.

"I've known this guy for twenty years," Doherty said.

Doherty refused to wait in the vestibule. So the trooper led Doherty and Daley into a room with a one-way mirror. There were five troopers staring through the glass, each with a pencil and a pad. But what Doherty saw on the *other* side of the glass made him furious. There was Maher sitting with a polygraph operator ready to strap him up.

"What are you doing?" Maher asked.

"We want to take a polygraph," the operator said.

Maher bolted out of his chair. The incident was beginning to bear eerie similarities to the Ciasullo case, in which the Queens chief of detectives thought Maher might have been involved in the attempted robbery. *They're trying to link me with Rifkin.*

"I ain't taking no fucking polygraph," Maher protested. Then he turned, pointed toward the glass, and shouted: "And I don't like all those guys staring at me."

The five troopers behind the glass jumped. Doherty could almost hear them thinking: *He's not supposed to be able to see us.*

"I want out of here!" Maher screamed. "And where's Sergeant Doherty?"

On the other side of the glass, Doherty turned to a trooper. "I want to call my boss."

Doherty was ushered into an office, where he called Robert Creighton at the Suffolk County district attorney's office.

"These guys pulled this shit without telling me," Doherty roared into the receiver. "It's completely out of order. It's not professional between law enforcement agencies. They treated me like I was harboring a criminal."

"Jim," Creighton asked, "is Kevin under arrest?"

"No."

"Then you're free to leave anytime you want."

Doherty hung up the receiver and charged down the hall into a lieutenant's office.

"We're leaving," Doherty informed him.

At that moment a major—whom Doherty knew from previous contact on a case—walked into the office.

"What's the matter, Jim?" the major asked. "You don't look too happy."

"I don't like what's going on," Doherty snapped. "Why wasn't I told any of this before I got here?"

"We play hardball around here," the major said with a smile.

"He's not going to take a lie detector test," Doherty said with a growl. "I can tell you that right now. Not under these conditions. We're getting out of here."

The major shrugged. "Your guy's already talking to investigators."

"What?!" Doherty was furious. "Take me to Kevin. *Now!*"

The major showed Doherty and Daley to a door.

"He's in there," the major said, then walked away.

Maher looked up as Doherty and Daley entered the room. When Maher saw Doherty's face, his heart began pounding. In all the years Maher had known Doherty, this was the first time he saw Doherty show any fear. Doherty grew even more concerned when he saw Maher sitting amid eight troopers, each of them firing questions. *Eight guys interrogating one suspect?* Doherty fumed. *What a Mickey Mouse operation!*

One of the troopers interrogating Maher asked him: "Were you ever in Joel Rifkin's truck?"

Maher's brow wrinkled in disbelief.

"What's the next question? Did I help him dump the bodies? What are you, out of your fucking mind?"

Maher leaned in on one of the troopers.

"But I *do* think there was someone else involved," Maher said. "A pimp named Peter B."

The trooper was unimpressed.

"We already looked into that," he said with a yawn. "Rifkin acted alone."

"How can you overlook the fact that the pimp's house is five minutes from where they found the body?" Maher asked, his voice raised. "Peter B. *was* involved in the murder of Mary Catherine Williams."

"We have no evidence to support that," a trooper countered.

"Okay," Maher said, "then give me a wire. I'll go talk to Joe Leo, Peter B., the prostitutes. They'll talk to *me*. Not *you* with the badges."

A trooper smiled wryly at Maher. "Our policy is that we don't work with informants who don't take lie detector tests."

"Oh, yeah?" Maher fired back. "Well, *my* policy is I don't work with cops who don't believe me."

There was a long, tense moment of silence.

"You want me to help you," Maher finally said, "I will. You want to sit there and give me a hard time, I'm getting the fuck out of here."

One of the troopers, using a conciliatory tone, asked Maher if he would mind looking at some photographs.

"Photographs of what?" Maher responded.

"Items we believe belonged to Mary Catherine Williams," the trooper said.

Maher nodded, and a book of photographs was brought into the room. As Maher looked down at the photos, his eyes watered.

"That looks like her belt," Maher said, his voice cracking.

Oblivious to Maher's emotional pain, one of the troopers asked: "Will you give us a written statement to that effect?"

"Sure," Maher half whispered.

After examining the photographs, Maher wrote the following statement on a deposition form:

On 08/19/93 at about 3:00/PM I viewed a book containing photographs of jewelry and clothing in which, at the State Police Barracks in Farmingdale, I recognized photo number 7 as displaying a set of white Rosary Beads. I know that Mary Catherine Williams owned a pair identical to these, and that they glowed in the dark. I recognized photograph number 13 as depicting a black belt that looks similar to a belt Mary Catherine Williams used to have. A key chain attachment depicted in photograph number 37 is definitely Mary Catherine Williams's. Photograph number 18 which depicts a crucifix and portion of Rosary, and this looks familiar to one that Mary Catherine Williams had.

And then, for the next *five* hours, Maher went through virtually every minute of every day from the time he first met Mary Catherine Williams until the day he socked Joel Rifkin in the face. The troopers were spellbound. Clearly, they had never seen anyone who could talk so much for so long and recall every detail.

Doherty watched the faces of the troopers as Maher told his story. True, the troopers were hanging on every word. Yet doubt radiated from their eyes. *They still think Kevin was involved somehow*, Doherty thought.

It was dark when Maher, Doherty, and Daley left the barracks. They were drained.

"This is it, kid," Doherty said. "They don't believe you."

Maher couldn't respond.

"We did the best we could," Doherty continued. "We gave them all the information. There's nothing more we can do."

But in Maher's mind, there was a great deal more he could do. For one thing, he could turn up the heat on the New York State Police.

After his grueling experience at the State Police barracks, Maher felt justified in contacting the *Daily News* and *New York Newsday*. Both ran stories about Maher's brush with serial killer Joel Rifkin.

The headline of the *Daily News* story on August 25 blared

VICTIM'S PAL SOCKED JOEL. The accompanying subhead elaborated by stating SAYS HE HALTED SLAY TRY.

> A man who claims he dated a prostitute apparently slain by Joel Rifkin says he caught the confessed serial killer trying to strangle her in a lower east side apartment and punched him out—weeks before she disappeared.
> "I whacked him right in the face," said the 39-year-old Kevin Maher.

While the article gave Maher's account of the incident between him and Rifkin, it also contained a two-paragraph reaction from the State Police, replete with a subhead reading QUESTION CREDIBILITY.

> Law enforcement sources believe key elements of Maher's account and that he knew Williams but could not confirm he punched out Rifkin.
> They cautioned that they feel the paid informer, who is working for the Suffolk County prosecutors, could be embellishing part of the story in an effort to gain notoriety.

Maher was not particularly happy with tone of the two paragraphs, nor was he thrilled with the charge that he was seeking notoriety. But he actually choked when he read the words "paid informer." *What are they trying to do, get me fucking killed?*

Doherty was incensed. It was unconscionable for one law enforcement agency to publicly identify the informant of another law enforcement agency.

Following the two newspaper articles, Maher was contacted by *The Maury Povich Show*, which was about to tape a segment with acquaintances and relatives of Joel Rifkin. Maher appeared in the studio on August 31 along with several guests, including one of Rifkin's coworkers, a former classmate, and the mother of Tiffany Bresciani, the first known victim in Rifkin's homicidal spree. The show aired in late September.

Maher was obsessed. Not only was he going to tell the world that Joel Rifkin killed Mary Catherine Williams, he also was going to prove it. To that end, Maher called the Manhattan district attorney's office and spoke with Tom Harkins. By now

Maher had become extraordinarily conversant about the case against Rifkin, which was evident as he laid out the situation to Harkins.

"The State Police fucked up from the beginning," Maher asserted. "They hold Rifkin for twenty-four hours without reading him his rights. Then they call his mother and say they arrested her son for traffic violations. Meanwhile, Rifkin gets to confession number seventeen—I believe Mary Catherine would have been number eighteen—and some fucking lawyer shuts Rifkin up. Which means that the only evidence not tainted is *my* evidence."

Harkins smiled. He was accustomed to Maher's leaps in logic.

"You should continue working with the State Police," Harkins said. "Continue gathering evidence."

"I'm not working with them," Maher reacted. "The reason the State Police don't care about this case is because the victims were drug addicts and prostitutes. I point out that this fucking pimp Peter B. owns a house in Westchester, they don't want to hear it. And what about the fifty-five-gallon drums Rifkin used to get rid of some of the bodies? You think one man can do that? Lift a body *and* a fifty-five-gallon drum and throw it in the river? You think *you* could do that? Rifkin had to have a helper. And I think it was Peter B."

Maher took a breath and then concluded his diatribe.

"I'll tell you something, Detective Harkins, I'm not letting this go. I'm going to find out exactly what happened to Mary Catherine."

"So," Harkins asked, "what do you want me to do?"

"Two homicides were in Manhattan," Maher said. "You have jurisdiction."

"To do what?"

"Give me a wire. I'll go down to Ninth Street."

"I don't know, Kevin. The State Police are the lead agency in the case."

"Fine," Maher said with a sigh. "But you can't stop me. With or without your consent, with or without your wire, I'm going there."

"Hang on," Harkins said.

While Maher was on hold, Harkins called the assistant district attorney who was handling Rifkin's two Manhattan homicides.

"Give him a Bluebird," the ADA said.

A Bluebird was a state-of-the-art recording device that had replaced the Nagra tape recorder in law enforcement surveillance. Unlike the Nagra, which required audiotape, the Bluebird could record eight hours of conversation on a microchip.

Harkins punched the blinking light on the line where Maher was holding.

"Okay, Kevin. You've got it."

THE FOLLOWING DAY, FITTED SNUGLY WITH A BLUEBIRD, MAHER WALKED into Joe Leo's apartment. Maher's only concern was that Leo might have read the *Daily News* article in which Maher was identified as a "paid informer."

"Hey, Kevin," Leo said, his tone friendly.

Apparently Leo hadn't seen the *Daily News*. But before Maher could get into a meaningful interchange with Leo, there was a hard rap on the door. When Leo answered the knock, two men stormed in.

"State Police," they announced as they flashed badges.

Maher smiled. *The fucks listened to me after all.*

"Joe Leo," one of them said, "we'd like to ask you a few questions."

"I'm too sick," Leo said. "Maybe tomorrow."

One of the investigators shoved Leo into a chair.

"Shut the fuck up," the investigator said with a growl. "I'm a New York State policeman."

Maher frowned. *The guy is going to beat the shit out of Joe. And I'm wearing a fucking wire.*

Maher walked over to the other investigator.

"Can I talk to you for a minute?"

"Go ahead."

"Not in here. In the hall."

Maher and the investigator walked out into the hallway.

"What do you want?" the investigator said impatiently.

"Do you know who I am?" Maher asked him.

"Yeah," the investigator said smugly. "You're Kevin Maher."

"I'm a CI."

"I know."

Maher raised his shirt, revealing the Bluebird. The investigator's eyes widened.

"What's that?" the investigator asked, knowing full well what it was. "You wearing that for some TV show?"

Maher shook his head. "I'm working for the Manhattan DA's office."

The investigator's eyes widened even more; then he walked back into Leo's apartment and whispered in the ear of the other investigator. The investigator blanched.

Maher left Leo's apartment and walked to the street. The area was filled with State Police. Maher climbed in his car and drove away, but he only got a couple of blocks before the State Police pulled him over. Several investigators and troopers surrounded Maher's car and demanded to see the Bluebird again. Maher raised his shirt.

"Is that thing still on?" one of them asked.

"No," Maher said, showing them the on/off switch.

"Give me that," another said.

"You ain't taking this," Maher fired back. "This belongs to the Manhattan DA."

The State Police insisted that Maher call Tom Harkins immediately. Maher got Harkins on the phone and then handed the receiver to an investigator. After a brief conversation, the investigator handed the receiver back to Maher.

"I'll meet you downstairs in front of Hogan Place," Harkins said.

When Maher met Harkins in front of 1 Hogan Place, Harkins had a concerned look on his face.

"I'm in trouble," Harkins said with a sigh. "The DA's in trouble. *Everybody's* in trouble."

"I told you I didn't want to work with the fucking State Police," Maher said as he unstrapped the Bluebird and gave it to Harkins.

The case was over now as far as Maher was concerned. If he continued to pursue it, he would create more problems for Harkins.

Several weeks later the chief of the State Police filed a formal protest with NYPD chief of detectives Joe Borelli. Calling the incident "a classic case of left hand not knowing what right hand is doing," the State Police chief blamed the breach of interagency communication on the Manhattan district attorney's office.

ON A WINTER DAY IN EARLY 1994, THE RIFKIN CASE STILL EATING AT HIM, Maher drove out to Suffolk County to see Doherty. They talked for a while in Doherty's office. Then Doherty walked Maher to his car.

"You know, Kevin," Doherty observed, "you've got to leave the Rifkin case alone. It's time to stop all of it. It's time you quit this shit for good."

Maher looked into the setting sun. As late afternoon transformed into early evening, swirls of hues and colors spread across the sky like celestial butterfly wings.

"Yeah," Maher said with a sigh. "I guess you're right. No one treats me like a *real* cop except you and Bobby. Everyone else treats me like a fucking snitch."

Maher and Doherty hugged tightly. Doherty suddenly began to laugh. So did Maher. They released their embrace and just stood in the parking lot, laughing.

"Why are we laughing?" Maher asked between outbursts.

"I'll tell you why we're laughing," Doherty said, catching his breath. "Because all this started with a rug. A fucking *rug.*"

"It was a good rug, though," Maher observed.

And then they laughed so hard that tears began to roll down their cheeks. Tears and laughter. Endings and beginnings.

"Listen," Maher said, "you interested in a guy who's selling guns?"

"*Get outta here!*" Doherty said, laughing.

Maher opened the door to his car. He started to climb behind the wheel but stopped with one foot on the floorboard and one foot still on the pavement. Both Maher and Doherty stood motionless for a few seconds, frozen in a fragment of time.

"Be talking to you, kid," Doherty whispered, fighting back emotion.

And then, as Doherty turned and walked away, Kevin Maher climbed into his car and, with nowhere in particular to go, slowly drove away.

Epilogue

IN LATE 1995, A DINNER CONVERSATION BETWEEN KEVIN MAHER, JIM Doherty, and Bobby Colaneri centered around Maher's desire to seek a private investigator's license in the State of New Jersey. However, the same 1971 felony conviction that had prevented him from becoming a cop now would disqualify him as a licensed investigator. Doherty and Colaneri offered to go to court with Maher in an effort to obtain what is known as a "certificate of relief from a felony conviction."

(While such a certificate does not overturn or expunge a conviction, it does allow a convicted felon to obtain various licenses.)

In addition to suggesting that Maher should have been given youthful offender status at the time of his arrest, Doherty and Colaneri intend to cite Maher's twenty-year cooperation with the NYPD, the FBI, the DEA, and other law enforcement entities. Should the court decide in Maher's favor, he would be free to obtain a license as a Private Investigator.

Kevin Maher currently works for a security firm. He resides somewhere in New Jersey.

Jim Doherty is still a detective investigator with the Suffolk County DA's office.

Bobby Colaneri is still a detective with the Carlstadt Police Department.

Beth Maher is the vice president of circulation for the *Economist* and lives in New Jersey.

Bobby Eschert is a fireman for the Wood-Ridge, New Jersey Fire Department.

Susan Remy, Maher's sister, resides in Westchester County, New York with her second husband Mike and her three children.

Agnes McNulty, Maher's mother, lives with her sister Irene in Marino Valley, California.

Burton Roberts is an administrative judge for the Bronx Supreme Court.

Detectives from the Manhattan DA's office: **Tom Harkins** retired in 1994 after more than 20 years in the Manhattan DA's office. He lives in Brooklyn. **Josh Wainwright** retired from NYPD April 24, 1989. He remarried in 1992 to his second wife Sandy. He is now show director at the Sanford L. Smith Art Gallery in New York City.

Morris Weiss served the maximum term allowable under New York State law and was released from prison in 1990.

Beverly Hodge was released on parole April 17, 1991. She now lives in Van Nuys, California.

John Hemmers was paroled May 31, 1994. He lives in Rochester, New York.

William Hand served 3 years for attempted bank robbery and subsequently served numerous other sentences. He is now out of prison and lives in the Bronx.

Ronald Scofield was released from prison in 1991 after serving 15 years. He lives in Orange County, New York.

Joseph "Mad Dog" Sullivan is serving a life term with a release date of 2094.

John Uribe served 3 years in prison and was released in 1991. He is wanted by the Immigration and Naturalization Services and remains at large.

Tom Slavanki is still with the DEA.

In September, 1995, **Joel Rifkin** entered a plea regarding two of the seventeen homicides to which he had confessed. He received two sentences of twenty-five years to life, which are to be served consecutively following the twenty-seven year sentence that was handed down regarding his first homicide conviction.

Beverly Merrill's last known address was in Wayne, New Jersey. Maher last saw her in 1992 dancing at a club called Shakers in Carlstadt.

Appendices

DISTRICT ATTORNEY
OF THE
COUNTY OF NEW YORK
ONE HOGAN PLACE
NEW YORK, N.Y. 10013
(212) 335-9000

RT M. MORGENTHAU
District Attorney

April 10, 1992

Jim,
Assure me
as his date
gets closer
BF

Also, let me
know ADA
handling oth—

Honorable James Catterson
District Attorney
Suffolk County

Attn: Robert Creighton
      Chief Investigator

Sir,

I am an Assistant District Attorney assigned to Trial Bureau 80 here at the District Attorney's office, New York County. I am preparing a case for trial in which the defendant is charged with the homicide of one victim and the shooting of others in a robbery which took place last year.

I am writing to you regarding Kevin Maher who was instrumental in securing for this office information and assistance which enabled us to make a positive identification and arrest of the defendant in this case. It is significant also to point out that Kevin came forward with this help without seeking anything in return for himself. He has had a seventeen year special rapport and record of cooperation with one of our Senior Detectives, Thomas Harkins, which began in 1975 with our Detective and a Senior Investigator on your staff, who was the Supervisor of Detective Harkins then, James Doherty.

Kevin's history of cooperation is remarkable in that only on the initial contact with him did he request any help from us back in 1975. Since then and only through his direct involvement were we able to make arrests, prevent serious injuries or death and obtain convictions in the following types of cases:

1. The planned homicide of one man by his partner in business.

2.   The planned armed robberies at residences throughout New York and New Jersey by a gang, including members of Organized Crime, who posed as policemen.

3.   The planned robberies of business people in their driveways at home arriving at night with the days receipts by a gang in Queens.

4.   The planned robbery of an off duty police officer who also had a jewelry business. A gang of five men abused him in his driveway as he arrived home one night. They were armed with handguns and a shotgun.

At great personal risk to himself and owing nothing to this office Kevin repeatedly gave us assistance over the years, the most recent of which is the case I cited in the opening paragraph.

Kevin has a matter pending in your jurisdiction. He was arrested and charged with Driving While Intoxicated. His next scheduled appearance on this matter is in May. The foregoing information is provided to you for the purpose of assisting you and the Court in determining the ultimate disposition of the pending case and hope you and the Court will take it into consideration.

If any further information regarding Kevin is required by your office on this matter please call me and/or the following:

Thomas F. Harkins   James Doherty
Detective   Senior Investigator
District Attorney's Office   Suffolk County District
New York County   Attorney's Office
(212) 335-9048

Respectfully and with appreciation,

Deborah Gelb
Assistant District Attorney
Trial Bureau 80
New York, New York
(212) 335-4147

STATEMENT

STATE OF NEW YORK

COUNTY OF Suffolk

Town OF Babylon

PAGE ONE OF 2 PAGES

DATED: Jul 7 17. 1993

I, Edward Maher , AGE 39 , BORN ON 04/18/54 .

AND RESIDING AT _____

HAVE BEEN ADVISED BY Senior Investigator Donald P. Delaney

OF THE New York State Police , OF THE FOLLOWING:

I HAVE THE RIGHT TO REMAIN SILENT, AND I DO NOT HAVE TO MAKE ANY STATEMENT IF I DON'T WANT TO.

IF I GIVE UP THAT RIGHT, ANYTHING I DO SAY CAN AND WILL BE USED AGAINST ME IN A COURT OF LAW.

I HAVE THE RIGHT TO HAVE A LAWYER PRESENT BEFORE MAKING ANY STATEMENT OR AT ANY TIME DURING THIS STATEMENT.

IF I SHOULD DECIDE I DO WANT A LAWYER, AND I CANNOT AFFORD TO HIRE ONE, A LAWYER WILL BE APPOINTED FOR ME FREE OF CHARGE AND I MAY HAVE THAT LAWYER PRESENT BEFORE MAKING ANY STATEMENT.

I ALSO UNDERSTAND THAT I HAVE THE RIGHT TO STOP AT ANY TIME DURING THIS STATEMENT AND REMAIN SILENT AND HAVE A LAWYER PRESENT.

I FULLY UNDERSTAND THESE RIGHTS, AND AT THIS TIME I AGREE TO GIVE UP MY RIGHTS AND MAKE THE FOLLOWING STATEMENT:

SIGNATURE

WITNESS

I can Read and write and completed the 11th grade. During February 1992, I met a girl named Mary Catherine Williams at the Z Bar on Ave 3, between 11th and 12th Street in Manhattan, NY. We developed a relationship and she was my girlfriend through September 1992. I would visit her at the apartment on the first floor behind the storefront at 439 9th St in Manhattan. There she would service customers as a prostitute until she disappeared in mid October 1992. I didn't see her again until Wednesday night, July 14, 1993 when I saw her photograph on television connected to the Bifkin murders. On Thursday, July 15, 1993, I contacted Suffolk County Detective Investigator James J. Doherty to advise him that I knew Mary Catherine Williams, that she was the girl I would visit on 9th Street, and that I was in possession of her address book. After hearing that Mary Williams was missing for two weeks,

n. Edward Maher
_____

During the first week of November, 1992, I went to her room in the 9th Street
apartment and picked up bags of her clothing and her address book. I felt that
I would hold it for her and when she returned, she would contact me, and I
would return it to her. On ~~Saturday~~ Friday, July 16, 1993, I saw a picture
of Joel Rifkin on page 3 of the New York Daily News. I recognize him to be a
person who would come to the 9th Street apartment to have sex with Mary Williams.
On a day in mid September, in the early evening, I was in a first floor apartment
with a girl named Alicia Wittington. I heard a scream from Mary Catherine
Williams apartment. I ran to the door of her room and banged on the door until
a man cracked the door. I forced my way inside and saw Mary Williams(street name
Kelly) sitting on the floor, with no panties on holding her neck. When I asked
her what happened, she explained that she had choked her. I punched him in the
face and beat his glasses. He left the apartment but came back about 10 minutes
later to retreive his glasses. Mary Catherine Williams left the apartment with him.
That man is the person identified in the July 16th, 1993 as Joel Rifkin. In
the prior four months, Joel Rifkin was a frequent visitor to the 9th Street
apartment to have sex with prostitutes. I often observed him smoking crack
cocaine with the prostitutes there. On one occasion, I saw Rifkin smoking
crack with Alicia Wittington, Mary Williams, and Peter (a Pimp). I have not seen
Wittington since October 25, 1993.